John O'Groats

Drumnadrochit

Loch Lomond

Lockerbie

Lancaster

Stoke-on-Trent

Birmingham

Weston-Super-Mare

Okehampton

Land's End Truro

FROM LIGHT TO DARK

FROM LIGHT TO DARK

The Story of Blind Dave Heeley

Foreword by Sir Ranulph Fiennes

Dave Heeley and Sophie Parkes

First published by Pitch Publishing, 2016

Pitch Publishing
A2 Yeoman Gate
Yeoman Way
Worthing, Sussex
BN13 3QZ
www.pitchpublishing.co.uk

Front cover image: MDS2015©WAA/CIMBALY

Reproduction of the poem 'The Quitter': by courtesy of
Mrs Anne Longepe

A CIP catalogue record is available for this book
from the British Library.

ISBN 978-1-78531-119-2

Typesetting and origination by Pitch Publishing

Printed by Bell & Bain, Glasgow, Scotland

Contents

Acknowledgements

There have been a great number of people who have given their time to the writing of this book. Dave and Sophie would like to thank: Tim Andrews, Jane Camillin and all at Pitch Publishing, Steve Dourass, Steve Dugmore (Duggie), Tony Ellis, Peter Emmett, Sir Ranulph Fiennes, Raphael Fraga, David Gagen, Adrian Goldberg, Mark Green, Annie Heeley, Rob Lake, Dave Long, Eric MacInnes, Karl Moore, Rosemary Rhodes, Darryl Webster and Garry Wells.

Don't be fooled into thinking that writers enjoy quiet seclusion when putting together their memoirs. Oh no – this book has been compiled during the course of weekends, weekdays and evenings; in the early hours and the more-sensible hours; in between training stints; around film crews, holidays and speaking engagements. This book has survived Sophie's car crash and has been subsequently edited one-handed. This book has been pored over by adults and children, alike.

Dave would especially like to thank his wife, Deb, and his children, Grace, Georgie-Lee and Dannie, for their relentless love and support.

Sophie would like to thank Chris for his calming influence and patience; her parents, Pat and Loz, for being constant sounding boards; and her brother, Matt, for always making her smile. Thank you for the additional, otherworldly help you've all given her this year. She would also like to thank Deb, Grace, Georgie-Lee and Dannie for being so welcoming and letting her infiltrate their home. Finally, she would like to say a massive thank-you to Dave for being so thoroughly entertaining and a joy to write for. Sophie will never look at life quite the same way again.

Foreword

I N 2003, my good friend Dr Mike Stroud persuaded me into running seven marathons in seven consecutive days, on all seven continents. It was to be a world first and it took some organising, but we believed we could do it.

Our chances of starting the marathons – let alone completing them – seemed somewhat scuppered when I experienced a heart attack that left me in a coma and in need of a double bypass just 14 weeks ahead of the start date, but thankfully my recovery was quick and I was back to training.

But, heart attack aside, Mike and I hadn't anticipated the intensity of the challenge. It wasn't clocking up the mileage that was the problem – we had done enough marathons in our time to keep to sensible paces and to watch out for the wall – but it was the heat, the cold, the altitude, the wind, the constant dehydration, uncooperative muscles, an old back injury and the jet lag brought on by lack of sleep through ever-changing time zones.

And even with our luxury of British Airways-sponsored first-class flights and the odd sumptuous hotel that the profile of our challenge made possible, it was still seven days of discomfort, which sometimes could be classified as downright pain.

So when we returned, like jubilant, staggering war victors, and I received a letter from a chap from West Bromwich telling me he fancied having a crack at the same thing, I thought he was completely and utterly mad. Back then, Dave Heeley didn't call himself a runner – he had done one or two London Marathons, I believe – but that was about it. He didn't have the experience and knowledge that Mike and I had built up during the course of our careers, in medicine and the armed forces respectively, and to top it all off, he told me that he was blind.

But in conversation with Dave, I detected a certain challenge-hungry madness, a determination to do something that others gawp at, to push the body and mind to its utmost limits. Dave's blindness adds another layer of complexity that must be taken into account – though Dave is so eager and able that, after a while, one forgets he even has a disability at all. In fact, I would go as far as to say that his achievements put many able-bodied athletes to shame.

After Dave and his guide finished those punishing seven marathons, we kept in touch through the occasional e-mail and telephone call, but I wasn't at all surprised to learn that in 2015, when I hoped to be the oldest Briton to complete the gruelling Marathon des Sables, Dave was also in training to do it. And, of course, he and his two talented guides not only completed it, they also raised thousands of pounds for a worthy cause.

I'm sure Dave will continue in his endeavours well into his twilight; after all, his fitness outstrips many younger men. And even when his legs can no longer carry him, I am certain that the causes in which he believes so passionately will continue to be trumpeted – that's just the kind of man he is. A true inspiration.

Ranulph Fiennes
August 2015

Preface

'You'll have to write it all down, Dave.'
'When's the book out?'
'Where can I read more?'
'Have you censored any bits, Dave?'

I HAVE regularly been asked to write the story of my life, especially since undertaking the challenges for which I have become known.

But where the hell do you begin? How do you pick your opening gambit?

When I think back to my early life and my proudest moment, it was easily 14 May 1970: the day I won the 1,500m in five minutes and 13.09 seconds to become the town champion and break the record. It instilled in me a lifelong love of running, albeit across longer distances and in pursuit of more significant personal achievements.

Or I could easily start the book on the day, not so long ago, that I eloped to Gretna Green with the love of my life, Deb, or my presence at the births of my three daughters, Grace, Georgie-Lee and Dannie.

If I wanted a fast-paced opener, like a scene from an action movie, I could tell you about the time I drove a tank in the

Scottish Highlands or the occasion I steered a fast car around Brands Hatch, or threw myself off steep cliffs in Corfu in the name of fun. Or maybe a humorous anecdote, something unexpected – like the time I was lost in a snowy Ostend, Belgium, dressed only in a belly-dancing outfit.

Maybe the first few pages could be devoted to one of the 'big ones', picking up the pace during the adventure of a lifetime, running seven marathons in seven consecutive days across seven continents, or the ten days I dragged an ever-growing team of weary cyclists and runners from John O'Groats to Land's End through ten marathons and 700 miles of cycling, when fundraising opportunities presented themselves mid-pee and failing brakes shook our nerves to the core.

I suppose the most obvious place to start would be that day in 1968 when Mom and I visited the Birmingham Eye Hospital. I can remember that moment like it was yesterday. The consultant shut the door, sat down and said to me, 'You've got a disease of the eye, young man, called Retinitis Pigmentosa.' I must have looked blankly back at him. That was a term I hadn't heard before. 'You're going blind,' he clarified.

I remember the consulting room. It had big, high windows. As he said it, I looked out of one of them. I noticed that the sky was blue. I could see the sun. A bus went past on the street below. I was confused. I wasn't blind; I could see. At ten years of age the realisation just didn't dawn on me. So perhaps that isn't the place to start. After all, it was only later – when the career I had banked on became a no-go – that the diagnosis hit me like a sledgehammer. It was only later when I realised that my entire lifestyle would have to be adapted, shifted, tamed.

I actually tried to start this story, initially, as many people do, with my birth. I looked up a weather report from November 1957 and thought this would set the scene for readers, contextualising my arrival in West Bromwich. I took it seriously, reeling off four pages with the weather report as its foundation, and, after a hushed couple of hours, I printed off pages for Deb, my fiercest critic, to read. The next thing I heard was not the sound of astonished gasps or proud sobs. No, instead, all I heard was the aggressive, greedy whir of the shredder. 'What a load of rubbish,' she said, bluntly. She was right, though. It was.

This time, hopefully, I've got it right. It's a strange thing, to sit in your comfy chair and wonder whether your memory can serve you right, piecing together your life bit by bit, from being a kid right through to old codger days. I've cringed, shed a tear, smiled and laughed out loud, frowned and wondered how the hell…?

And with so many people asking me to write my story, *challenging* me to write it – well, you know how I like a challenge. I simply thought it had to be done.

1

I T WAS more commonplace, back then, to be born at home as I was. The home in question, 60 Elizabeth Road, West Bromwich, was, at the time, cutting-edge: a Smith house constructed from steel and brick, with three bedrooms and two living rooms, a kitchen and two toilets, one upstairs and one outside. Smith houses were seen to be a revolutionary way of providing affordable housing quickly, although I think you'd struggle to get a mortgage on one these days. As building regulations were relaxed in the 1950s to stimulate house building, there was a housing boom, with hundreds of thousands of new homes built each year across the country. My family home was part of that.

When I think back to my first 22 years of my life, when I lived at home, I'm immediately reminded of the cold and damp: there was no central heating, and it was always a case of straight-out-of-bed and get dressed – there was no hanging about. In the winter, there was always a race to who could get to use the inside loo first. The inside loo was marginally warmer than outside and had the better toilet paper, too. It was horrible, that hard, shiny stuff, not like the soft tissue paper we get today, heaven in comparison. But still, it was far better than the damp, inky squares of newspaper hanging by a nail in the outside toilet.

We were only allowed in the front living room on special occasions, certainly at Christmas, when Mom always had a big fire going. In fact, sometimes the fire got overbearing. We'd sit on the settee closest to the fire but as we warmed up and the flames grew, we'd begin to slowly rotate around the living room, a bit like musical chairs, until we were further away and by the window. Of course, you couldn't turn it down and I often wondered how Santa made his entrance. He must have carried a fire extinguisher. Still, we always got our presents scorch-free, and that was the main thing.

So I, David George Heeley, plopped out on Sunday 24 November 1957 at around 12.20am, weighing in at just over 7lb. Apparently I had big blue eyes and no hair, and soon proved I could eat and sleep a great deal – some things never change! I'm sure it must have been like the old films we used to see: the midwife shouting to the father-to-be to bring boiling water, hot towels, a bowl. But yet, years later, when I was present at the birth of my own daughters, there was none of this at all. Perhaps the boiling water was just for a cup of tea.

My first actual memory was seeing my baby sister for the first time. Sharon was born on 8 September 1961 and I had a quick glance at her, peacefully sleeping next to my mother in bed, before I was whisked away by my Auntie Dot, my mom's sister, and Uncle Ivan to Blackpool for a fortnight's holiday. I can remember standing on the platform at the old West Bromwich station, right there, where the Metro station is now, and the steam train blowing its whistle and smoke belching everywhere. It was a brilliant holiday, where everything seemed to revolve around me. I was given bread and toast each morning at the hotel kitchen to feed the seagulls, I met Harry Corbett and had my photo taken with a life-sized Sooty. We went to the theatre to see a play about a lion and I can still see that lion in a rowing boat. I'm not quite sure what it was doing there to this day.

I can also remember the pain on the backs of my ears as my wire-rimmed glasses cut into them. They were my first pair; I'd had them from around the age of three. Back then it was presumed that kids didn't have poor eyesight, that it wasn't a concern until something proved otherwise. But my parents had picked up the telltale signs: as soon as I could walk, I walked straight into things, like doorframes, the edges of the settees, discarded toys. My first glasses were like two pound coins, plastic with wire rims that wrapped round your ears. The wire repeatedly cut through the skin, leaving my ears red and raw. I tried to keep it from my auntie as I didn't want her worrying, especially on holiday, but she found out; grown-ups always do.

Only a few days after I was born, my parents, George and Annie Heeley, and I moved out, to our own place. But my dad's dad, Grandad Heeley – otherwise known as the 'Nightingale of Dudley' on account of his sweet singing voice – died on New Year's Day. We promptly moved back in again, to keep Granny Ag company. That made five of us in that house: Mom and Dad, me, Granny Ag and Uncle Gill, dad's younger brother. Six when Sharon came along. People didn't seem to move around so much in those days, and generations continued to live together under one roof, with other extended family often only down the street or across the park. I liked it, having everyone around, and it meant you often knew your neighbours, and your neighbours' neighbours. I suppose it made it safer, more community-spirited. Few ordinary folk had cars, and trains and planes were expensive and didn't go quite as far or as regularly as they do now.

Granny Ag was the name on the rent book and she ruled the roost. She still ran the coal business, with one of Dad's brothers, Uncle Ernie, lugging the coal, and I loved to accompany him in the wagon. Gran had run a shop before compulsory purchase forced their move to the house on Elizabeth Road but that didn't stop her; she continued selling produce from the new place. Mom always said it was like living in New Street station: there was always someone knocking the door, whatever time of the day or night, for potatoes, pop, bottles of beer, Davenports in those days.

My grandparents on my mom's side were Granny and Grandad Clee. Though I didn't see them daily, I did go and visit them as often as I could. In fact, when I was allowed to ride my bike out by myself, it was Granny and Grandad Clee I'd go and visit, often calling in to Auntie Dot's first to pick up meals she had prepared for them. Maybe I was the original meals on wheels! Granny Clee became, in the latter years, the breadwinner. She worked in the factories – it was all factory work round here back then – and she worked hard in the warehouses at Walsall Conduits and Conex Sanbra, where they made pipes and compression fittings and put the components together. She even had a spell operating overhead cranes at a company called Cashmores, but would often clean the 'big houses' for extra income when she needed it. It was hard, physical work and she was old school, as hard as bloody nails. She had a hip problem for years, but hip operations weren't the rite of passage in the 1940s as they are for many old people today. She just frowned and got on with it.

Grandad Clee could have been a teacher, I'm told, but he was prevented due to poor eyesight. He took a job as a dustman instead but he was eventually forced to give that up, too, due to his aggressive blindness. When Grandad Clee gave up work, he attended the Queen Alexandra College in Harborne, Birmingham, where he learnt the art of basket weaving. In those days, he used hot pitch to make the baskets and he burnt his fingers regularly. But his baskets were beautiful, and he continued to make them from his garden shed. The college also taught him everyday life skills, helping blind people cope better as they aged and their disabilities became more profound. When I visited them as a kid, I always marvelled at him frying bacon and eggs, feeling his way around the hot hobs and sizzling pans. Back then, I didn't realise I'd be doing the same, years later. I can't recall him ever complaining about his condition, or wondering why he had been singled out for blindness.

In fact, people did forget that Grandad was blind, a tribute to his skills and get-on-with-it mentality. Back in the late 1950s and early 60s we used to have terrible fogs, real pea-soupers. There were times when people would lose their way, their senses dulled by the pollution, and Grandad would whisk them to where they needed to go. He never told them he was blind and they never knew; after all, it would have sounded crazy, the proverb in action.

My dad, George Thomas Heeley, was born on 14 May 1933 but the midwife attending the birth didn't think he'd survive the night and told Granny Ag to prepare herself for the worst. But she needn't have worried, as Dad was always a fighter. He was one of five brothers – Arthur, married to Beryl; Norman; Ernie, married to Auntie Margaret; and Gilbert, or Gill, married to Auntie Chris – and their only sister sadly died in infancy.

Dad and his siblings didn't have it easy back then. He would roam the same fields as I would do, 30-odd years later, looking for adventure and a game of football with the other lads in the area. But by the time he was 14 years old, he was expected to contribute to the household. In fact, it wasn't an expectation – he had to. So, like his parents and brothers, he began to work the coal, delivering with a horse and cart. When his older brother, Ernie, was called up to national service in the army, he had to keep the coal round going, pretty much single-handedly: up at four in the morning to sort out the horse, then get the cart hitched up before bagging up the coal and getting off on to his rounds. No wonder he was built like a barn door, as I would find out years later, to my peril.

Dad always worked long hours and, like the other members of my family, experienced heavy labour. I've known him to hold down two jobs, one during the day that he'd finish before heading off to his second at night. He worked very hard to support us, and would rarely take risks in case it would jeopardise his young family. In the latter years, he was a fitter, fixing anything that had moving parts such as engines and motors. He was a very practical man and common sense and experience got him through his working life.

In 1951, Dad was called up to do his national service. He joined the Royal Horse Artillery as a tank driver and two years later, he was given what was seen as the ultimate privilege – he was chosen to represent his regiment in the Coronation Parade. I don't think there are too many people from West Bromwich who could say the same, and I'm told it was a very proud day for the family. In fact, Uncle Ernie went right out to buy a television – black and white, of course – so they could try and catch a glimpse of Dad. London, along with the rest of the country, came alive that day and celebrated. I think it was much needed after the end of the war only eight years previous.

Mom was born Annie Elizabeth Clee on 1 March 1934, St David's Day. Mom was one of three, alongside Auntie Dot and her younger brother, Fred. Like everyone in those days, Mom finished school and went straight out to work, working all her life. Just like Dad, she often had two jobs at once, and she only retired in 1995, just after Dad died.

Mom worked at Conex like her own mother had, and like many of our family and our neighbours did, and she operated the machines. At 16, early into her working life, she suffered a horrific accident. She wore her hair very long, which she piled on top of her head in a turban. And, well, you can only imagine. She told me it happened so quickly: one moment she was working away, and she barely noticed the few strands of hair that slipped out of the turban. Before she knew it, the machine had caught hold and mercilessly ripped out the vast majority of her hair from her head, from back to front. She was off work for 12 months, convalescing, and was awarded £100 compensation. From that day until now, she doesn't like her head to be touched.

It was not long after Mom's accident that she met Dad for the first time. They 'stepped out briefly', as she says, but then Dad was whisked off to do his national service and they split for a while. It was a couple of years later when they met again, when she was asked to the Great Bridge Palace cinema, and romance flourished.

Money was tight but my parents still liked us to have pleasure when we could. We somehow always managed a holiday, whether it was a caravan somewhere in Britain with various aunties and uncles, or sometimes even the Costa del Sol. Auntie Dot and Uncle Ivan, having no kids of their own, would take Sharon and me with them from time to time.

Sharon and I would fight like siblings do. My particular bugbear was the fact that she would borrow my best jumpers and t-shirts and wear them for her favourite pastime: horse riding. The smell of horses! It took at least two washes to get rid of that smell. I'll always remember one Saturday night disagreement. I can't remember what it was about, but it must have been serious as, in a moment of madness, Sharon pulled the leg off the old coffee table and hit me over the head with it! With pain there is often a natural instinct of retaliation. Incensed, I thought about my reciprocal move, but Dad's voice chimed, 'Don't you even think about it,' and I was forbidden to move. She got away with it – typical younger sister.

She and I have always got on, though. I used to drive her mad with my persistent losing of the contact lenses I had treated myself to when I was 18. I'd always lose them when I got home from the pub and rather than risk the wrath of sleep-deprived parents, it was Sharon I dragged from her bed to help me find them. Thankfully, Sharon and I continue to get on well today, and I have a great relationship with her husband, Mark, and my only niece, Hannah.

Though our typical house was on a typical council estate, we were actually incredibly lucky with the amount of green space that surrounded us. The area was known as Greets Green, as it still is, but the open spaces were just known as The Fields. I could skip over the back fence and I'd be there: grassy banks and hills, perfect for playing and hiding. As clichéd as it sounds, me and the other kids did play cowboys and indians, we did pretend we were in armies, and we did go tracking on our bikes and trolleys. In the summer months, we were like latchkey kids, only coming home for dinner or when the sun was setting. In the winter, we got out our sledges. I always remember snow, proper snow, that lasted for weeks. But then people always say that – is it the trick of nostalgia?

The brook that zigzagged through the area was shallow enough to paddle in or look for fish but I later learnt it was actually a section of the River Tame. I got a little wet more than once, with a good telling-off to go with it. I didn't have the patience to sit and fish in the pond just adjacent to the river, but as the other local lads did it, I found I had to, too. So there we were, whiling away hours and hours with a worm suspended into the water from a piece of string attached to a stick. The sticklebacks fell for it every time. I much preferred it when we made rafts so we could float across the pond, or when it iced over in winter and we could play on it.

Over to the left of us was what we used to call the 'cawper', which was left over from the brickworks that had once been there. There were still great banks of stones and piles of dust which became, to us, some rough, barren cliffs and dirt tracks: perfect for bikes and some of the older lads even had motorbikes which were great fun when we could get a ride on the back. If we weren't climbing them, we were jumping off them, on foot or on bike.

We liked to try and come up with ingenious ways to make money. On the fields, there were some paddocks that belonged to a small riding school. And as soon as the coast was clear we'd get up there like a shot, buckets and shovels in hand, to collect up all the horse muck. We made a small fortune around the estate, selling manure to anyone who was growing vegetables.

Though there were also a few occasions when we had to shell out for some new buckets when we were chased off by the owners of the fields.

Another great money-spinner was newspaper. Of course nobody really recycled then, so we took it upon ourselves to load up our trolleys with an estate's worth of newspapers, knocking on the doors like religious missionaries. As soon as we'd got as much as we could carry, we'd head up to the paperworks and make a few bob. We always had great fun jumping in the huge vats of paper – Health and Safety officers would go bananas at that these days. Actually, Dad would have back then, too, if he'd found out.

There was a tip opposite the fields, Sheepwash Lane Tip. Anything too big or cumbersome for collection by the bin men was dumped there and we always had a good rummage through to see if there were any overlooked jewels. Anything of any worth – copper wire, copper piping, lead, brass, metal of some description – we'd lug up to the scrap metal merchant, or the tat yard as we called it, in exchange for a few coins. I'll never forget the day that a lorry-load of Etch-A-Sketches appeared there. They were the toy of the moment and they were all at varying states of disrepair, but word soon got round and all the estate's kids were soon down at the tip, sifting through to find the best ones.

Thankfully, there were also safe, sensible places to play, too. In the middle of the estate, still there today, I'm pleased to say, is Farley Park. We enjoyed all-weather and grass tennis courts, a bowling green, a playground complete with swings, slides, seesaw, and what we called 'the witch's hat' which went round and round and in and out. But it was the football pitches that were most in demand.

Anyone who owned a football then was automatically popular. Actually, you didn't need to own a football, just a book of Green Shield stamps that could be exchanged for a football up at the stamp shop in Dudley. It was a chore trekking all the way up there, just for a football, but as soon as you were back, the game was on. Sometimes it felt like we were always running up to that shop in Dudley – balls were forever being impaled on the park railings or getting lost in the undergrowth.

My years at school certainly hold some memories. On reflection, it's a period where you can really see your own personality emerging, your character developing as a result of your experiences. It's also a time when things begin to change, and I remember my name changing from the age of five. As soon as I started school, I wasn't David any more. I became 'four eyes', 'bunk eyes', 'milk bottle eyes', the Milky Bar Kid, some other names that, even as early as five, I can't put into print.

Greets Green Junior and Infant School was situated on Whitgreave Street and just a stone's throw from our house. It was a cluster of Victorian buildings, originally opened in 1872, with large, high-ceilinged classrooms, and visible cast iron pipes running throughout which serviced the old, heavy radiators. Polished wooden floors gleamed underfoot. A few years after I left, the school closed, the buildings too old and tired to keep the kids warm, dry and safe, and a new school opened round the corner in its place, on top of the old cawper. Newtown Primary School officially opened in 1972.

My memory of my time in the infants is very vague. I can't remember starting school exactly, but I do remember we had plenty of toys and two rocking horses in the first class, the nursery class. The rocking horses were large and one was missing a head. I always ended up on that one, for some reason. Mrs Shooker taught us to read and write our first shaky words. Apparently I had real difficulty in writing in a straight line – purely because I couldn't see the lines on the paper.

My experiences at junior school are more vivid. I can remember all the teachers, starting with Miss Westwood, then Mrs Bissell, moving on to the old battleaxe, Miss White, and in the last year before senior school, Mr Grocut. The headmaster was a big, strong-looking man, Mr Summerton, and there was a rumour that he was an ex-regimental sergeant major. I don't know if this is true or not, but it certainly explained his appearance: tall and stocky, rather menacing with a handlebar moustache covering his mouth. He was as strict as a sergeant major, too, and quick with punishment when deserved. I had my hands slapped a few times and my legs more than once, but I'm sure I deserved it. One particular game we – or I – always got in trouble for was running the gauntlet to the toilet block outside in the playground. We were only supposed to go there when we needed to use the facilities, but kids being kids, this was the challenge to earn peer glory. I never saw Mr Summerton hanging around until it was too late.

As smaller infant kids we had watched the juniors playing their games in the playground. The most exciting was British Bulldog, and as soon as we reached junior school, we couldn't wait to get stuck in. The chosen one had to get from one end of the playground to the other without being rugby-tackled to the ground by the bunch of menacing ruffians in the middle. My first go at this game taught me a painful lesson. There were only six or so kids waiting to cross, one of which was one of the cocks of the school, the self-confident kind. Slowly, one by one, the six were picked off until the cock of the school remained. He found himself trapped against the wall at the midpoint of the playground. We encircled him like a pack of wolves. I can't remember his exact words but with one fist clenched, he dared us to tag him. Which one of us would dare? You guessed right. On impulse, I reached out and touched him. As a reward, I got a swift punch in the ribs before I found his fist perched under my chin. He snarled a few words of wisdom and I knew not to try my luck again.

My academic endeavours at Greets Green Junior School always took a back seat. It was never going to be the times tables, alphabet or geography lessons I was going to remember; it was always the sporting memories which would shine through. It was at Greets Green that I had my first swimming lessons, but it was the more social occasions at the baths on the weekends with the bigger kids that honed my skills – especially when one of them threw me in to the deep end and it was either sink or swim. Thankfully, I swam! I managed to get into the school swimming team and though I was never fast enough to win any races or daring enough at that age to perfect the art of diving, I found my place: style swimming, which suited my capabilities. To my astonishment, the first year I competed, I came second in the final.

Though the idea of diving scared the living daylights out of me, there was a special headmaster's badge for those of us who managed to dive from the high board. Of course, it was a coveted badge and we all wanted one, so I let my desire get the better of my nerves and put myself forward. It was just me, that week, going for that particular badge. My knees knocking and my legs trembling, I left the pool and climbed the ladder. I didn't know if they were, but I felt that everyone was watching me, waiting for me to wince and climb back down again. I was ten and not very tall, but nevertheless, the water looked a long way down. I glanced over at Mr Summerton, who was standing there with his self-satisfied grin peeking out from under his moustache, his formal suit including fob watch in the waistcoat pocket looking sharp and out of place at the poolside.

Everyone stopped what they were doing. They waited. They watched. Oh to hell with it, I thought, and dived off, arched like a swallow and headed slightly to the left of the pool – towards Mr Summerton, it seemed. I hit the water with an ungainly thump, stomach first.

I heard the roar of approval from my class-mates as the wind flew out of me. It was a spectacular belly flop and as I looked over at the headmaster to see whether it still qualified, I realised I had managed to soak him in the process, too. He didn't seem to mind, though. The next day, I was awarded my diving badge on the stage at school.

CHAPTER 1

I wasn't the best footballer in the world, despite the practice I'd get on the estate with the other kids, but I scraped into the school team which I felt to be quite an achievement. We all looked forward to Friday lunchtimes when the teachers put up the team sheet on the noticeboard. I played right-back in those days but I'm sure the rest of my team thought it should have been 'right back in the dressing room'. Still, me and my glasses were on the team. We weren't a great team, and in the last year of junior school, we only won one game all season.

I was a much more enthusiastic supporter of football. There was no doubt that I'd be a Baggies fan. My home-town team, my dad's team – I'm pretty sure I was wrapped in blue and white stripes the minute I arrived into the midwife's arms. I couldn't possibly name my favourite game or goal; there's been so many high points – and low, of course – over the years that it's impossible to pinpoint favourites. But I've had the pleasure of bumping into a few players during my lifetime. Occasionally, Baggies great Ken Hodgkisson would come and show off his skills to us kids rattling a football round the playing fields. Later, I had an unbelievable moment when Tony 'Bomber' Brown came to my warehouse business with his City Electrical Factors hat on – he was a rep and wanted to sell to me. Having one of my greatest idols standing at my office door really was something else. I'm not sure many fans of Premier League clubs these days would ever encounter anything remotely like it – David Beckham as an electrical sales rep? I don't think so, somehow.

In later years, Jeff and Lorraine Astle opened the Albion Lounge at our local, the Sow and Pigs, which was certainly a coup for the community. And latterly, I've enjoyed the camaraderie of a long-haul bike ride with Brendon Batson, shared a drink and a joke with Bob Taylor and Cyrille Regis, to mention just a few. That club means the world to me: it's certainly been my salvation when things haven't been easy. Through thick and thin, win or lose, the Baggies will always be my club.

Of course, one of my best Baggies moments was that day in 1968, the summer before my last year at junior school. The 1968 FA Cup Final featured my beloved Baggies against Everton. My Uncle Ivan had managed to get a ticket to the final and was willing to take me to Wembley and blag me in. But Dad wouldn't let me go. 'What if you can't get David in?' Dad had said, over my head. 'Then you'll have to miss it, too.' Ivan hadn't considered that and he decided to go along without me. I didn't blame him, but it meant I had to make do with the telly and Dad.

But I'll still never forget that game. Sitting there as you do, nose right against the telly, willing the ball into the net, King Jeff Astle, our legendary striker – and one of few strikers who has actually scored in every round of the cup – hit the ball.

A rebound.

He hit it again with his left foot and it sailed sweetly into the back of the net. At this point, like many other houses in West Brom, our living room erupted. Dad was eating his dinner of faggots and peas. Dad and I yelled in unison. As Dad flung his arms upwards, his faggot flew off his fork and hit the ceiling. We'd won the cup! We beat Everton 1-0, and that faggot stain remained on the ceiling for nearly two years, until Dad got round to redecorating.

I fared much better at running than football. I was the second fastest kid in the school over 100 yards, always beaten by Malcolm Mills. On every school sports day he would get first, I'd get second. He was almost six inches taller than me, though, so I didn't worry about it too much. After all, that's what appealed to me most about running – it was an event for individuals, and I was always comfortable with the notion of competing against myself, trying to better and shatter my last time.

I looked forward to athletics at secondary school, with access to better facilities and more impressive athletes to beat. It wasn't far on the horizon.

CHAPTER 1

My final year at junior school was certainly memorable. There was my last junior school Christmas party, which was pop and sweets heaven until the walk home. It was dark and cold, and visibility was poor, even for someone perfectly sighted. Right opposite the school was an old brewery and here I'd usually cross the main road before cutting across the wasteland. But this time, as I neared the road, I saw a familiar hump lying in the middle. It was Bart, our family dog. He was a Heinz 57, a mongrel, but he was our mongrel. Something had hit him. I didn't know if he'd died on impact or been left to die, but by the time I reached him, I could see he was gone. I cried my bloody eyes out and ran home.

But there was something else memorable about my last year at junior school, in 1968. Given the significance of the moment, given its lasting, huge impact on my life, it's funny that I can't remember either the day or the date, only that I was ten and senior school was very much on the horizon. My annual eye test loomed on the calendar. This time, though, I wanted a change. I suppose I wanted a second opinion. I had come to learn – well, to admit to myself – that my eyesight wasn't getting any better. In fact, it seemed to be getting worse, no matter what glasses I wore. I had presumed, as young kids do, that Keeler's was the only opticians in the world; when it became apparent that there were other branches, other companies, I decided I would go elsewhere. I was getting to be a big boy now, you know. I wanted to assume some responsibility for myself. I suggested Stephenson's Opticians in Great Bridge and Mom agreed. I made my appointment and turned up by myself, punctual.

On opening the door and walking in, I fell straight over a chair leg. 'You have bad eyes, son,' the optician announced to the room with a smirk. Red-faced, I feigned a reciprocal smile. The optician sat me down and set to work. He didn't say anything out of the ordinary, he didn't seem shocked or saddened by what he saw. He didn't even give me a new prescription. 'Just hand that to your parents,' he said, pushing an envelope into my hand. 'Things might be on the mend,' I remember thinking, as I walked home.

Six weeks later, Mom and I were in the consultation room of the Birmingham Eye Hospital. The consultant came in and shut the door. I was diagnosed with Retinitis Pigmentosa; in layman's terms, I was going blind. I asked the consultant how long I would have sight for but, until I wrote this book, I didn't realise that at that moment Mom had shaken her head, indicating to the consultant that she didn't want him to tell me the truth. I don't remember his answer.

Still, to me, it didn't make sense. I could still see. Mom and Dad didn't seem to understand more, either, as they didn't offer any more explanations – though they probably had more of an idea of what lay ahead for me because of Grandad Clee. And that was it. There was no crying or lamentations, no conversations in hushed tones behind closed doors. I was going blind, and that was that. Life would carry on, regardless.

The next day at school, though, I was asked where I had been. I told them I was going blind.

'Wow!'

'Bloody hell, Dave's going blind!'

I became a school celebrity. No one else they knew had this complaint, I was a one-off. I enjoyed the attention. As I passed through the week, the news travelled through the school.

'Dave, are you going blind?' Kids stopped me in the corridors, at the playground gates, even kids I didn't know that well. They looked into my eyes with a new curiosity. They didn't pity me; they wanted to know more. But because I didn't feel any different to what I had yesterday, the day before, last week, I can honestly say the implications and the understanding of my diagnosis hadn't really sunk in.

And it wouldn't for a long time to come, so life went on as normal for me and my glasses. After all, the transition to senior school seemed a much bigger, more significant event at that point in time.

2

'What's it like to be blind?'

I'M OFTEN asked questions about being blind, and that's the most common of all. I don't mind answering but the answers aren't always what people want to hear. After all, the truth is that being blind is bloody awful.

Blindness is a very lonely experience. Even in a crowded room, the blind person is at a disadvantage to everyone else; you're last to the joke, last to the action on the screen, last to the compliments about your friend's appearance. People don't mean to do it, it's human nature to forget, but there might be times when the person sitting next to you is mouthing to their friend to get them a drink, or pointing to something mid-sentence to provide context to what they're saying. It often means I can't quite work out what's going on. Then there's the nodding or waving to someone across the room, a thumbs-up or a wink of approval mid-conversation... it's all natural human communication, but for the blind person, it's impossible, lonely and frustrating.

It's actually the frustration that is most unbearable. A simple second of sight would often alleviate it all. For example, when the computer packs up talking to me and I can't work out what it needs to get going again, or after sanding down a chair leg when I want to know whether the marks are removed and I can go ahead and oil it.

Of course, it's certainly no one's fault, it's just part of being blind, but it usually means waiting until Deb gets home… a few hours' wait to complete a simple task that just one second of sight would solve – pressing one button on the computer or glancing over that piece of wood. There are times, even now, after 30 or so years of complete blindness, where frustration makes me feel like screaming.

There are bigger moments of frustration, too, of course. Just to have 30 seconds of sight to see my daughters would be worth the world.

Many tell me that I must get used to being blind, that it's something I've become familiar with over time. The truth is, though, that you never get accustomed to it – every time I run into a post and end up in hospital with stitches holding my forehead together, or cut myself making a sandwich, is an aggressive reminder that blindness is never something I can get used to.

Instead, I've had to accept the fact that blindness is here to stay, and there's nothing I can do about it. As I say, there is no point worrying – after all, worrying is known to cause hair and tooth loss and I can't afford to spoil my good looks! My mirror doesn't lie; mind you, it doesn't work, either.

Some people find it incredibly difficult to converse with a blind person. I actually find it quite amusing: many decide to talk to me through my wife, or whoever is accompanying me at the time. Some will avoid any kind of communication with me altogether, or talk over-enthusiastically, as if to compensate for their own sight somehow. 'Blind people aren't renowned for cannibalism, you know,' I want to say. But it's not necessarily their fault; they are just focusing on my disability and find it difficult to comprehend. Like I might do with a Villa or a Wolves fan.

CHAPTER 2

It's these kind of instances that motivated me to spend a chapter helping readers understand my disability as I see it – no pun intended. I don't intend to speak for all blind people, as my situation will vary considerably to the next blind person's, but I do hope that my exploration of the topic will help others feel more at ease with blind and partially sighted people.

Firstly, it's a fallacy that all blind people can't see; the varieties of blindness and levels of sight loss mean that blind people's conditions differ dramatically. Some might be partially sighted, and that could mean central, peripheral or tunnel vision. As many people will know from visiting an optician, there are different levels of sight, so some people might be able to see across the road, while some might only be able to see a few feet in front of them. Amazingly, some people see additional things like shadows or might be affected by the light. When I had sight, streetlights, especially when reflected on a wet road, were a lifesaver. And when it snowed, I positively gambolled down the road, as the reflections were fantastic.

Then there is, of course, total blindness. I am now completely blind, but I try not to let that impede my lifestyle. In fact, my independence can exasperate my friends and family. There are the times when I presume we're home and get out of the car, only to hear Deb shriek that we're at traffic lights. Or when we park up somewhere and I automatically get out and wander off, in no particular direction. 'Where are you going?' Deb will ask me, when I have no idea where I am. 'I don't know,' I have to admit, as she tells me to turn the other way. Of course, my mates like to remind me that although I might be blind, I never pick up an empty pint glass!

According to the RNIB, four people an hour in the UK begin to lose their sight and, as you can imagine, there are a multitude of reasons why this might be. Retinitis Pigmentosa, or RP as it's more commonly known, is what I suffer from, but then there's glaucoma, molecular degeneration, oxygen starvation at birth, many hereditary diseases, accidents... I certainly am no doctor or optician, and though I might be blind, I can't tell you the hows and therefores, most certainly not the whys. What I can tell you about my condition is that my grandad was blind and, being hereditary, the disease was passed to me at birth. Thankfully, though, it seems to have stopped there.

RP is an umbrella term for a range of retina disorders, where abnormalities in the retina's photoreceptors mean that the retina gradually stops working. Generally, for the sufferer, it means an incremental loss of sight that can begin from birth or develop over time. Not all RP sufferers are completely blind; as with many conditions, it varies from person to person. For me, my experience was very gradual. I describe it to people like this: on Monday, I could see over the road; on Tuesday I could see the kerb; Wednesday the privet hedge; Thursday the end of the drive; on Friday I could see the front step; Saturday the front door, and Sunday, nothing at all. Though of course, this didn't occur over a week, but over a good many, frustrating years.

It's not the cause I'm bothered about, particularly; it's the cure. Oh, how I dream of some kind of miracle cure… I've put myself forward for a few medical trials in the past in the hope that I can contribute to research. I am certain that there are scientists out there making progress every day, gaining a better understanding of the eye and its complicated mechanics.

Despite the prevalence of blindness in society, it does feel as though blindness is pushed to the bottom of the priority queue, in terms of social services and government bodies, anyway. The charities and support groups are a godsend, I'd never knock their tireless support, but in terms of how the help is dished out financially, blindness does seem to come at the bottom of the pecking order. I often wonder if that's because blindness is a quiet, discreet condition. It's not life-threatening – well, providing you've got access to a guide dog when you decide to cross those busy roads on the way to town – and it isn't always obvious that someone might be blind. My eyes look absolutely fine, so I'm told, so no wonder I cause confusion at times.

In fact, sometimes I cause downright embarrassment, like the time I had arranged to meet my friends in a pub I didn't know too well. I was waiting at the bar for them to arrive, but unbeknownst to me, the barman was standing directly opposite, anticipating my order. Suddenly an irritable, sceptical voice boomed, 'Do you want serving, mate?'

'Sorry,' I replied, 'I didn't know you were there.' I hoped he got the message.

'I've been standing here for five minutes!' he scoffed. 'Are you blind, or what?'

'Yes,' I said, simply.

He probably hadn't noticed the dog sitting by my side or the lead in my hand, but then the realisation hit him.

'Mate, I'm so sorry; I didn't see you walk in with the dog. Oh mate, what can I say? I didn't mean to! I wouldn't have! Christ, mate, I'm so sorry.'

His voice softened instantly. He was utterly humiliated, so I tried my best to assure him that he hadn't offended me, that I knew it was a genuine mistake.

Then there was the time that Karl and I were out running a half-marathon together. Karl was diligently guiding me, describing the scene as we passed through. Then we overheard two runners in front of us.

'You all right, mate?'

'I would be,' he grumbled, 'except for the constant bloody BBC commentary going on behind me!'

As is to be expected, he was pretty mortified when Karl told him that I was blind. He dropped back and ran alongside me, adding to the commentary himself to make up for it. I then had two blokes jabbering on, telling me what they could see!

That's the thing about blind people: you might see a white stick, a guide dog or a pair of oversized dark glasses, or you might not. There are no rules that blind people have to obey.

And my cockiness, my refusal for assistance, hasn't helped, either. On holiday in Cyprus, I decided that I knew the layout of the hotel well enough that I could find the toilet without my white stick. From the table, I walked forward to touch the bar and followed it round until I found the stairs down, second door on the right as memorised – bingo!

However, as I made my way down the stairs, I became distracted by a conversation with someone coming the other way. As I left the bottom step, I missed touching the first door, so the second became the first. I counted one, and then at two turned in right. The door to the loo should have been on the left, but as I searched for a handle, I realised it had gone. I began to fumble around each wall, searching for a door in. I checked, then rechecked.

Suddenly, I heard a voice I recognised, which soon turned into laughter. Thankfully, my friend Joe had found me, and went on to explain that I was actually in the lift. I was so grateful that another hotel resident hadn't, at that moment, called the lift as I wouldn't have been able to explain myself. 'I'm blind, not drunk!' doesn't sound very convincing in a lively hotel bar late at night in Cyprus, does it?

Quite often, people tell me of their 'experiences' of being blind. They might tell me of the time they stumbled round their bedroom in the dark when a bulb had gone or attempted to find the gas stove when a power cut hit. But, of course, when they open their wardrobe, they can pull out the right shirt they were looking for, or they don't burn their finger while waiting for the water level to come to the rim of the cup. I've encouraged friends and relatives – even business people as part of team-building days – to do certain things blindfolded to give them an idea, like the Go Ape day I held in Grizedale Forest. The participants completed the course as usual, but some tackled the last section blindfolded, and it was incredible to hear their reactions. Deb's report was particularly insightful. She found it difficult to follow the instructions of the sighted guides as there were so many other verbal instructions taking place, making it confusing. But it was her final comment that hit me.

'I can take my blindfold off, but Dave can't,' she said. 'I've lived with Dave for years, I hear about his trials and frustrations. But that really hit me.'

My friends and I have run a race as the Three Blind Mice – me, Garry and Tony wearing mouse onesies with oversized sunglasses – to raise money and awareness, while Garry has run three races blindfolded.

But the truth is: you can't imagine how your life is turned upside down until you suffer that affliction. You can't experience it until you have it. And I wouldn't wish it on my worst enemy.

Over time, I've found the best way to explain the blind experience is this simple analogy: from waking to arriving at work.

You wake when the alarm clock tells you to, and you throw open the curtains to see it's another fine day. Immediately, you get an idea of the day ahead. You glance at the lawn and make a mental note to cut the grass at the weekend. You throw open the wardrobe and wonder what to wear, settling on a different shirt and trousers to yesterday so your colleagues don't suspect you wear things twice before washing. Downstairs, you click on the kettle, say good morning to the kids, notice how quickly they're growing up. You pick up the envelopes and newspaper lying on the doormat, flicking through to see which are junk and which are dreaded bills. Then it's coat on; open the garage to pull the car out, reversing carefully out in to the street with a quick wave to Mr and Mrs Jones who are already picking up the leaves on the lawn. A check in the rear-view mirror and you can accelerate away.

Driving through town, you spot the florist which reminds you to buy that plant for your mom before the weekend. What happened to the old shoe shop? You can't remember it becoming a phone shop. The lights are changing to amber, will you make it? Oh, that lady's bottom has caught your eye… gentlemen, eyes on the road. The roads seem to get busier and busier, despite all these cycling and walking campaigns. Oh, speak of the devil, watch out for the cyclist!

As you pull in to the car park, you're scanning for any spaces that will allow you a quick exit later and spy one, pulling into it neatly. You nip through the factory door and clock in, run up the steps to reception and put your security pass in the door, punching in the numbers on the keypad.

It doesn't really matter what job you do – receptionist, shift worker, radio presenter, managing director, nurse, policeman or fireman – but now, imagine that same hour or two in the morning and close your eyes. You're blind, just like me. Do you think it would change the day much?

Let's compare it to my start to the day: no blue sky, no long grass to remind me it needs cutting which is a bonus, I suppose. Clothes are picked out by my wife, so let's just hope she hasn't got the devil in her and she sends me out in unusual colours! Like the time she packed me off to a talk with one of the girls' princess-themed lunchboxes. There's no newspaper, nor any bills to read either. Don't think I get away with that, though; they are soon read to me as a reminder that they are there. I don't have a garage to open and obviously there's no car, while getting a job is hard enough for sighted people at the moment – imagine what it's like for the disabled. Jobs are extremely limited for those who are blind or partially sighted.

But the very worst thing of all is not seeing your kids growing up: that wonderful first painting in nursery, their spidery, uncertain handwriting as they put pen to paper for their first spellings. I have to brace myself as I fear the worst is yet to come. I won't see them looking beautiful at their university graduations or as they walk down the aisle on their wedding days, and I could only guess what their own children will look like when they introduce me for the first time. It's

CHAPTER 2

thoughts like these that plague me from time to time. It's thoughts like these that make me take myself off and have a private, quiet cry.

But though I can't see my daughters, it hasn't prevented me from being a hands-on dad. In fact, Deb often says she reckons that my involvement with my daughters' upbringing has been greater than a lot of dads, such has been my determination. There was the time that I tried to put Georgie-Lee into the bath, only to be confused as to why she wouldn't let me, her little legs curling upwards and away from the water. I called Deb up to investigate, only to be told that she still had her socks on. Even as a baby, she knew those socks should not go into the bath water. Or another bath-related story: the time that I was bathing Georgie-Lee and Dannie and couldn't understand how they had sneaked Maltesers into the bathwater. Deb had to be called for again, and it was then I learnt that some accidents had occurred… why Maltesers had come to mind, I don't know. A handful of what seemed like melting chocolate balls changed the bathtime routine in a hurry – at least I knew something wasn't quite right!

We had a homebirth with Dannie, actually, and I had even been given the opportunity to cut the cord, which filled poor Deb with horror. She made sure the midwife knew to give me strict instructions, especially with my left and rights, and not to cut until told!

When Dannie was three years old, she and I were tasked with changing the light bulbs in the kitchen. It was clear, once Dannie sent me giddy with her instructions, that perhaps she also needed to brush up on her lefts and rights. She instructed me to go left, so I did. Then left again. And again. And then I realised the problem when she said, 'No, Dad, the other left!' After some time, I gave up and found the best solution to be to touch every light: if it was hot it was fine. I could hear laughing from the other room, and Deb called through, 'And don't forget the balloons!' It had been Grace's birthday a month prior.

They were only hanging along two walls in the kitchen, so how hard could it be? Dannie's approach this time was to tell me, 'They're over there!' Perhaps needless to say, it took longer than expected and even Dannie got fed up, grabbing my hand and physically pointing it to the very last one. Joint effort! 'To listen to you two was hilarious,' Deb laughed.

Grace has also fallen foul of my blindness, which we like to remind her about, now and again. Coming home one evening in her car, Grace saw me walking along the street with my guide dog. Automatically, without thinking, she waved and flashed her lights at me, and then sent me a text to tell what she had done. Then there was the time that we were on holiday in the Lake District and I was at the front of a shop queue, the rest of the family waiting for me outside. Grace said loudly, 'Oh, it's just a blind bloke, holding everybody up,' which a woman in the queue did not take kindly to. She berated Grace, telling her to have more respect, and didn't let up even when Grace explained that the blind bloke in question was her dad! I guess living with me as a dad has demonstrated to the kids that I'm normal and jokes can be made.

I like to help out at home and surprise Deb where I can. Like the time when Deb's dad, John Burford, wallpapered the spare bedroom. He had done a fantastic job, as always, but I thought that while the room was free of furniture and carpets, I would give the new wallpaper a coat of paint. I called Deb at work to ask which cans contained the emulsion but when I told her why I wanted the emulsion, she told me categorically not to touch the new wallpaper – the anaglypta paper was beautifully coloured already, and didn't need painting. Reluctantly, I headed back to the cupboard where we kept the paint to put the tins back in and close the door. But as I did so, one tin toppled over. I went to right it and clean up, but soon realised it wasn't emulsion, but Hammerite, the stuff for painting metal. It quickly stuck to my hands, the carpet, door handles, even the phone as I panicked and called Deb again.

'Stop! Stand still, don't move, and I'll come home now,' she said, infuriated. I would love to know how she explained her abrupt disappearance to her boss. How she hasn't throttled me over the years, I don't know. She has often said it would be easier with ten kids than one Blind Dave!

My blindness can certainly cause hilarity – usually at my own expense. I've always tried to be discreet about my gradual loss of sight over the years, but there have been times when friends have witnessed certain moments that have given me away. For example, I will never forget the time I was out one Friday night for a work's social at the Tower Ballroom in Edgbaston, a very popular nightspot. Walking through the foyer, I nodded and said hello to someone who looked vaguely familiar; it was probably someone I'd seen in another department. Immediately, my mate piped up, the beginning of a laugh bubbling in his throat, 'Do you know him then, Dave?'

'Looks familiar,' I replied, dubiously, as we made our way to the bar. My mate couldn't control his laughter. His eyes creased up with tears. I frowned, what had I missed?

'You – you –' he sniggered, 'you just said hello to yourself in the mirror!' Had I ever felt such a prize Charlie?

Then there was the time that I went to Amsterdam on a business trip, with colleague, Ron Sherwood. As unbelievable as this sounds, flying in and out on the same day was far more costly than booking a weekend trip, so, in order to visit our new contacts in the Netherlands, we settled for a weekend in Amsterdam. Of course, there are some fantastic sights to be seen in that infamous city, and Ron had lots of fun describing the women in the windows of the red light district: women of all shapes and sizes, wearing all manner of clothes, or, at times, a complete lack of clothes. On one particular street, Ron was invited to look a little closer, and he went to town in describing this particular lady, the little she was wearing and her pose. We gathered quite an audience, to the annoyance of security. At first, the woman didn't quite understand what was going on.

As soon as she caught sight of my white stick, however, she made the connection – quite literally. Bounding out of her door, she unclasped her bra and thrust her huge breasts in my face, saying, 'Now can you see, English?'

Ron told me that the look on my face was enough, and we were politely moved on by red light security.

Blindness has often got me into scrapes – quite literally. I remember coming home from the pub with a pal, cutting through a grassy area I knew pretty well in the daylight. We were walking and talking but suddenly I stumbled and I couldn't feel solid ground beneath my feet. I gave a grunt. I'd fallen, I thought, but I was still standing. I was confused. More so, when I heard my friend stop and shout, 'Dave! Where are you?' He sounded further away, above me, somehow. 'Hello?' I called, 'Over here!'

Not that I knew where 'here' was. I could hear him shuffling about, ostensibly searching for me. But soon enough he found me – down a manhole. I was only glad it wasn't a mineshaft!

I suppose the night blindness was the first worrying indication that the diagnosis was correct and my sight was fading fast, and would continue to do so. After escorting a young lady home one night, again post-pub, I found myself confronted by the plastic, heavy-duty bollards and cones that indicated roadworks were taking place. But under that blanket of darkness, I couldn't work out what was either side of the fence, and where terra firma lay. I decided to test it, pushing my foot through the barrier. It felt all right. I would just need to hop over here and then I'd be well on the way… but my instincts had been wrong and I plunged into a muddy trench, easily six feet deep and four feet wide. Pipes stretched out across the bottom made it incredibly difficult to get a foothold and scramble back out, up and over the bank.

Eventually, I made it back to the bus stop to find my friends. They presumed I'd been in a fight, as my shirt and my brand new beige trousers were streaked with mud, my hands scratched and my fingernails blackened. I felt my cheeks redden as I told them the truth but there was no sympathy – understandably, they found it absolutely hilarious!

After a pint or two, I often fall foul of the pranks played by some of my oldest friends. Even after 30 or so years, I can be found in the pub most Monday and Friday nights with two of my closest friends, Bret Meeson and Tom Walker. Bret's favourite prank is to set me off on a conversation then quietly nip off to the toilet without telling me. I'll be there, talking away to the facing vacant chair until his silence gives him away. For them, it's a joke that never wears thin.

One time, I was walking home from the pub, accompanied by Bret. I heard the sound of someone walking by, and Bret got me by the arm and whispered, 'Look at the anatomy of that young lady,' or words to that effect. I did as he said, and turned my face in the direction of the woman, as he had done. I don't know why, considering I couldn't see a thing, but it seemed like the natural thing to do. But with both pairs of eyes off the ball, we weren't concentrating on where we were going and I walked clean into a lamppost. It hurt, but not wanting to show weakness, I carried on. 'It's all right, you can rub it now. She's gone,' Bret whispered. But the lamppost had split my face from eyebrow to cheekbone and there was a lot of blood – all for a second's glance at a lady's backside, which I couldn't see anyway.

Tom has also used my services at times. Like the time when he had a new floor installed in his living room. He found that the wooden floorboards were not as level as he would like, so we set to put them right. Beneath the floorboards was a void so his idea was to level from the top and insert pieces of slate where joists met brickwork beneath. However, there was one slight problem: there was no light under the floor. Tom decided his job would be to level from the top, while I, not needing any light, could get to work underneath. The things he was prepared to put me through, rather than get new batteries for his torch! And with the instructions I was getting from up above, it was like the blind leading the blind!

My mother-in-law, Joyce Burford, has also taken advantage of my blindness. Joyce is better known as 'Broomstick' since the time she asked me to get her two new brooms from the warehouse and I asked whether one was for riding and the other for charging up in the shed. When Broomstick was recovering from a hip replacement, Deb and I thought it would be easier, and more comfortable, for her to live upstairs at our house. With my blindness, she could recuperate at her leisure, close to the bathroom and without the worry of having to get dressed properly. That was until I discovered, quite accidentally, her knickers hanging on the bathroom door handle, left there, presumably, so she wouldn't have to bend down.

'Whose the bloody hell are these?' I laughed, her drawers in my hand. 'You could fit two pounds of spuds in these!' Poor old Broomstick – I've never let her live that down.

But sometimes my disability isn't funny at all. Some people can be cruel and decide to take the mick. I might be heckled or teased. I'm sure they're not completely heartless, but I suppose some don't understand the real implications of what they choose to say.

There was one time, though, that I managed to turn this on its head. Again, it was another night, another visit to the pub. A chap came over to me at the bar and asked me, 'If you're blind, mate, then how can you tell the time?' This was not intrigue. He had an audience and there was something mocking in his voice.

'Blind or not, I can still tell the time. Why?' I responded, not sure where this was going.

'How can you tell the time if you can't see the clock?'

I couldn't resist. 'Did you ever see the film *Crocodile Dundee*? He could tell the time by looking at the sun and where it was positioned in the sky,' I began. The guy sounded interested, and prompted me to continue. 'Well, I do the same with the moon. Before I came into the pub, I glanced up and noted the position of the moon.'

I had him, hook, line, sinker. 'Go on then, tell the time,' he urged. The pub was noisy and I pretended to scratch my ear, sneakily pressing the button on my speaking watch. It was 10.05pm, it told me. He hadn't noticed.

'It's just after ten. Five past ten,' I said, pretending to think hard so as not to arouse suspicion.

'Bloody hell, mate,' he replied, clearly impressed. 'That's amazing!' He promptly circulated the pub, telling everyone of my amazing feat, while I left with a smile on my face. He didn't seem to notice that being blind, there was no chance I'd be able to see the position of the moon and stars.

For the most part, I would say blindness has turned my life completely upside down. I feel it has robbed me of a perfectly normal life. I've often been left wondering whether I could have made it as a professional sportsperson, or what my life would have been like as a serving soldier. I've stewed over the other things I could have done had I just been allowed to see. For a time, my condition removed ambition. It gave me headaches and heartaches, caused stress and upset.

But as time crept on, and my sight got worse, I tired of feeling lonely and negative, of that constant nag of worry, of bitter regret. I knew I had to change.

And boy, did my life change. I began to look forward to the future, and I can wholeheartedly say that I now live an exciting, fun-filled life. Every day holds a different adventure, and there's always something different to focus on. Using my blindness as motivation, I know it has enhanced my life and I've been prompted to do many, many things that I wouldn't have dreamt of if I'd been sighted.

Blindness has made me realise that life is still for living, regardless of a disability, that disability will not curb my hope for the future. Bring it on!

3

SEPTEMBER 1969 marked my first day at George Salter High School. When I started, it was a new chapter for the school as the fences segregating the girls and boys had come down and it was to become a mixed comprehensive. Today it's an academy and my two youngest daughters go there. I'm still involved, too, but this time as a governor.

On my first day, we were funnelled into the hall and assigned to a house, Harry Potter style. I was put into House H. As had been the case at primary school, I was no great excitement academically, but I settled into a new school routine, made some new friends and retained some old ones, kept out of the way of the older lads and admired the older girls.

But I did look forward to PE lessons and quietly vowed to get on to some of the school teams. I entered the inter-house cross-country competition, an event in which the whole school – from first-years right through to fifth-years – competed. In my first one I came in tenth, which I didn't think was bad for a glasses-wearing 11-year-old. And that made the teachers sit up and take note: I was invited to join the school cross-country team.

I'll always remember 14 May 1970. Firstly, it was Dad's birthday. Secondly, it was the first time I'd be representing the school in athletics at the annual school championships.

CHAPTER 3

I had been picked as first reserve but as I got to school that day, I was told that the boy I was standing in for hadn't turned up. I'd be going to the Hadley Stadium, Smethwick, in his place. Mr Dyson told me that I'd be running the 1,500m. My stomach flipped over and turned itself inside out. I couldn't wait to feel the track, a real athletics track, beneath my Dunlop pumps.

But I had to wait until the end of the day for my event. As I saw the bodies hurtle past me, representing rival schools, my excitement – and my nerves, if I'm honest – grew. I was just a little lad, an unknown little lad in my football shorts and socks, my George Salter running vest and, of course, the glasses. What I would get out of it, I didn't know. I mean, I wanted to win, I knew that much, but I told myself that was stupid – there were kids here that had done this every year, that knew what they were doing. This was my first ever competitive race.

The gun went off for the start. After two strides, I was in the lead. I came round past the stands for the first time and I heard my school pals shouting. They were shouting my name! I can't remember if my face actually grinned, I was probably too busy concentrating, but I was certainly smiling inside. I can remember the race even as I write now: I felt relaxed, but energetic. Three and three-quarter laps of the track. Keep going, keep going. As I could hear my school friends again, they were yelling something more specific. They were trying to tell me something. I glanced back. A lad from another school was literally on my shoulder. Not on your life, mate, I thought. That was enough to shift me up a gear. The bell chimed innocently: one more lap to go. I let my legs go, they seemed to know what to do.

I ran through the finish line. I'd won! I beaten the second-place runner by nearly 200 yards, at a time of five minutes and 13.09 seconds. I'd won! I was the town champion for the 1,500m! The other kids from school gathered round me, thumping me on the back. It turned out I'd also broken the record for the fastest 1,500 metres at that level. I later appeared in the *Sandwell Chronicle*.

'So this is what Olympians felt like!' I thought to myself as I received my certificate. I didn't have the nerve to face the crowd and wave, my arms stretching high over my head, so instead I nodded and smiled, nervously. One day, I told myself, one day it would be for real. But what I was looking forward to most was getting home and telling my dad, especially as it was his birthday.

As I burst in, he was already having his tea. I babbled what I thought was the greatest ever news, a great time, just over five minutes! Dad listened and put down his fork.

'Is that the best time you could do? Couldn't you have run any quicker?' At first I thought he was joking, but I soon realised he was serious. It was not the response I was looking for. Dad, being Dad, never showed any emotion and over the years, I realised it was just his way of making me try, compete, even harder. It certainly had the desired effect: I always thought about him in competitions.

I was the talk of the school the very next day, though, which more than made up for it. Even the older kids came over to congratulate me. I was over the moon. But the best prize was the fact that I was asked to represent the town for both cross-country and the 1,500 metres – great in itself, but the races would take place in the afternoons. I had a get-out-of-lessons free card!

On 24 November 1970 I became 'The Teenager'. I continued to train hard for running. It was something I took seriously, even joining a running club. I just loved it. If I had to go to the shops, I ran; when I went to school, I ran. I used to run every morning, and every afternoon. To slow me down, my friends used to make me carry all their bags. I also loved running because I didn't have to worry about seeing anything in particular. I loved football, but it became a bit of a problem when I had difficulties seeing the ball. Some referees insisted that I took off my glasses to play, despite protestations that I was much better – and safer – when I had them on.

I didn't play for the school football team; I simply wasn't good enough. Out of school, though, I joined a local team, Newtown Rangers. Many of the kids from the estate played for this side and eventually we enlisted some of the lads from school, too, so it wasn't a bad side. We played both Saturday mornings and Sunday afternoons, and our arch rivals, our derby team, were Greets Green United. We had some great clashes. In one particular game, I scored once to take us to a three-all draw. With ten minutes to go I scored another, the winner, with my left foot which, considering I was right-footed, wasn't bad.

There were times, though, when my performance suffered due to my sight. With a dark brown leather ball, black boots and mud-streaked pitches, I had no hope. I began to beg our manager, Bernard Langley, for a white ball, the kind that we're used to seeing today. But back then, they were expensive and I was told that club funds couldn't run to that kind of expense.

Little did I know that he was trying to find a way round it. One Friday night, before training, I called in at his house and he threw a white football at me. 'I thought we couldn't afford a new ball,' I said, ecstatic. It turned out he hadn't bought a new ball – he'd found a special type of paint that could coat leather. I was overjoyed, and couldn't wait to try it at the next day's game. But guess what? The very next day, it flaming well snowed! We still played – it would have taken a hurricane to call off our games – and I simply had to hoof at everything. In the air I had more of a chance and I even nodded one in just before half-time, to make it eight-nil. But I finally had a white ball – and it snowed! I'm sure it could have only happened to me.

It was around this time that I took on a paper round, keen to make some real money after all the years of flogging tat and manure with the other kids on the estate. I was very lucky to get the round where I knew everyone: our street and the two neighbouring. I very much wanted the money, but I hated those early mornings. I'd hear Mom or Dad call me from downstairs and I'd be up, dressed and out the door in two minutes. When I occasionally covered other rounds, if the lads were ill or on holiday, it was a struggle to find the right houses as I couldn't see the door numbers properly. But the weekly tips were a great bonus and the Christmas tips made it all worthwhile. I remember saving specifically for a brand new pair of football boots, as all my previous pairs had been hand-me-downs. They cost six quid. I must have been 13 and my paper round had brought in £5, so Dad, satisfied I'd grafted, stumped up the other pound. I was delighted. Dad helped when he could. He made me a purpose-made pull truck to lessen the load, but my sight still managed to get the better of me – I had many instances of swerving to avoid oncoming cars or tripping and landing in flowerbeds or impaling myself on fences.

It is perhaps no surprise, given my love of running and football, that I was bike mad, back then; in fact, anything with wheels. I had roller skates, a pedal go-kart, hand-me-down bikes. But Christmas 1970 marked the arrival of a brand new bike, an RSW Mark 2 in metallic brown. It had small but chunky wheels, three-speed twist grip, disc brakes, with a large carrying bag on the back, just right for the meals on wheels to Nan's. In a typical turn of events, though, Christmas 1970 was the snowiest Christmas for years and it took forever to clear, meaning I had to wait days to ride my new bike, give it a spin. The last day of snow, though, I was ready to go. 'Not too fast, it's icy,' Dad told me. What does Dad know? I thought to myself, these wheels will be fine. But he was right, of course, and as I turned left at the VG store, the bike and I parted ways, horizontally. Fortunately, there was no damage to the bike, only to me, so there was no reason to mention it to Dad, either.

That bike did some miles with me over the years, and it saw a few towns. It never came on the paper round with me in the morning though; it was too precious for that, it wouldn't have taken all the propping up against fences and the lying down on gravel. That metallic body needed protection.

It was around this time I had my new bombproof glasses. Over the years, I had progressed from the wire-rimmed, Milky Bar Kid glasses, to the hard plastic type – though they weren't hard enough, and broke if you only blew on them. As I told Mom, it had nothing to do with falling off my bike or out of trees; they were just too flimsy for the outgoing, adventurous, clumsy kid! The new glasses were jet black and made from a kind of nylon and they certainly took some breaking – in fact, I never did break them, despite twisting them, sitting on them, and wearing them to play football.

It was also around this time that I joined the Army Cadet Force, the Royal Corps of Transport, based at Carters Green in West Bromwich. From an early age, I had decided that army life appealed: it was active and outdoors, there was a great team spirit, and Dad's achievements during his national service had also impressed on me. I thought that once I left school, I would join the army. I hoped that the cadets would give me a good indication of whether it was for me, and if so, would stand me in good stead for the future. Ian Derby, or 'Dan Derby' as he was nicknamed, lived down our street and joined the cadets, too. For me, the cadets gave me a sense of independence and the courage to act as an individual. It was up to us to make sure our uniforms were clean and pressed, our brasses gleaming, webbing blancoed and boots polished. Surprisingly enough, I also enjoyed the pomp and ceremony that came with cadets, especially the weekend camps: when some 500 cadets marched on parade, it certainly did give you a real sense of pride.

At annual camp in Aldershot we had some great experiences. A regular army camp, us cadets loved to play the regular army lads up something terrible – though my motto was to play them up from a distance, a long distance, because they could be quick and once you were caught, that was it. A few of the cadets were hung upside down from the rafters. As their training had taught them to do, they took no prisoners and gave no mercy.

Despite the discipline, I loved the camps. We would be up at six for a shower before cleaning and tidying the billet, sweeping and mopping, with beds stripped and made up properly for inspection. Our kit would be inspected, too, so it had to be laid out, ready. If the NCOs were feeling lenient in the morning, we were allowed to go to breakfast without redoing the billet but some liked the authority, their power, and could make you do it again and again. I felt, though, that it made us respect and appreciate what we had, and to learn to treat other people and their property better.

The regular soldiers, when we weren't playing them up, took us out on exercise, teaching us to read maps, strip down certain weapons, clean them and put them back together without any nuts and bolts left over. We would be transported in the large army trucks to army locations where we were taught observation skills: taking in the surrounding environment, listening and watching. I could feel my senses heightening, and it didn't matter so much that my sight was poor, my listening could be just as valuable. In fact, there were no medicals in joining the cadets, it was open to all. I was so relieved that I wouldn't be subjected to rigorous eye tests, and prevented from doing the things I really wanted to do.

The best part of all was slapping on the camouflage cream, sticking branches to our hats and then running around like lunatics, acting out a battle scene and shooting rifles with a magazine of blank rounds; in other words, behaving like kids in the most dreamlike scenario ever – with the real equipment and uniform!

I remember firing live for the first time. At Cannock's firing range, I shot a 303 Lee-Enfield rifle in a lying position from both 100 and 200 yards. It was an absolute thrill, being able to control that noise and power. Now I think it's hilarious: there

I was, shooting live rounds at a target I could barely see! There was always an adult with us, giving instructions, so, thankfully, the only thing I could seriously hurt was my own shoulder if I didn't hold the weapon properly.

During another weekend camp on Cannock Chase, we took part in reconnaissance and field manoeuvres. There were around 200 cadets in total and a dozen of us, Dan and I included, were picked out to play the enemy. The aim was for the enemy dozen to find positions on Cannock Chase, get hideouts ready for night time and occasionally fire blanks so the rest of the squadron would be able to plot where we were hiding. It seemed like we had it easy: we found a hill which was covered in bushes and shrubbery, perfect for concealing us from our attackers and the wind which we had noticed was picking up, chilling our skin beneath our many layers of stiff uniform. We turned in for dinner and waited for nightfall, knowing that we'd be making our way back in the dark. Thankfully, Dan knew how poor my sight was, especially in the dark, and he knew it'd be his job to guide us back to our shelter.

As the wind subsided, the rain came. Unfortunately, our natural canopy didn't do much for rain protection and we were soon soaked through. The little hollow we had so keenly taken began to fill up with water and before long we were sitting in water. We kept firing at random, but we couldn't hear any attackers. We sat in miserable silence as the ice-cold water leaked down our faces, our hands numb but still able to reach for the trigger. 'Is this what war would really be like?' I wondered. If so, it didn't seem particularly dangerous. Unless hypothermia and gangrene took hold. Even the sounds of our gunfire seemed mute, wet and despondent.

'What the hell are you two still doing here?' barked a voice. We jumped out of our sodden skins, our arses sploshing in surprise. We turned round, guns cocked. It was the adult sergeant. 'It's nearly midnight, the others returned to barracks over an hour ago!'

The fact that they hadn't found us, I found myself thinking, was surely testament to our skill in hiding? I kept my thoughts to myself as we were marched back to barracks, ordered to shower before bed.

Not all of my sporting or outdoor activities gave me pleasure. In fact, many gave me enormous pain, but it was never quite enough to put me off trying something. Like the time I tried ice skating. A few of the lads from my street and I headed to Silver Blades in Bearwood and eagerly we pulled on our ice skating boots and hobbled down to the ice. None of us had been before, but we weren't intimidated – we were just keen to join the speeding mass of bodies, elegantly circling the ice. It looked easy! But as soon as I took a step, I was on my bum. I hadn't realised how cold and wet it was – it was real ice! Undeterred, I stood up again, but before I'd even moved, I was down again. I'd heard the myths of novice ice skaters having their fingers chopped off by passing blades so I knew to keep my fingers tucked in when I went down, but I was cursing not having brought gloves. A man came over and helped me up, telling me to tighten the boots as much as I could and then have another go. It worked! I thanked him, pleased I could finally stand. My friends and I began to see who could stand for the longest.

Our perseverance and communal coaxing began to pay off and after an hour, we were able to shuffle and slide around the rink. We were slow and ungainly. There were the inevitable crashes into other skaters and the barriers around the rink until we perfected the art of turning and stopping, but soon we were circling with the others.

By dinner time we were like foals on our feet – steadier and keen to explore and experiment. All skaters were called off and the rink was raked before experienced skaters took to the rink to be put through their paces, and show us how it was done. By the time it was over and we were allowed back on to the ice, it had played to our collective ego and boosted our confidence. Though the rink was packed full of enthusiasts, we found that we could dodge and weave, and I started to be able to get up a good head of speed. Round and round I went, seemingly getting better and better. Then I was challenged to a race – one of the lads was just as cocky as me, and we were always challenging each other to something. It was the third lap that caused the trouble. I was in the clear lead. I wasn't Robin Cousins, or anything, but I was finding my feet and I was winning, I was glides ahead of him. Suddenly, though, I tripped. Well, at least I thought I had. I was flying through the air, catapulting face first across the ice, landing on my chest with a heavy thud and sliding like a sledge when my head hit the barrier. Stopped.

As I tried to piece together what had happened, ignoring the throb in my head and the bruise on my chest, a woman came over and began to berate me for interrupting her lessons. 'What are you doing?' she kept saying. I had no idea.

Then laughter. My friends were killing themselves, bent double, their laughs amplified by the space and the hard surface from which I was desperately trying to pick myself, hand on head, legs shaking.

'Did you not see the rope?' she asked. I didn't know why she had asked me that; I couldn't see a rope even now. They pointed and as I squinted, I made out the silhouette of a thin rope lying across the rink like a dead snake. It had been set up to section off a portion of the rink for the skating instructor's lessons. I staggered away and vowed never to ice skate again. I would stick to wheels from now on.

As you progress through secondary school, from nowhere, clothes suddenly become important, hair is shaven back or gelled or styled and girls seem to feature more on the agenda. We became a bit more urban, I suppose, hanging around town, rather than the fields in which we'd mucked about as kids. But it was a strange time: I wasn't sure if I was a kid or adult, whether I was friends with my parents or governed by them. I think my parents wondered the same. I'll never forget the time when, in front of my mates, I pretended to square up to Dad, trying to be jack-the-lad.

'Go on then, put one on my chin,' I said.

He did. One minute I was standing by the hall door; the next, I was lying against the front door, 12 feet away, nursing my chin. Dad laughed and asked if I wanted another one.

In late 1973, I ran my last cross-country race for the town. It wasn't that my running wasn't good enough, or my enthusiasm was waning. No, far from it. It was simply the fact that my eyesight was deteriorating rapidly and this last race, in Rugeley, Cannock way, proved the turning point. It was a cold, dry autumn day, perfect cross-country conditions, and for the first few miles, I was doing well and in tenth place. We had been warned prior to the race that the course would take in agricultural land and we were to keep to the perimeters of the fields, but of course, as soon as we were unsupervised, cutting corners to shave off time was commonplace. Fine, until we hit the cabbage field.

The front-runners had cut across the cabbages, the pummelling of their feet squashing them into the ground so that subsequent runners would find it easier – but only just. It was like running over footballs, consequently hard work on the legs and ankles. As one field was completed, the course took us through an opening in the hedgerow marked by two upright posts. The low autumnal sun was bright, restricting my vision even more than usual and though I spotted the upright posts, I hadn't noticed the bar over the top, a bit like a crossbar. I ran clean into it at speed, knocking myself out in the process. When I came round, there was no camaraderie. It was a case of picking myself up, dusting myself down and perching those loyal glasses back on my nose and carrying on. I made it to the finish line in 29th place and vowed that would be my last for the town.

I didn't tell anyone that was the reason, though. How could I? I didn't want to admit the problem to myself, but I had done and that was enough. With a sick feeling in my stomach, I began to prepare myself for what I had been told was coming, but what I desperately hoped was not. Everything I loved to do, everything I was good at, chiefly sport and being active outdoors, was going to be taken away from me.

So I decided to leave Newtown Rangers, too. The team was moving to play in an over-16s league of which I would have loved to have been a part: the team played together well, and I had some great friends there, not to mention some gentle rivalries. But I had noticed that it was becoming increasingly difficult for me to see the ball and there were only so many excuses I could give. I was becoming a liability, letting the side down. I told the rest of the team that I had commitments elsewhere, other teams and other sports, and hoped that with less than 12 months at school anyway, there was little chance I'd see them regularly so it seemed sensible to creep away, nursing my disappointment internally.

Still, there were some things I wasn't going to miss, crap eyesight or not. I'd never been abroad without a relative and I'd never been skiing, so naturally, when the chance of a school ski trip came up, I begged and pleaded Mom to let me go. The pleading paid off and in my final year at school, me and a few from my year, plus kids from five or six other schools, flew from Birmingham to Munich then took the coach to Austria. It was a long old journey, but as fifth-formers, we had the privilege of gaining an extra day for only £1, for some reason – what a bonus! I wish I could get the same deal these days!

When we arrived at the hotel, we found that we weren't the only British school kids enjoying a ski trip and after being allotted our bedrooms, we decided to introduce ourselves to the other guests. Immediately my name changed again. How brazen they were! They had no idea who I was, where I was from, what I was doing, but they knew I wore glasses and that was enough, 'Hello, four-eyes!' I did make the point that my name was Dave but it was no use. I shrugged it off easy enough.

I supposed it was like being ginger; just one of those things that kids would always pick on.

The early starts didn't bother us; it was exciting and we were desperate to get out on the slopes and get the skiing under way. The slopes we were due to learn on were right opposite the hotel but we were told that there hadn't been as much snowfall there as normal – meaning we would have to be transported every day up to the location of the Olympic slalom. Another bonus, I grinned to myself. This was working out to be quite the coup. Though the land was farmed in the summer, by winter it was an impressive sports playing field, with great mountains I was itching to sample. It took my eyes time to adjust, all that gleaming white and sparkle with little contrast, but once I was taken to the summit, the views were fantastic: mountains encased the whole place, with traditional ski lodges dotted about, linked by ski lifts and pulleys. Although very sunny, it was quite cold. It felt strange to be both coating my body in layers of clothing and sun block. Although guess who sat on his sunglasses on the very first afternoon and broke them? Yes, you guessed it.

On the first morning, we learnt how to put on the skis, then how to stand up. It was a damned sight easier than getting started with ice skating – until we were coached in the art of the 'snowplough', turning toes in and knocking knees so that we could stop when we wanted. Gently I went down the slope. I wasn't stopping yet. But I persevered: a few metres sliding down, side-stepping back up, then trying again. It took me a few attempts to get it right. In fact, all morning, myself and the rest of my class practised going up and down, up and down. By lunchtime, though, we were making headway and most of us could move downward, sliding along the slope without falling over and stopping when required. We were proud of ourselves and our instructor decided then was a good time for a breather.

After lunch, we found we had some time to kill – kill nearly being the operative word. Four of us thought we'd put our newfound skills to the test: going up on the ski lift and coming down on what we were told were the nursery slopes. Gleefully, we realised that there wasn't an instructor or teacher in sight, from whom to ask permission or to stop us either, so in for a penny, in for a pound… we went for it.

We had to buy a ticket to use the ski pulley so we joined the queue. When our turn arrived, we paired off and held both sides of what I can only describe as a stick attached to a rope. As we held on, it began to pull us up the mountainside. Just as we reached the peak, only 100 yards or so upwards, we learnt from the other skiers ahead of us that we should let go. As I approached the top, though, I should have realised it was never going to be plain sailing. I misjudged my footing, still alien in these alarming, rigid clown boots, and slipped, landing on my front.

I then had to crawl the last little rise, over sheer ice, which took a good ten minutes, much to the annoyance of the lift operator and the other skiers. Still, I got there eventually and the four of us lined up at the top, side-by-side, ready to descend together. It looked scarily steep, I admitted to myself, but it was only a nursery slope. It was better that my nerves had kicked in, it was just human nature. But if this was a nursery slope, I dreaded to think what my first descent down a proper slope would feel like.

Off we went. I hadn't travelled for more than six feet when my feet left the slope, my body taking the brunt as I hurtled ungracefully downhill. In a desperate bid to save myself, my arms went outwards, my poles skywards, so that I took the other three with me. All I remember were arms, legs, boots, poles, arms, legs, boots, poles on repeat until we stopped. The bottom. It wasn't long before we received a dressing down, either, firstly by an Austrian ski instructor and then from our teachers, who were quick to join in on seeing the mêlée.

'You are quite lucky to be alive,' the Austrian said, straight to the point. 'What do you think you were doing?'

'We just thought we'd try out the nursery slopes,' one of us replied, the voice small.

The teachers were quick to point out our major mistake. My gut feeling had been right: this wasn't the nursery slope; it was far too steep for that. The nursery slope started at the other side of the mountain and gently sidled off for a mile. We had gone down the best part of the mountain. Lady Luck had been with the four of us that day. We didn't even feel like laughing it off.

But learning a very hard, humiliating lesson on the first day pulled us into line and for the next couple of days we knuckled down to learn to ski properly. We didn't progress on to the (real!) nursery slopes until about three days in, by which time we had finally finessed the basics. Although I did feel for one of the younger kids… it could have been me, though I was incredibly relieved it wasn't. On the second morning, just as he was becoming accustomed to the ski pulley, he slipped where I had and broke his arm. I'm certain there's a serious injury every school ski trip, it has to be a rite of passage.

My fearlessness and sense of adventure meant that skiing and I got on very well. I was enjoying myself tremendously. That's not to say I was any good, it wasn't something which came naturally to me, but I loved the feeling of being able to glide gently around the course, the fuzzy adrenalin rush which hit as I slid down hills and through ravines. But there's always a case of falling off the horse, and one morning I managed to hit the top rail of a fence as I was racing one of the others back to the log cabin. The fence had been hidden by the snowfall, buried right past the top rail. I'm sure anyone with better eyesight would have noticed the difference in shapes, but I didn't. My skis stopped suddenly and I was catapulted facewards into the snow. My opponent took his opportunity and left me, the snow already melting on my salopettes as I picked myself back up. That was just the challenge I needed and I flew after him, catching him up just before the last hurdle – a hill followed by a bridge. We had been told that in summer,

CHAPTER 3

the bridge crossed a small stream and gully, but covered in snow and not spotting the bridge correctly could mean a quick, snowy descent into the icy gully. It seemed that Lady Luck was with me again, as he misjudged the bridge entirely and fell into the snow bed. And me? I skied right past.

By the end of the week, we were allowed to give the slalom route a go. My goodness, I came down there with a good head of steam! Mind, not quite like the experts, as they came past us like we were standing still. On the final day, we were taken in to Innsbruck for present shopping before one final spell on the slopes. However, by the time we got back from Innsbruck, the snow had begun to come down so thick and heavy that we had to settle indoors for our final afternoon, visibility had become so poor. Only then did we realise how lucky we had been with the weather all week, as we bid an internal goodbye to the slopes and boarded the coach for home.

It was such a long journey home that we heard the same records over and over again. I will never think of 'The Air That I Breathe' by The Hollies without the associated stink of a coachload of cooped-up teenagers and the dazzling white of snow and ice. It made number two in the charts in 1974 and it seemed to be on the radio every five minutes.

February half-term was over and we were back at school. The remainder of the year and of my time at school seemed to fly by. Though I was sitting eight O Levels, it was sport that continued to be my focus and I won the West Bromwich Schools 1,500m track event for the fifth year, leaving school as defending champion – although even that race wasn't without incident. One of the lads, who I had partnered over the previous season in the town athletics team, came screaming past me on lap three. I wondered what was going on and kept up with him, following yards behind. As we came to the last lap and the bell, I managed to eke past him and ran to victory. When I approached him afterwards, he told me that he had misjudged the amount of laps and had presumed on passing me that it was the final circuit. I commiserated with him, but secretly I was pleased – it had spurred me on to my benefit.

Then I was forced to swallow my pride and stick to my promises in our final inter-house cross-country. Another lad, Suresh Patel, and I, decided that for the final race we would come in together. It seemed a nice thing to do, to commemorate our time as running partners. But half a mile from the finish Suresh faltered, allowing a lad from the year below to overtake. 'Take him, Dave, go on, take him,' Suresh urged. Promises are promises, though, and I refused. I'd stick by him to the finish, coming in an equal second and taking a great deal of ribbing in the process.

In early July, once all O Level exams were finished, the school held its first inter-house athletics competition, marking out a running track which didn't have the conventional circumference of 400 metres but 200 metres, meaning we had to run twice as many laps. The track events were held over two days: the first for sprints and relays, the second the long distance. By then I'd specialised in long distance, and was the school cross-country champion, so I cheered on the sprinters. We were delighted when our house, House H, won the 100m relay final – a spectacular way to finish! But the race I was most looking forward to was the 1,500m on the second day. I felt I needed to redeem myself. Though it was my first ever athletics event at school, and my first 1,500m run at George Salter, it also turned out to be my last ever competitive run.

As we stood on the line for the last race of the day, there were a few jibes, a few mutterings for my scalp. But there was no way I was promising to run with anyone on this one; I was looking out for myself.

The gun sounded.

As is to be expected, too many went off too quickly, and I sat back in sixth place. I waited until lap six to make my move. Slowly I upped my pace, taking the lead and enjoying the pleasure of overtaking the lad from the year below who had beaten me at the cross-country. I won by some 100 metres and I do believe there was quite a smile on my face as I crossed the finish line.

Back in the 1970s, school-leavers didn't have the proms and balls that kids do today. Our last week of formal, compulsory education was eventful in its own way: there was the obligatory exchange of flour and eggs, blazers ripped and ruined, a few of the teachers' cars decorated in one way or another, plenty of promises to keep in touch. There were some heading off to further education with university in mind, but I knew that wasn't for me. I didn't have the inclination. Providing I got the O Level results I needed, I already had a job lined up, but I was still quietly holding out for the armed forces – after all, nobody had said no yet!

I fully realise that many can't wait to be shot of school, to be out there with independence and the chance to make money. But I felt sad that it was coming to an end. Although sport had always been my focus, I couldn't deny that I'd learnt a great deal at school that I never would have elsewhere. On a social level, too, I'd met and mixed with kids with different backgrounds to me, from other parts of the town and other cultures; I'd gained confidence and hopefully developed a bit of common sense, too. And, hilariously, I'd become known as a swot or a teacher's pet because I always sat at the front of the class – and all because I couldn't see the flaming blackboard! I thought I had disguised my problem very well, to the point that many didn't know the severity of my poor eyesight. At the time, that was what I set out to do: I wanted to be accepted as a normal kid in a normal world. I didn't want extra time in exams or large-print textbooks. I wanted to squint and get on with it.

THE summer between finishing school in July and starting full-time employment in September 1974 was strange. I played out with my friends on the estate, playing football, getting into the kinds of trouble I suppose we always had, but there was the excitement I felt for impending independence and freedom, but also a kind of nostalgia for the days that I knew wouldn't come again. It was a definite chapter, closed for good.

So when I walked through the gates of Smith Corona Marchant, on the Birmingham Road, West Bromwich, I was nervous, excited, enthusiastic… in many senses I felt grown up – I had found the job myself; Mom hadn't even known I'd got the interview – but then I reminded myself of the bag of sand-wiches, made by Mom of course, and the brand new Tootal tie and the glasses and I felt like an imposter. The security guard pointed me in the direction of the personnel department where I was treated to a plethora of forms to complete and then I was introduced to the busy factory. That was an experience. The noise was tremendous, with machines clattering and voices shouting above the din. Radio 1 filled the factory with music and there was a metallic smell of sweat and machinery in the air.

Yes, this was pretty different from school. My first job, as a commercial trainee, had begun. But, much like beginning school, I earned a different name from the off: some jokers in the office took a shine to my thick black glasses and nicknamed me 'Joe 90'. Eventually the 90 was dropped and I was known throughout my entire career at SCM as 'Joe'. If somebody new or official asked after Dave, my colleagues had to be reminded. 'Dave? Dave who? Oh, you mean Joe!'

Commercial trainee was a pretty loose title, meaning I was to be trained in most office environments: cost accounts, financial accounts, the purchasing department (which actually became a favourite of mine), wages, stock control... in fact, any office duties I would be instructed in, with day release at college and hopefully some qualifications at the end of it. It seemed like a good plan, and the thrill of earning my own money soon kicked in.

In 1974 I was earning the princely sum of £11.49 a week. Rich or what? I felt like it. After paying Mom a fiver a week for bed and board, I managed to save the rest of it for going out, which I did practically every single night. I also managed to put aside a small sum to treat myself to a new bike. During the day I hadn't noticed much deterioration in my eyesight; it was in the evening and night time when the lack of light merged everything into one impenetrable mush that gave me real difficulty. So, as long as I didn't cycle at night, I reasoned, then a new bike would be fine.

I took myself off to the little bike shop in Great Bridge and invested in a brand new ten-speed racer. Admittedly it was the colours that attracted me – blue, purple, yellow – and with ten gears, it was like owning a Rolls-Royce. Boy, I could get some speed up! Immediately I began to ride to work on it, but as soon as I experienced the muddy, wet morning commute, I vetoed the idea.

I decided to take my first long ride on it during my first day of holiday from my new job. Uncle Gill and Auntie Chris had recently moved to Sedgley so I thought it was time I paid them a visit.

As anyone who knows Sedgley can testify, Sedgley Hill is long, steep and perfect for adrenalin junkies like me. I hit the hill and changed to tenth gear, flying downwards with the wind tearing at my ears. It was one of those unusual moments: the traffic lights, two sets, were both on green and I shot through, a big grin on my face as I tasted the speed of my brand new bike. I wondered whether I should carry on to Dudley Port, or turn left, taking a short cut into Great Bridge. I didn't have much time to wonder though, and the short cut won. I took the corner beautifully, still moving along at a fair lick, instinctively ducking my head under the low bridge even though it was miles above me. Up ahead, I saw a lady on the pavement, her hands weighed down with bags of shopping. She seemed to look directly at me, notice the speed at which I was travelling, and still decide to cross. I couldn't stop, I couldn't swerve. It was too quick. Thud.

Speed stopped. Everything seemed to happen in slow motion. The woman and her shopping went every which way, the bike halted, dead. I was thrown straight over the handlebars but I don't remember the impact. The next thing I remember was coming round, propped up against a fence. Somebody was asking if I was okay. There were potatoes and cabbage leaves strewn across the road. The old lady seemed to be fine physically, but she was furious, loudly picking through the vegetables and assessing each one before putting them back in her bag. She was terrified that the mirror she had just bought was broken, but she didn't dare open the box to check.

Instead, she accused me, berated me for not looking where I was going. Two passers-by contradicted her; they had seen the whole thing and she had stepped into my path. She hadn't been looking, or she hadn't realised at what speed I would be coming through. I was in a daze as this noise continued, the traffic building up behind us, some stopping and getting out of their cars, others having enough and pulling around to avoid the potatoes and cabbage leaves. Then, my luck. Her husband happened to come round the corner, hitting a run when he saw his dear wife was in the midst of the carnage, finger pointing and bags split. Despite the protestations of my hero passers-by, he grabbed hold of me and unceremoniously marched me right round the corner to the police station. I had to carry the bike, the forks bent right back into the frame. My pride and joy.

The police started doing their job, taking statements. One copper took me outside and asked if I was all right, telling me to buy the lady a new pair of tights and everything would be fine. I didn't tell him that I was more worried about facing my dad. Still, one consolation? My glasses were intact. Sadly, the bike was ruined. The frame was beyond repair so I had to order a new one that took ten weeks to arrive and cost me £50. After that, it never seemed the same and I ended up selling it for £25, thinking that had better mark the end of my cycling career.

My next big investment was the decision to have new glasses – yes, the old faithful were to go into retirement. That seemingly indestructible pair, in all its thick black nylon glory, had been on my face since I was 13. They'd seen some life – some action – I can tell you. I think it was more a case of vanity, than anything. I was coming up to 17 and I thought it was about time the specs, with their 3/8 inch-thick lenses and their look of National Health, were replaced. I'm sure they had made me look like Mr Magoo. Instead, I treated myself to some with gold rims. I wanted to look the part – hey, maybe they would even help pull the ladies! But if my colleagues noticed the difference, it didn't help me shake off the nickname – I was still Joe to them.

That Christmas, two of my friends from the street, Geoff Harvey and Keith Perry, or 'Pez', suggested we spend Christmas in Blackpool. Mom wasn't particularly happy, but I was enjoying my newfound freedom and this seemed like a good plan to me. Keith's mom, Dos, was a widow and she took herself off each Christmas with a group of friends. Keith suggested we join them, and we did – three youths and the rest old codgers!

We arrived at the hotel on Christmas Eve and got straight on the beer. Being the youngest, Keith's mom had put us in the attic room so we hurriedly plonked our cases on each bed to claim it, then headed back to the bar for beer and dancing. By the time we took ourselves off to bed, we realised that there was no bed linen, just a scratchy duvet and lumpy pillow.

'Sod it,' I said to the others, getting undressed and diving beneath the quilt. But it was itchy and uncomfortable. There was no chance of sleep without sheets and a duvet cover.

'Come on,' I said to Geoff and Keith, 'let's go and find the laundry room.'

Why we then decided to go downstairs as we were – in nothing but our y-fronts – rather than get dressed again probably had something to do with the amount of beer we'd put away since arrival. We tiptoed downstairs, the bar still noisy with drinkers, but Geoff nudged me and I slid down the banister like Mary Poppins, landing spread-eagled on the floor in my undies. As I scrambled to get up, the door opened and out poured the widows. They all shouted and made a grab and I was up those stairs three at a time. They were like animals, laughing and chasing, and the three of us were back in the safety of our room in a flash. I got my sheets eventually, but it took some bartering!

Christmas morning in Blackpool was certainly different to what I was used to. Blackpool itself was different, too. The Pleasure Beach wasn't open… no sun either, but that didn't matter. Everyone around the place seemed genuinely full of Christmas spirit and the other guests at the hotel were friendly and talkative. The bluster of the seafront had the welcome effect of blowing away our hangovers on Christmas morning, before the hotel provided Christmas dinner and the obligatory post-dinner doze in front of the telly, *The Wizard Of Oz*, if my memory serves me correctly.

The festivities continued in the evening, and Christmas night saw the airing of my brand new suit, made to measure from Burton in Great Bridge, courtesy of Mom and Dad. It was dark brown pinstripe and I wore it with a crisp white shirt and Tootal tie. I thought I looked the business, and I was ready to hit the town. We decided we would go out and find a club, coming back to the hotel for last drinks. We had been recommended the Hotels and Apartments Club so in we went. It was teeming, being one of the only places open on Christmas night, but it wasn't quite what we expected. We'd anticipated a band or a disco, but this place was in the middle of hosting bingo. Still, they served a decent pint and we stayed, much to the dismay of the punters. They were taking it so seriously and our noisy laughter wasn't what they had in mind.

Boxing Day night was to be fancy dress.

'No way, not a chance,' Geoff said, taking himself off for a pint. Keith and I threw ourselves into it, though. The merry widows had decided we would be the brassiest pair of Blackpool tarts they had ever seen, and got to work: short skirts, tights and even make-up. They made one big mistake though – they removed my glasses!

After a few pints, the fancy dress was judged by the hotel proprietor and neither of us won. Then the conga started, gaining momentum and growing followers as it wove out of the hotel and into the hotel next door. I simply clung on to whoever it was in front of me as we traipsed up one side of the road, crossed over and down the other, going up through lounges, kitchens, across gardens and driveways, in and out of bedrooms.

But, as it started, it had to end and each participant discreetly made their own way back to their relevant hotel until I was standing by myself, alone. I hadn't a clue where I was, the path our conga line had trodden confused and convoluted. It felt like Hansel and Gretel, but without the breadcrumbs. And the worst thing? I hadn't a clue of the name of our hotel. I hadn't remembered seeing a sign, and it wasn't posh enough to have its name emblazoned across dressing gowns or hotel stationery. I stood there, wondering what to do, all the bodies passing me by in a blur. It was cold in my short skirt and my toes were murdering from the heels. I could understand why women wore tights in the winter, though I knew I'd definitely be sticking to trousers in the future. It was freezing. Thankfully, after a while, Pez's mom, Dos, had realised I was missing and had come to look for me. I welcomed the familiar warmth of that hotel when I arrived back.

As 1974 came to a close I couldn't help but reflect back on what an important, prominent year it had been, perhaps one of the most pivotal of my life. I'd left school and started work. There were still two major ambitions, though, that I wasn't sure if I'd have to give up. I decided that, in the early part of 1975, I'd tackle them once and for all.

The first was learning to drive. I'd always said that as soon as I'd passed my test, I'd buy a brand new car to share with my dad. Dad had an allotment and often on a Sunday, we'd go along with him to help maintain it, dig it over. He had a black van and when I was up there, he'd allow me to drive it along the dirt track, probably all of 200 yards. One time, one of the lads asked me if I could read the number plate of a parked-up car in front. I told him no and Dad was astounded. He later spoke to a driving instructor who confirmed that I'd never hold a driving licence. When Dad relayed the information back to me, I had to accept it as fact. There was no point pursuing it.

Still, it hasn't ever really stopped me from having a few goes, here and there. One time is probably best forgotten, but I'm going to tell it anyway. One of my old customers, John Maloney, became a good friend and drinking partner. He and I met in the pub one night after work and before we knew it, 1am had arrived and Baz, the gaffer, was rocking on his heels. Time to go.

'Will you be all right to drive?' I asked John.

'No, I'm legless.'

CHAPTER 4

'Shall I drive then?' I asked, wondering what the answer might be. To my astonishment, he was delighted and handed me the keys.

I began to wonder how far I could take this.

John's van was sitting outside. I found my way to the driver's seat and climbed in. Still nothing.

'Where do I put these?' I rattled the keys.

'In the ignition,' John gruffly replied, irritated.

'Where's the ignition?'

John didn't seem surprised at my questions, just annoyed. He had got to that point of a drinking evening where his focus was on one thing: bed. I put in the keys, turned. The engine came to life.

'Which way?' I asked.

John told me to reverse out, then to follow the white lines. What bloody white lines? I giggled to myself. He told me to go left so I did but soon we bumped and buffeted. We were on the pavement.

'STOP!' John cried suddenly, as though his senses were returning. 'Get out!'

'But I thought you were legless?'

'I'm sober now!' he said, fumbling frantically for the lever and bounding out of the passenger seat.

The following night, we thought we would make amends and went back to the pub.

'But I'm driving back,' John said, sternly. It was far more sedate that night, with John sticking firmly to the shandy. Later, like a reprimanded child, I quietly sat in the passenger seat in the same spot we had parked in the night before. John reversed straight into a lamppost, taking out the side of his van in the process.

Deb will happily swap seats with me and let me get behind the wheel, providing we're on private ground. We went to Borth once, Deb and I, and Deb took us out in the car along the beach. It was a red Peugeot we had back then, quite a big

69

car, and I enjoyed feeling the power of the car beneath my hands and feet.

'Okay, so the sea is getting closer now so I'd stop, reverse and pull yourself round,' she said. I did as I was told. But there was no reversing to be had. The car was trying its hardest, I could hear the wheels spinning obediently, but we were stuck. The sand was too wet. We were sinking. I tried again. Rrrrrmmm-rrrrmmmm. Again. Rrrrrm-rrrrrmmmm. Nothing.

'The tide's coming in, Dave, get out and I'll have a go,' Deb said, sounding more nervous than I'd have liked.

Deb tried, too.

'You've gone too hard, Dave, you've dug us in,' she said loudly over the whirr of the wheels. We were going nowhere.

I had no other ideas. I opened the door and ran to the front of the car, groping for the number plate then beneath, the underside of the bonnet. I bent my knees, gritted my teeth and heaved. It worked.

The adrenalin, and regular weight training, meant I managed to shift the car to the side, just enough to feel the traction on firmer, new sand. Deb, gentler, soothed the car into acceleration and slowly but surely, away we went.

Thankfully, driving doesn't always end in such difficulties. On 10 December 1994, just after my 37th birthday, Deb arranged for me to drive a car at Brands Hatch. What a treat! When we arrived, we were ushered into the outbuildings near a practice track, somewhere that's not used for official racing, and I was introduced to the car – dual control, of course, but unfortunately I can't remember the make. It was impressive, whatever it was.

'Right, I understand you want to drive a car,' the instructor said, to the side of me, 'and you want to drive it as fast as you can?'

'Yep,' I replied. I was already grinning.

'Well, on this track, we're only permitted to do 70 miles per hour, but you're going to be in control.'

He drove us on to the official racetrack and we swapped places. Of course, he knew I was blind, but there were no real questions asked. Deb had obviously explained that I could actually drive, that I knew how to.

We started up and I put my foot to the floor. The instructor kept his guidance to a minimum, just 'a little bit to the left, a little bit to the right.' It was fantastic. We took on the famous Graham Hill Bend and the instructor told me to wind down the window so I could feel the pull of the air, the full experience. It felt incredibly fast. Once we pulled over, he whispered, 'We actually got up to 93 miles per hour then, but I can only put 70 on your certificate.' I couldn't believe it! I'd driven at over 90 miles per hour!

Towards the end of the allotted hour, the instructor pulled me over and explained there was a row of traffic cones ahead and he would try and guide me through. We made it through no problem, and then we tried it in reverse. This wasn't quite as easy, and one cone succumbed to my wheels, but it wasn't bad, considering.

Once the hour was up, we swapped seats and the instructor drove us back to the outbuildings – well, he did once he'd overcome his little problem.

'Blimey,' he said, as the car stuttered and sighed. He restarted as quickly as he could. 'I'm the instructor with the blind chap and I stall the car!' It was pretty funny. I imagined his face reddening by the second.

Then I learned that Deb had also booked me a few laps in a Lotus, a proper racing car. I wouldn't be allowed to drive, but I could enjoy the ride as a passenger with a professional driver at the wheel.

'We've got no speedos in these,' the driver explained, 'but I do know that we'll be touching 160 miles per hour.' He was very matter of fact. Sitting in the back, I could feel the full force of it, the pull and the sway. Those three laps flashed by in just a few minutes. It was incredible.

Another birthday treat – this time the big 4-0 – saw me fulfil an ultimate ambition. When Dad did his national service, he was a tank driver, so I suppose I've always had a bit of a thing for tanks, wondering how and what it would be like to be in charge of such a monstrous piece of metal. When I was in the army cadets, we had a trip to the tank museum in Bovington, Dorset, and I had sought out the two types of tank that Dad would have driven. I suppose I'd mentioned to Deb, over the years, that I'd really like to get those tanks moving, to experience what Dad had.

But when Deb told me that my 40th birthday would be spent in Scotland, I had no idea why. I certainly didn't think it was anything to do with tanks. She told me I'd find out when we got there – which was particularly intriguing, as we had to get through an eight-hour drive to reach our destination, as it was just outside Aberdeen in Banchory. And lo and behold – the owner of the rather plush hotel we stopped at only happened to be a very enthusiastic supporter of Guide Dogs for the Blind! I asked her where I could spend Peter, or let him go to the toilet. She knew exactly what I meant.

'You can spend Peter wherever you like; on my lawn or in my flowerbeds, we can clean it up,' she said.

But still I had no idea where Deb was taking me. We rose early on the Saturday morning and set off. With the passenger window open, all I could hear was the lowing of cattle and the rattly vibrations of the sheep. We were truly in the middle of nowhere.

'If you've brought me all the way up here to milk a cow, there's going to be problems!' I said to Deb as another cow boomed from the roadside. Deb said nothing.

I thought I'd perhaps hit the nail on the head when we pulled up in a farmyard. I could hear the hens scratching and clucking, and there were more cows shifting from foot to foot, stamping and sighing. 'What's going on?' But Deb still wouldn't let a thing slip.

72

CHAPTER 4

The air changed as we ducked into a barn. There was a fire roaring and we were greeted with mugs of coffee.

'You haven't got a clue what you're doing, have you?' a cheerful Scot piped up, delighted at my puzzled expression.

'No, but we're going to have words if I'm milking cows,' I said again. He laughed.

He took my hand and placed it on cool, substantial metal. 'Do you know what this is?'

I imagined a John Deere tractor, racing green with huge, earth-clogged wheels.

He moved my hand. 'Try this. What's that?'

My heart stopped.

'It's a gun barrel! It's a tank!'

It was. It was a tank.

I climbed in and clamped earphones to the sides of my head, and Deb jumped in to the back. The cheerful Scot accompanied us and he told me to do exactly as he said. I vowed I would. And off we went! I pulled and pushed levers, prodded buttons, and the tank went up and down, flattening everything in its stride. I only realised its capabilities when I swapped places and took a seat in the back.

'I'll now take you where you've just been,' he said.

Suddenly, the tank thrust me upwards, then forced me back down. There were times when I lurched up vertically; others when I was thrown to the side. I could feel every peak and trough, as though we were climbing in and out of multiple crevasses.

My stomach flipped and twirled. In the front, I hadn't felt anything like it, as the driver cabin moved with the tank, holding its position. Deb took a turn, and took us across the same course. I couldn't quite believe the sensation, what the tank could tackle. At the end of the day, the cheerful Scot told me that it had been a pleasure to show me the ropes. I'd listened to what he had said, which seemed to have been an unusual thing.

'Most sighted people do whatever they like, and we soon end up in a ditch or halfway down a cliff.'

I told him that I didn't have much choice but to follow his instructions exactly and he laughed. It had been a wonderful experience, and much better than milking a cow. I think I gave Deb a massive kiss.

Despite all that experience, I will never own my own driving licence. The subject did allow me to play a trick on a student researcher at the Birmingham Eye Hospital, though. It was around 1975 or 76 that I began taking part in experiments and research, in a bid to help future generations. One particular day, a student researcher began to ask me questions about my eyes, my sight and my experience of Retinitis Pigmentosa. 'Have you ever held a driving licence?' she asked. She thought it was one of the questions she had to ask; daft, when the answer was blindingly – excuse the pun – obvious. I thought I'd shake it up a little.

'Yes,' I replied.

'You have?' The intonation of her voice was hilarious. She was shocked; there were no two ways about it.

'Oh yes. My dad's once, when he was changing his jacket!' Needless to say, she wasn't amused.

My second major career ambition, of joining the army, was also teetering on the brink. My old friend Dan Derby had gone into the army at 16, as a junior leader. I didn't want to follow suit, I wanted to go in as a regular, at 18. While I was working at Smith Corona, I went up to the army careers office at Carters Green. I told a sergeant my predicament, that I really wanted to join the army but I had poor sight. He asked me what I did, and how I got about. I told him about my running, my football, how I wasn't prevented from doing much, really. I had impressed him.

'Blimey!' he said. 'It's unlikely you'd be able to join the Parachute Regiment or fire a weapon, as you need 20/20 vision for that.'

CHAPTER 4

But. There was a but.

Either kindly or truthfully, he told me that I might be able to make it into the Catering or Medical Corps.

My little brain started twitching then. If I could just get in and show them what I could do, then who knows where I could be transferred? That spurred me on. He duly booked my army medical and I went home with a smile on my face and hope in my heart.

The army medical centre, then, was near New Street station in Birmingham. Fitness was tested, as well as general health, so I was put through sit-ups, press-ups. I was asked about colour blindness, I was asked to look at a chart and read. They never once said no, they never once said yes. As the day progressed, I thought my luck was in.

I went in to the doctor's office at the end. I was asked further questions, all the questions that any individual applying for the army would. I wasn't a special case. I began to feel hopeful.

'Right, sign here,' the doctor said, sliding a piece of paper towards me on the desk. I signed on the dotted line. '**You're exempt**.' There was no softening of his words, no fatherly slap on the back in commiseration. 'Go to the reception and pick up your bus fare.'

I took a deep, silent breath to restrain the tears. I blinked furiously. Blindness was going to rob me of everything I wanted in life, I could feel it. It was happening, it was coming. There was nothing I could do – no matter how healthy or fit I remained – and no miraculous medical recoveries on the horizon. Stick your bus fare, I thought bitterly. It was then I realised that what that original consultant had told me was true. It wasn't a good outlook. I was going blind.

It was only when I was at home, in my bedroom, alone, that I allowed myself to cry. Why did this happen to me? I cursed myself inwardly, thumping the bedroom wall with the rage I could feel pumping through my veins. I was going blind.

I would be blind like Grandad Clee.

5

SCM was a fantastic place to work. I was mothered and spoilt by the women, hidden and fed tea and toast when colleagues came looking for me, and I spent many of my evenings in the pub with the lads. It was through many a night at the pub that I learnt that SCM wasn't quite as fantastic as I'd first assumed. Some of my mates were earning considerably more than me – £26, £28 a week – at their places of work, other firms in the area not far removed from what I was doing at SCM. I was only earning £12.

'Why don't you come and work with us? There's a job going,' they told me in the pub one night. My ears pricked up.

'In the warehouse?' I asked.

'Yeah, forklift driving,' they said. How I laughed! How the bloody hell would I do that?

But they were serious.

'Don't worry about that, we'll sort that out. We'll look after you: we'll drive the truck, you can do the warehouse bit.'

It was a funny time, my early 20s, because I was seeing and not seeing: I was seeing things that weren't there, and not seeing things that were. I could look at a desk and see a pen; blink and the pen would disappear, but I could put my hand out and feel it. It was strange how my eyes worked – or didn't – and I had come to rarely trust what I saw before me. For many people in the same situation, I am certain that kind of experience would be frustrating, and the individual would exercise restraint in their daily lives: perhaps they would become over-cautious or fearful of doing the things they had previously done.

But I didn't want to start curtailing my life. I still had, even in my 9-5 working life, an overpowering sense of adventure. I'd always be the one up for going somewhere new or trying something out. So though my eyes playing tricks on me enraged and infuriated me, I learnt to battle past it, to muddle through. I saw myself as a bit of a pinball, bouncing from one thing to the next. And sometimes it made me more reckless than ever. After all, I was already losing my sight – what else could go wrong, really?

I decided to take the job at the BICC warehouse and pretty much double the money I was getting at SCM. For the first six weeks the lads covered for me beautifully. All I had to do was navigate the stuff into a box, load it on to a wagon and off it went.

But the inevitable day dawned: I was to drive the forklift. For me, a forklift truck was something that you sat on, with two forks that came straight out in front and would be used to pick up a pallet, or something similar. I'd never experienced a forklift truck with not only forks, but also two fixed stanchions. The idea with this truck was that you sent the forks out, past the stanchions, picked up your item then reeled it in to rest against the stanchions.

Well, nobody told me that.

The supervisor asked me to try a wooden drum, a great wooden wheel used to wind in the cabling we provided for the BBC's enormous cameras. My colleagues had spent the best part of eight hours coiling up the cabling around this one particular drum. I puttered the truck forward and, squinting with concentration through the minute windows that my peripheral vision could afford me, managed to hook my forks through the drum. Magic! Slowly, I went to lift and… bang! Something had gone wrong, but I couldn't see what. Helplessly,

I turned to my supervisor. The drum had caught itself on the stanchions and when the forks had risen, it had fetched the top clean off. This BBC cable, all 300 yards of it, catapulted itself to freedom.

Though the supervisor was furious, I was given the benefit of the doubt; beginner's bad luck.

A couple of weeks later, I was told I needed to get back on the truck; after all, I was a warehouse man *and* a forklift truck driver. Here we go, I thought.

The supervisor invited me to do a bit of training first, to familiarise myself with the truck. I was asked to go forwards, backwards; lift up the forks and lower them back down. I didn't want to do it, I knew it spelt disaster. But I had to save face and get on with it. Back then, there was no way I would admit any kind of visual impairment, let alone my future prognosis.

I sat on the truck in front of a long corridor. I lifted the forks up four feet in the air – which I later found out was the wrong thing to do anyway, as the forks should always stay close to the ground when on the move – and I went down the alleyway, stop start, stop start.

Suddenly, there was an awful noise. An inevitable noise: breaking glass, screeching of metal. The foreman's office had been there – even I had seen it – but the next minute, it wasn't. I've got this cartoon vision of the office clattering to the floor like a house of cards, filing cabinets sinking like tower blocks exploded by dynamite. I imagine people jumping at the sound, before scratching their heads and puzzling over what just happened.

'You shouldn't have had the forks in the air!' I was told by a multitude of voices, exasperated and accusatory. 'You shouldn't have hit the foreman's office,' I muttered to myself.

I was just so pleased the foreman wasn't in it. It didn't matter that I was being howled at, or that I knew this meant the end of my job. I just thanked my lucky stars that man was elsewhere in the factory at that moment in time.

'Why didn't you tell me you have a problem with your eyes?' my supervisor implored, astonished. It was too obvious to hide this time.

'You didn't ask me,' I retorted.

Thankfully, Dad helped to sort me a job just next door at Fordath and I was back to phone, desk, chair. My forklift truck driving days were over.

I worked at Fordath for about 12 months and it was all right, but it wasn't what I wanted to do. I looked for another job and found myself at Rudders and Paynes. It was a well-known timber merchant in the area and what a place! It was absolutely brilliant. I started as a stock controller but took enquiries on the phone, too. I began to understand how the company ticked, and how they sold their suspended ceilings and within two months, I joined the sales team. And I was good at it, too! It really felt like I'd found my calling: customers started to gel and commissions came in, the sales team worked together like clockwork and we turned over some phenomenal amounts of money. Slowly, I began to do the purchasing, too, so I was buying the stuff in, then selling it out. I met some great people through my job: suppliers and their reps, the regular customers, all sorts of people from all over the country. And do you know what? I actually looked forward to going to work. When it was time for clocking off, I was surprised. Already?

Though I loved the job, I still struggled with getting up in the morning. Oversleeping was a regular occurrence and I frequently had to leg it down the hill and through the industrial estate to make it in on time. However, one morning I was later than usual. It was about a quarter past nine, and I couldn't risk running past the director's office and into reception. I'd be seen.

Instead, I decided to take my chances with a direct entrance to my desk – through the window. I could do it, I reckoned. I just needed a little help from my mate Geoff.

As I neared the window, about seven feet tall and almost a person's height from the ground, I just about made out Geoff's face at the window. He pulled up the sash window quietly, muttering something through gritted teeth. He was probably warning me to be quiet, I decided, so I went for it: pushing open the window and hauling myself up, puffing, panting and crawling on my belly through the opening. I was proud of myself; this would be something to tell the lads at the pub. They'd never believe it.

But as I looked up, elbows grappling with the windowsill, I noticed my boss, Mr Neades, the company director, sitting in my seat.

'Morning, David,' he said, without so much as a raised eyebrow. 'Most folks come through the front door.'

'Yes,' I stuttered, not quite sure what to say next. Thankfully, he walked off, shaking his head.

'I tried to tell you!' Geoff said, smiling.

Though Rudders and Paynes was a place of practical jokes, we cared about the work, too. While I was there, I pulled off the biggest contract they had ever had in suspended ceilings at that point: 20,000 square metres. I pulled in this discount, managed to get another discount, took the order and I was supplying – and they hadn't even got a credit rating on the company. Mr Neades came out again.

'Dave, have you checked the credit rating on this company?'

'Well, I guess they're good for it…' I began.

'Twenty thousand square metres? Do you know how much money that is?'

'They're a big group,' I said.

He told me that the company only had a £2,000 credit limit.

'This is going to be about 60 grand!'

'Well, I've supplied it,' I smiled.

'What?'

Thankfully, it all went through smoothly and the company paid up, good as gold. Mr Neades didn't complain then, did he?

Trade and industry is never stable, though, and the company merged and found new premises that would have taken me three buses and a train to get there every day. I couldn't physically do it, so I moved on to another company, Sheffield Insulations, where I was tasked with putting together a ceilings department from scratch before being poached by another company, Firsmere Engineering, where I did the same. I was there for a couple of years and it did well.

I think it was fair to say that my personal life, however, was as unstable as my working life, but without the peaks. I'd met Beverley in 1976 and we married in July 1980, when I was 22. We were just too young, and I think it's fair to say that I prioritised drinks in the evening over any kind of marriage vow. I suppose that was a rite of passage then, though; everyone seemed to marry young. We lived first in Wednesbury, then back in West Brom at Hilltop. Though we had some great times, the marriage fizzled out, and by 1982 we were separated, though it took until 1985 for the divorce to come through.

A year later I met Graham Fox through my good friend Roger Makepeace. Graham had run his own business already and we decided to give our own business a go.

Heeley Interior Systems was born in 1986 and lived for six fruitful years. We dealt with suspended ceilings and their associated materials: tiles, metal and light fittings, and so on. It was a time of serious work – and serious play. Graham and I took on multiple roles: we were managing directors, salespeople, labourers, caretakers and cleaners, deliverymen, suppliers and purchasers. We were chalk and cheese, Graham and I, but I suppose that's what makes a good partnership. We started, on the first day, with fitting the phones and nothing on the books. By the end of the first year we were turning over £1m; by the time we finished it was £3.5m.

It was hard work but I loved it, the variety of it all, the people I met and became good friends with, the thrill of the chase of a good deal. I'd worked on Christmas Days, I had been in at 2am loading vans for customers. I even took supplies home on the bus – not easy when you're blind. We had a great customer base and supplied materials into the fancy hotels in Birmingham, such as The Hyatt and The Swallow, along with the NEC and the ICC. We did well, by and large, and it was fun to say that I was a millionaire on paper. I found the industry fantastic to work in; fast-paced and good fun. I was respected and frequently asked for advice, by customers, suppliers and competitors alike. And nobody knew the extent of my poor eyesight. In fact, when a Porsche was parked outside our premises for the first time, most believed it to be mine, until one of our car-mad employees explained otherwise. People within the industry didn't even realise I couldn't drive.

Our team was small and compact, mainly because I kept the role of overseer-and-doer. I had a large desk covered with telephones and from seven in the morning until seven at night, I took call after call. Quite often, I'd get home and they would call at home, too. And when mobile phones came about, I was never off the thing. But I didn't mind: Heeley's was my baby. I lived and breathed it, so the saying goes.

Though work took up a great deal of time, it didn't stop me from socialising. I managed to combine business with going to watch the Albion – clients would offer us their executive boxes at times – and if I finished work at nine in the evening, then I'd be sure to spend the last few hours of the day in the pub. Of course, that didn't correlate very nicely with any kind of domesticity, and my second wife, Pat, who I married in 1988, soon tired of my behaviour. I was a complicated bundle of behaviours back then. Buoyed by the success of the company and my enjoyment of my working life, but beleaguered by impending blindness that I refused to admit to, I numbed my highs and lows with drink, never knowing when enough was enough. Never violent or aggressive, mind. I was self-centred, but refused to acknowledge my real self, if that makes any kind of sense. I'd actually registered as blind the year before Pat and I had married, even though I could have done a decade earlier, but it did little to encourage me to take stock – instead, I think

I became more reckless. I adopted the attitude that I couldn't see, so what worse could happen? Though my first daughter, Grace, came along in 1990, the marriage suffered, stumbled and staggered into the 90s.

It wasn't helped by the fact that Heeley's came to a premature end: a combination of bad luck, bad eyesight and bad debt. I got taken for a lot of money, almost £500,000, when 13 of my top customers went under and we couldn't come back from that. By then it was the first recession of the 1990s, and the banks started pulling in all the construction overdrafts. Instantly, overnight. I had a large corporation tax rebate on the horizon and so I went to the bank, asked them to leave the rebate alone and give me three months, six months, and I could pull it off. The bank agreed to help me, but as soon as the rebate appeared, they took it from underneath me and I was left with nothing.

I was helpless, and deeply concerned. I felt sick and struggled with sleep. It was like reliving my prognosis all over again, and coming to terms with the fact that I would never be in the army. In fact, it went so far that when the bank called the liquidators in, it felt like a great cloud had been lifted.

Pat and I eventually divorced, and I moved out and into a flat by myself.

But there was hope in the form of Deborah Burford. I met Deb in the early days of Heeley's. In fact, the company had only been in operation for about two months when 19-year-old Deb came in one day with her boss, Mick, who I knew well. She was new to the industry, and new to her company, Pergola, and Mick was keen to show her some of the people she would need to get to know. My office was cramped and in the middle of a warehouse, and I remember taking a shine to her instantly. We always clicked. She tells me now that Heeley's was one of her better customers, and I often saved her bacon. She had to report on her sales figures regularly, whether meetings had resulted in a possible, probable or definite sale. Deb would often ring me up and gently plead, 'I've put you on my report this week; we're definitely going to get that sale, aren't we?' I didn't mind helping wherever I could. In fact, we spoke to each other regularly, arranging deliveries and supplies. After my first divorce, I knew I had a shine for Deb, even then, but I didn't know her situation. Her company was based in Coventry, so I presumed that was where she lived. Chatter between us revolved around work and jokes – banter, I suppose. It was only later I would find out she had lived in the vicinity, and had grown up pretty much down the road from me.

About six months in to the life of my new company, Deb turned up unannounced.

'I've come to take you out for lunch,' she said. It was a regular thing, our suppliers buying their customers lunch. It wasn't a romantic gesture, but I wished it could be. I really did fancy her, and I reckon she knew it.

I wanted to. But it was just me and my business partner then, and he was out doing deliveries. I had to stay at the office. There was no one else to look after it. My hopes for a romantic lunch were dashed.

And funnily enough, when Heeley's finished, Deb found herself in a similar situation: a divorce rumbling on in the background, and redundancy due to the economic climate. We decided to join forces to form Open Spec, combining our knowledge and contacts gained through our years in the industry. We managed to bring on board some of our previous customers and build up our customer base again. Deb focused on selling and administration, I brought some of the Heeley's team with me.

But it wasn't easy. It was around that time that all the bigger companies, the global conglomerates, were buying up all the smaller independents and we struggled to compete. If Heeley's had still been going, I'm certain we also would have been bought out – it was the culture of the time, it was the way it was going. Open Spec tided us over for a couple of years, kept the wages rolling, but I must admit that I never felt quite as hungry for it as I had done with Heeley's. It had knocked me, that was for sure.

So when Deb and I saw the warning signs, we decided to cease trading, rather than keep going until the bitter, inevitable end.

Of course, by then, around 1994, we had become a romantic partnership, as well as business partners – although, it must be said, it wasn't all roses. My goodness, there were some rows. And it was mainly down to the fact that I was a demon with the drink. The pub ruled my life: I played on the crib and dominoes teams – they wouldn't let me on the darts team, for some reason – and I always had to be back there for last orders. I was selfish, very self-centred, and I think that's how I dealt with my blindness – by hiding it, of course. In the early days, Deb certainly didn't know the extent of my sight problems. There were times when I wondered how we stayed together. But together we stayed, and did things back to front with the children arriving first and an elopement to Gretna Green following in 2005. Our moms were the only ones in on it, and subsequently organised a big party for everyone else when we arrived back home.

The businesses had consumed much of my adult life – even in the pub, I was drinking with clients, suppliers and colleagues. So when we lost the businesses, I was at a loss what to do with myself. I still had the Albion, but other than that, I suddenly had time. Free time.

So it wasn't long before Deb and I were on to our next business venture: Loveable Characters. It was an idea that had gestated over a few months and we had five animal characters – a mouse, rabbit, pig, frog, and teddy bear – each of which would feature on a range of wooden furniture and utensils, such as toilet roll holders and children's furniture. We had the prototypes developed by Deb's dad and were in the process of raising funds for warehouse space and machinery, with a deposit down on a space at the very end of the road where we now live. Our team consisted of Deb, Deb's dad, who was a retired specialist toolmaker, and me, a blind bloke. The business was at the forefront of our minds, and we found that every person we met, every conversation we had in the pub, was focused around our new opportunity.

The pub where I used to play crib and dominoes was frequented by lorry drivers, many of them northerners on a stop-off, and it wasn't long before I was sending photos of our new Loveable Characters round the pub. Des, one of the northern truckers, was taken with them.

'I reckon I could sell a few of these for you,' he said in earnest. Why not? I thought, handing him a price list.

Later, he called to say he had got some orders in and relayed them over the phone. We set about completing the order before bundling them into Deb's car and taking them out to his wagon parked up nearby, a week or two later.

Deb had told me there wasn't a soul in the car park, save for Des' lorry, and gave me full permission. She wanted in on the joke, too.

'Are we going to the pub then, Des?' I said, once the orders were stowed away in his lorry. 'Do you want a lift?'

I jumped into Deb's car, into the driver's seat, wound down the window and poked my white stick out – just for extra comic value, of course. Des hadn't answered, obviously working out how he should reply, when I started up the engine, put the steering wheel into lock and put my foot down. The car circled and circled, as I called out to Des, 'Don't you want a lift? Let's go to the pub, Des! It's all right, I can drive you!'

'No way!' he called, 'No thanks! I'll be fine!'

'What's the matter, Des? Don't you want a lift?' I tried to sound as manic, as enthusiastic, as I could. It had the desired effect: Des was horrified.

Deb and I didn't stop laughing about it for weeks, especially when Deb described the look on his face.

Though it didn't put him off, and, on this occasion, the orders went ahead – but it wasn't to last. In fact, in essence, the company never really got off the ground. Deb worked her socks off to apply for a Prince's Trust loan but our three-strong team can't have seemed strong to the assessors, as we were turned down. All other options came to a dead end. We had to give up the idea, and later cursed our misfortune when we found similar products in the shops. We knew it had been a goer in principle.

I began to feel nervous and uncomfortable. I was blind and I had no work. For the first time, I had to sign on. I was referred to Roy Short and EmployAbility, his organisation that works to get disabled people in to employment.

Roy Short lived locally to me and, so I'm told, had enjoyed a career as an engineer until it was cut short – he was diagnosed with Retinitis Pigmentosa and went completely blind at 28 years of age. Suddenly thrust into the dark, Roy must have been frustrated with the lack of opportunity for disabled people as he founded two charities, Ideal For All and EmployAbility, and campaigned tirelessly for disabled and disadvantaged people in the Sandwell area.

Admitting I was disabled – well, that was still not really something I was prepared to do. But disadvantaged? There was no denying that I was not sure what work I would find next. Now that Heeley's was a chapter firmly closed, I realised that work was not going to fall into my lap. I would need to make the next move, but I had no idea what it should be. Who would hire a blind bloke, used to being his own boss?

Roy Short, and his EmployAbility team, had a few suggestions. It meant going back to basics. All sorts of interviews took place to assess my skills, to understand how my lifestyle was hindered by my condition and what I could do or learn to better support myself.

Firstly, I was summoned to the EmployAbility offices for cane training. I was put through my paces with that long white cane: tap, tap, tap. But I didn't take to it. What did I want a cane for? To me, it was another blind stereotype, another thing to add to the blind person Top Trumps – generally, things from which I desperately tried to steer clear. I smiled, nodded, probably looked a bit pained and promptly stuffed it in a drawer when I got home.

Next it was suggested that I go along to support sessions for blind people. There were a few different groups in the local area, and Deb and I decided to try one out that met on a Thursday night. I wasn't enthused by the first session, but thought I would go again, just in case it had been an anomaly. At the end of the second session, though, I confirmed to Deb that I wouldn't be going back. It was stifling. The people there, though they meant very well, cocooned themselves in their own little blind worlds. The last thing I wanted to do was cocoon myself: I wanted to do everything I had been doing for the previous 30 to 40 years. It was just this small thing called blindness getting in the way.

I did, however, relent at the recommendation of a guide dog. Perhaps it was because I had grown up with a dog, or perhaps it was just curiosity – how did it all work? Could a dog really see for a human? Or, by then, I might have felt guilty at the lack of enthusiasm I was showing to Roy and his team and acquiesced to try something, anything. Either way, I found myself on the receiving end from a visit by Kevin Mundy, from Guide Dogs for the Blind.

The first meeting was an informal chat; the second and Kevin brought Peter, the Golden Labrador Retriever, with him. This wasn't to be a chat, though: straight away, I had to get involved. I swallowed my pride, hoping that my neighbours would be at work or the supermarket; anywhere but their front windows, watching as poor blind Dave muddled past, his life in the hands of a strange mutt.

Except the first try-out on the street didn't even involve Peter, who was back at home, being fussed over by Deb. No, my first experience of a guide dog was actually with Kevin himself: he held the harness as I was asked to latch on to the handle. The pair of us, the harness and the ghost dog, trundled down Great Bridge High Street and I have never felt a bigger berk.

Later, Kevin helped me to fill in some forms and checked over my flat to make sure it was suitable for a dog. I would be applying for a guide dog. It would improve my life no end, Kevin told me, give me my independence back. I felt pretty independent as it was, I told myself, defiantly – knowing full well he was completely right.

A few weeks later, Kevin, along with Peter, arranged to come back.

'When you go for a walk around the block, where is it? What's your "block"?' Kevin asked me, so I explained. I have a pretty good memory of the area from my childhood. Lucky, really.

So we set off.

And completed it so quickly, we had to do it twice. I was used to that route taking an hour and ten minutes, my toes feeling for kerbs, my hands for the familiar railings and splintered fence posts. With Peter, under Kevin's scrutiny, we sailed round the block, swerving every lamppost, tree and telephone box which I had come to know so well, and we were back in 12 minutes.

'I don't believe you,' I said, firmly, 'you've just taken me to the top and back.'

So we did it again.

Needless to say, I was sold. It was fantastic. Round the block, in 12 minutes!

'So are you interested, then, Dave?' Kevin asked, nonchalantly.

'Too right I'm interested!' I replied.

'Good, because I think this dog's for you. He's available, so when do you want to come in and train?'

Blooming Nora. Can you imagine? I'd gone from not entertaining the thought to an eager recruit in just a few weeks.

Training involved a residential in Leamington Spa, the charity's then training headquarters. There were 14 of us, and many were taking a course for the second or third time with their new dog. I hadn't realised that training had to be undertaken with each new dog, no matter how accustomed the human was with the whole procedure. I would be in it for life: this was the start of something new, and lifelong. I was completely baffled and hadn't a clue what to expect.

I was shown to my room and settled in before being given the grand tour of the complex: the dining room, the students' lounge where we could help ourselves to a cup of tea. There were a few unusual rules I had to remember, too: walk on the left hand side to avoid any collisions; tread mats denoted corridor junctions; and doors had to be tapped before being pushed, just in case there were any blind folk on the other side, unaware of your presence. I had never done anything like this before. If I wanted to go through a door, I found it and opened it. The training facility was like diving head first into the blind world, a world in which I'd previously refused to participate.

The feeding, spending and grooming rooms for the dogs were just as organised. To deem it a purpose-built facility was an understatement: they had thought of everything, and it was absolutely spot on.

Finally, our hands itching to get on with it, we were issued with our kit: the harness and reflective gear, and the grooming tools.

Towards the end of the first day, we were introduced to our dogs. Of course, I had already met Peter, but to him, I was just another human, another set of alien smells and sounds. It was his trainer, Karen, who was his master. Slowly, gradually, I would need to replace Karen as chief. I was asked to sit quietly in my room as the trainers brought him in, let him off his lead, and departed, the door closing behind them. Peter came to sniff me inquisitively, but then it dawned on him – Karen had left him alone. He cried quietly at the door, and I imagined the wag of his tail slowing, the hope in his eyes fading. I made a fuss of him, hoping to placate him, reassure him.

On the second day, it was all about the dogs. We were shown the correct way to feed and groom them, and to check for health concerns by feeling their paws. The trainers demonstrated minor first aid, too – after all, an unhealthy dog would be no help to us.

And then the real fun started: harness on. We started off with short routes about the campus. There were cars driving up and down the driveway; there were other animals roaming about; all in a bid to ensure our dogs would be unflappable in the face of everyday life.

We took the dogs – or the dogs took us – for walks across Leamington, Warwick, Nuneaton; places I didn't know if I could see, let alone when I couldn't. When Peter and I qualified, three weeks later, I came out of the training centre completely transformed. It was something so simple in essence: a man out walking with a dog, an understanding between the two. Many people share that. But my new dog wasn't a dog – he was Peter, my Peter, my guide. I could get from A to B, I could take a leisurely stroll, and I would be safer and quicker than ever before. I doubted I'd ever been so efficient or so confident. Even as a child, I'd bumped into things that loomed into view too late or tripped over kerbs that I had sworn hadn't been there before.

After we had qualified, and the three-week course had come to an end, we were given strict instructions: 'slowly, and surely'. No leaping into the thrum of the nearest city centres; no trains to London. Our new relationship, with our dogs were exactly that: new. Trust and respect would be built gradually, reinforcing what we had learnt in Leamington. The charity came out to visit us once a month, then once every few months. They kept a firm eye on us and we were told that if we encountered any problems, we were duty bound to report them.

Deb found watching Peter and I quite daunting at first. She was surprised at the pace we kept up, and felt our paths across the pavements perplexing. Whereas sighted people cut corners and find the quickest way to cover the ground, guide dogs are taught to walk straight forwards at all times. When a corner comes in to view, the dogs go right up to it and then turn at a right angle at the very last minute. She cringed and winced, waiting for Peter to lead me head first into a brick wall, a lamppost, a ditch, or something. But every time, Peter did as I hoped he would, leading me to safety and keeping my precious face scratch-free.

Deb was perhaps less surprised to learn that Peter liked the pub as much as me – we were a complete match in that respect. He couldn't walk past a pub without slipping in through the doorway, often without me fully realising until I was propping up the bar, pint in hand. In fact, the very first time Deb watched Peter and I at work, after our return home from Leamington, he took me across the road, left and to the first available warm public house. Perhaps he liked the people, the sound of the jukebox, the smell of the beer, I don't know. I remember being ill and asking Deb if she would mind walking Peter for me. She obliged, but when she arrived home an hour later, she was bemused.

'Do you really go into all those pubs?' she asked, incredulous, reeling off a list of local establishments. There were a few unfamiliar names, and many I definitely didn't frequent. Peter had pushed his nose in to every single one on their route. He had seemed puzzled when she hadn't followed and instead dragged him away.

Though he had some recognisably human traits, and I began to rely on him like a friend, Peter was most definitely a dog, too. In fact, if he had been human, he'd have been in the nick. Early on in our relationship with Peter, we thought it might be sensible to see how he fared around cats. I brought him round to Deb's house one morning so he could pay Deb's cat, Cindy, a visit. I needn't have worried about the cat; that was the least of our concerns. As soon as I let him off the lead, he leapt out of the house, into the next-door neighbours' garden, their fishpond, their house. He was a tornado! It took us half an hour to catch him, and we were only successful once he was distracted by the neighbours' teddy bear… up until that point, Deb's interaction with her new neighbours had been a friendly wave through the living room window. Peter certainly broke the ice. And the teddy bear.

Peter was also an excellent scavenger and thief, and he always knew to tackle the most vulnerable. Like the time Deb's Nan Lyylia was quietly anticipating the delight a succulent piece of Black Forest gateau would bring. Whoosh! Peter stole it deftly from her hands before she had even a forkful.

He certainly made a name for himself outside the family, too. During a long weekend break in Windermere, close to Hallowe'en, we made the mistake of unclipping his lead next to the lake. He was in. He had spied the largest swan of the lot and doggy-paddled in hot pursuit of him. We stood at the lakeside, shouting and hollering his name, some other tourists joining in. Deb lost sight of him.

'What are we going to tell Guide Dogs?' I breathed, incredulous. 'That we've lost the bloody dog?'

Two lads went off to fetch a rowing boat when there was an almighty watery ruckus. Peter came bounding out of the lake as fast as he had gone in. Deb managed to grasp the collar but he wouldn't slow his pace for anyone. Deb skiied behind him. It was *Tom and Jerry* to the last.

Sadly, that wasn't the end of his Windermere escapades. Later that evening, in the bar, somebody piped up at my elbow.

'Your dog's eaten all the cobwebs!'

Peter had hoovered up every artificial Hallowe'en decoration he could find. Cobwebs, skeletons… he'd even made inroads into the pumpkin. On realising his time was almost up, he bounded into the kitchen, nosing out every morsel he could find.

Perhaps the biggest commotion Peter caused was at the zoo. He quite literally rattled the cages of a number of the more interesting animals: lions roaring at the cage-side, monkeys so unimpressed with his presence that they began to throw their business at him. We escaped into the elephant house where Peter was as quiet as a mouse – until one of the elephants trumpeted some straw at him. He gave that elephant what for, barking at the top of his voice. It sent the elephants wild – and the rest of the visitors out of the enclosure as quickly as possible.

Most presume that guide dogs are never off-duty; that they are highly intelligent creatures with an empathetic sixth sense, always the second pair of eyes for their defenceless, hapless humans. And truth be told, Peter's work on the lead was incredible. But off it? He was a naughty, naughty dog. Deb would ask me after the latest mishap – a birthday cake from the table-top, a cuddly toy ripped to smithereens, a showdown with a swan – 'Are you sure he's a guide dog? Are you sure?'

So not only did I have to become accustomed to sharing my life with an animal with a naughty disposition and boundless energy, but I had to quickly adapt to his working 'personality', too.

In the early days of my relationship with a guide dog, I found it difficult to comprehend that my life was in the hands of an animal – how did it *know* its responsibility? Did Peter really equate a speeding car on the road with my death? Did he know to avoid a lamppost in the street because it would be painful to me? And it is something I still consider to this day. I tell myself that a guide dog can't really *know* in the way a human can; that it doesn't make the links between danger and death like we do.

But I am certain that there is something more than rigorous, repetitive training and reward by food, I'm sure of it. There has

CHAPTER 5

to be some amount of loyalty or empathy there, some kind of mutual understanding, that's more than just a bowl of dog food at the end of the day – after all, why would a dog do that, all day every day? It seemed like a lot of work in exchange for food alone. Did Peter get some enjoyment or reward out of it, too? Or did he simply know nothing else, having been conditioned into guiding since birth?

The mechanics of working with a guide dog, the prompts and instructions, also take a bit of acclimatisation. Now it's just second nature, but like learning any new skill, it was confusing in the beginning and took up a great deal of brain space.

Guide dog prompts are universal, so if I was to learn in another part of the world, it would be almost identical. Guide dogs are almost always taught to walk to the left of the blind person. The dog is trained to take us to the kerb where they will automatically sit – unless it's a German Shepherd, which usually continue to stand as they find it more comfortable. It is the person's duty to stand at the kerb with their right leg trailing slightly, which lets the dog know that you are listening, ready to move off. The dog will not move until you give the command 'forward', and then, if the coast is clear, you and your dog will cross the road.

Turns require a tap of the leg and a foot pointing the way you want to go, and the dog will always try to remain between the person and the road – or as far from the road as possible. There are instructions for every manoeuvre, just as there are when learning to drive a car or ride a horse, and remembering them became a daily test.

I have since learnt that when people leave the training centre, they relax the rules and become more instinctive – just like a driver would, by driving with one hand on the wheel and one on the gear stick, or whatever. But I decided I would be strict, and keep to the tried and tested formula as much as I could. For the first year, I made sure that I didn't let Peter off the lead in our local park: I was told it would cause problems later as he would become distracted when I asked him to walk past the gates.

A guide dog is taught to stop if a car is coming, and only to move off if the cars are at a standstill or if there are none around. But as the dogs become accustomed to using pelican and zebra crossings and walking in front of stationary cars, those noisy engines somehow seem less hazardous. I'm told that it's the first thing they forget. Sometimes I will just test my dog, to see if he is awake and on duty. If a car is coming and I command him to go forward, he should stop – and if he moves, I can be a bit vocal! In fact, a woman once told me off for raising my voice at one of the dogs.

'He's done wrong,' I told her, patiently, 'he's taken me into the road. If your life was controlled by a dog, I'm sure you'd do the same.' She wasn't convinced and huffed off, her face inevitably a picture. But I maintained that I was doing just as Guide Dogs had taught me.

It's funny: though I know that guide dogs are wonderful creatures, and I owe my quality of life and independence largely to my guide dog, I also know they make mistakes – they are animals, after all, working animals.

We had Peter until he was around six years old, when it was found that he had an ulcer. The vet thought that it was unfair for him to keep working when he had a medical condition that could have been caused, or at least exacerbated, by stress and so he was retired. I will admit it: I was truly devastated when I had to let go of Peter. I had come to see him as an extension of my left arm. He had accompanied me absolutely everywhere. However, I knew there would be a good home waiting for him; there is always such a long waiting list for retired guide dogs. Although I always wondered what Peter's new owners made of him!

I had a gap of three months before my next dog, Carla, came along. I was lost. I hadn't realised how dependent on him I had become, and how difficult life could be without a guide dog.

I had to try and manage with a cane, which I had never taken to in the first place. When I left for the pub, I'd find that Deb would ring ahead to ask the lads to watch out for me – and to ring if I didn't appear through the doorway!

When I was introduced to Carla, the training process started all over again. Though every dog is trained in the same manner, every dog is different, just like every trainer is different. It is imperative – for health and safety, for the wellbeing of the dogs and the owners – that we become familiar with each dog's foibles, and the dog adjusts to its owner and its new environment.

But Carla was simply fantastic. Another Labrador Retriever, she will take some beating. In her temperament, her diligence, she rarely put a paw wrong. She was even bridesmaid at our secret wedding. When we lost Carla to cancer, my heart was broken. We had her through six months of chemotherapy but it was to no avail and I was with her when the time came for her to be put to sleep. I'm not embarrassed to admit it – I cried my bloody eyes out.

Then came Wicksy: if he had been one of the Seven Dwarves, he would have been Dopey. And Seamus? He's a lovely dog, a German Shepherd: playful, friendly, nosy, but the main thing is he's good at his job. Seamus hates being left at home, he always wants to be a part of what's going on. They say that German Shepherds actually make the best guide dogs, better than Labradors, because they are so intelligent, but they are often retired earlier due to hip problems associated with the breed.

Having a guide dog is certainly not for everybody. Some of my fellow trainees returned home from Leamington to find that their dog simply didn't fit their current lifestyle; that they found keeping another life happy and healthy too much of a burden.

But me? I was instantly enamoured with the whole concept: I adored the dog; I found the charity to be inspiring, the trainers studious and dedicated, the support robust and well-rounded; I was grateful to get back a real slice of independence, as Kevin had promised. It wasn't the same as being sighted, nowhere near, but it did reduce some of the laboriousness of everyday life. It was far better than bouncing down the street from lamppost to fence post. And I could slink off to the pub any time I liked.

A charity had effectively changed my life. Guide Dogs for the Blind made it possible for me to stand tall and feel proud, full of confidence. I was no longer the hunched figure trawling the footpath; instead, I strode out with a sure-footed, four-legged friend. My mobility was assured. It was the perfect recipe for adventure and my social life was second to none. Without a guide dog, I feel like someone who has lost their glasses or a kid without a mobile phone. My only regret was not having a guide dog sooner.

It got me thinking. What could I do for the charity? How could I repay them?

It was an easy decision, really: the charity needed, as most charities do, considerable funds to operate. I would fundraise, in the hope I could contribute and enable other people to receive the service I had.

I'd never really fundraised before but I held my first event at The Nag's Head in Great Bridge. I just did what I knew best – how to party! We held a disco and a raffle, and once all the silver had been counted, I was delighted to find I'd raised £1,150. I enjoyed throwing myself into something, and making a difference.

Around the same time as I was being prepared for accepting a guide dog into my life, Roy and his colleagues at EmployAbility persuaded me into going back to college.

I couldn't believe that I knew nothing of Queen Alexandra College, a learning establishment for people with disabilities, which was practically on my doorstep. Moreover, it turned out that the QAC had been the place where my grandad –

remember Grandad Clee? – had been taught life skills and crafts. I was to attend a six-week taster course, to sample what the college had to offer for people like me: schooldays long since gone, a medical condition worsening.

I did the lot: carpentry and woodwork, literacy, computing and touch-typing, and my scepticism soon ebbed away. I truly enjoyed it, and realised that there was something out there for me. I could do something else. I could do *something*; I had skills. And I was the classic mature student, as I got top marks in everything!

When the six weeks came to an end, I was offered a place at the college for a three-year course, covered by the local council. I was delighted: no longer on the dole, I'd have the chance to study for three years.

I had dabbled with a bit of braille on the quiet while I had Heeley's, I suppose to prepare myself for the worst, but I hadn't really taken it seriously; more a curiosity, a novelty, than anything else. But at the QAC, I took it up properly, as a core subject, learning grade one and grade two. And do you know what? I won Student of the Year for braille! It's something I still use today, and unsurprisingly, it's also managed to get me into hot water. Take the Christmas card I brailled for Deb one year, for example. It was on a rather suggestive theme, in all honesty, a private, rather saucy, moment between lovers that I presumed would be safe from prying, sighted eyes. But how wrong I was – it was soon found out by a visitor to the house who was perfectly braille-literate!

I also plumped for craft, design and technology, which mainly consisted of carpentry and woodturning, and computing, alongside the obligatory English and maths.

At the time, many of my fellow students were blind, too; perhaps even so much as the majority of the college intake. But my situation was markedly different, easier. Many had further complications; they were deaf-blind, or had additional learning difficulties. Nowadays the college population is very different, it is much more mixed. I think this is largely to do with the impetus to ensure that blind people without any additional needs attend mainstream schools where possible.

The layout of the college was easy to follow and it wasn't long before we knew our way around. Braille and textured flooring helped us to understand any changes. As there were only around 200 students at the college when I was enrolled, lecturers and students were on first-name terms. It was – it still is – a friendly, sociable place. The bulk of the student population was aged between 16 and 21 so I naturally migrated to befriending the older, mature students. I was delighted to be invited, in 2009, to become a governor of the college, the first ever former student to be asked.

Needless to say, I had a fantastic three years. At school, I hadn't been bothered by learning; I just wanted to be on the football pitch or the running track or swimming pool. But this time, I had a gnawing, nagging feeling of curiosity: I just had to learn. I had some fantastic lecturers, one of which, Gordon Gray, the carpentry lecturer, I am still in touch with. His knowledge was extensive. And considering he was a sighted bloke, he made sure that his knowledge was transferable to people who couldn't see. The room, too, was set up perfectly: one kickstrip round one part of the room denoted that there were benches in the middle; the other kickstrip told us that the lathes were nearby; everything was brailled up. And what I enjoyed most was that it wasn't dampened down or diluted just because we were blind, or had other disabilities. We used the real machines and produced real pieces of work, and that made us really proud. For some of my fellow students, that was probably the first time they had ever felt proud of something they had done. One of my lamps still has pride of place in our living room to this day.

The course came to an end in the summer of the new millennium, and I was feeling buoyed by my experience at college and renewed set of skills. I decided that I would set up my own business in carpentry and joinery. I was actively encouraged in my new venture by the college and the local social services, which kindly supplied one of their team to support me in the development of my business plan. He talked me through all the grants available and initiated me into the blind home-worker scheme, which would allow me access to a fully fitted workshop.

But then, almost overnight, the political landscape shifted and the fellow from the council was moved to another department, the grants were axed, the home worker scheme abandoned. Though I kitted out my workshop, and set up the machines just like I'd used in college, woodwork became my hobby – I just hadn't the finance to set up a new, viable business. A fortune teller I'd seen told me that I'd never make money from woodwork, and I realised she was completely right.

The workshop looks like an ordinary shed from the outside, but all the tools and machinery are placed precisely, so I know exactly where to find them. I think that people are perhaps surprised that I use the machines that I do, given that I can't see to operate them. I have a bench power saw, two lathes, pillar drills, a wood router. There's a rack of rounders, all in varying sizes, to turn square chunks of wood into round. I can lose hours in the workshop – days, if I was allowed – creating and designing.

I love coming up with unusual one-offs and no project is too big or too small. I can tell that visitors to our home are surprised at the quality of the things I've made. I can go through the house, pointing out my accomplishments and I can tell from their tone that they didn't expect a blind bloke to work wood so that it looks half-decent. I say that it's all down to Deb, that she's my biggest critic and wouldn't let anything that looks cobbled together sit in the house. 'No, that needs sanding down further, Dave, it's uneven here,' she'd show me, thrusting the wood back into my hand. She also keeps me motivated by creating the list of things to make. She's requested floating shelves, pelmets, television cabinets… I've also made bases for lamps, dishes, and a chess set, but my biggest accomplishment is the kids' bedrooms. I turned both Dannie and Georgie-Lee's bedrooms into a Winnie the Pooh-themed wooden fantasy land, a kind of castle with all the usual bedroom furniture but interconnected with slides, tunnels and secret hideouts. It always delights me to hear their friends, when they come over, request to play in their bedrooms. Alongside my braille tape measures, I have my own methods of getting measurements right: I use my arms, fingers and memory, and it works every time. In fact, I'm always surprised at its accuracy!

Of course, my DIY can go awry. Like the time I managed to cut through a plasterboard wall and the electric cable that ran through it. It threw me and the saw across the room, taking out all the electrics and a chunk of my saw with it.

It was my love of carpentry that first put me on the radar of Insight Radio, the RNIB's specialist radio station. Established in 2003, it became Europe's first radio station catering specifically for blind and partially sighted people and all the shows and features tend to have an angle on living with blindness – including *Blind Yoga*, which describes yoga postures for listeners to follow!

I was first interviewed on the station some time in 2007, and the presenter, Simon Pauley, thought my interest in DIY would make an unusual regular feature. I was pleased to oblige, and I have held a regular slot with Simon every Thursday morning for the past five years, as part of his *Morning Mix*. Sometimes we still talk DIY, but more often than not, it ventures into other areas of my life – including the writing of this very book.

But back to the early part of the 21st century. I was still jobless, but equipped with skills. I had probably just about come to terms with blindness – that it wasn't going away, but, thankfully, something else had caught my attention. I had a new passion, and I had to talk about it, persuade people to reach into their pockets for it.

6

IN the summer of 2001 I was standing at the bar of our local social club with my guide dog, Carla, at my feet, when Roy Steatham approached me.

'I'm going to do some fundraising for Guide Dogs for the Blind,' he told me.

'Oh really?' I said. He knew how important the charity was to me.

'Yes, I'm going to run the London Marathon,' Roy said.

'Well, I tell you what,' I began, without really thinking. I'd obviously had too many beers. 'If you are prepared to become my guide runner, I'll leave my guide dog at home and I'll run it with you.'

Roy thought for a split second. 'Yeah, all right then. I'm up for that.'

On the following morning, I awoke with a thick head.

'Do you realise what you said last night?' Deb asked.

'Yes,' I replied, simply. I had already made up my mind.

'You're going to run the London Marathon?'

'Yes.'

'But you haven't run for 30 years plus! You don't even own a pair of trainers!'

I didn't care; I could do it, I knew I could.

I mentioned the challenge to one of my best friends, Joe Whitehouse. He barely flinched and said he'd join Roy and I in the training. A week later, I borrowed a pair of trainers and a pair of shorts, and Joe and I went along to our local running track. Deb and Pat, Joe's wife, came along for moral support. We stood on the track and Joe passed me the end of a towel.

'Come on, hold on to this and let's try a lap of the track,' Joe said. Pat said she'd join us for one, too.

Blimey o-riley.

Off we trots, me, Joe and Pat, Deb watching from the sidelines with our newborn baby, my second daughter, Georgie-Lee, in the pram.

Next thing I know, Pat is telling me I did well. It's curious – she doesn't sound out of breath. She's finished before me, but I didn't feel her pass me. How did she get there before me?

'Sorry, Dave, I took you round twice, just to see how you'd do,' Joe said, meekly. The crafty sod. Still, it was no consolation – two laps of the track and I was knackered. I had 26 miles to run!

We stepped up the training. Two days later, we did our first road run, about a mile and a half, with our first proper running cord: a piece of canvas that Deb's Auntie Mavis had sewn up. For two or three weeks, we ran this route, slowly pushing it so we did it more quickly, before moving on to two miles. We went out most mornings, so our improvements were steady, and two months later, we were pushing ten miles. We had just shy of a year to go until the marathon, and it suddenly seemed like a reality.

The three of us hadn't looked into guide running. We didn't read any case studies or best practice. We just worked it out as we went along, and that's what I have come to tell new guide runners over the years. Sometimes I'm able to give hints and tips: Joe would normally do this at this point; Roy has found that when there's a kerb, that it's best to do that. It pays to have a guide runner who is quicker than me – whether they're fitter is a different thing – because I like to give it as good as I can; if they can run a marathon 15 or 20 minutes quicker than I can, then it's always going to be in their armoury. Guide runners need to be confident, quick to make decisions, because that fills me with confidence, too. They need to be watching my feet, watching the road ahead of us, but keeping their own feet in check, too.

I've had some good guide runners over the years, and I've had some better ones, but I couldn't tell you why they were better, what they did that was easier to follow. They're individuals, and have their own ways of doing things. I have to remember who I'm running with, as some will say, 'Right we're going up a kerb, then down a kerb,' while others will just push and pull me with the cord. But it definitely affects my performance: I'm waiting for the running cord to go tighter to signify that I need to be alert, come closer, or that I need to be pulled left or pushed right. I'm always on guard to hear the next command, the next instruction. As a result, I think that's what helps me to forget that my legs are running, that my thighs might be aching or my knees might be twinging. If I'm honest, I never feel like I can't do it, that I can't go on. I think it's because there's too much going on around me that I don't really worry about what my body's doing.

Roy suggested that we try an organised half-marathon, just to see how we got on, so we booked on to the Wolverhampton Half in the September. And amazingly, we finished it in less than two hours and I felt great! Well, apart from the fact I couldn't walk right for two days afterwards, but aside from that, I had my sights firmly set on the London Marathon seven months away.

But I hadn't officially applied, and I wasn't sure how to go about it. As I made enquiries, I began to feel panicked – runners would hear from October onwards whether their applications had been successful. It all sounded much more complicated than I had realised. I had to get a move on. As I wasn't a member of a running club, I was advised to go via the charity route, so I called Guide Dogs for the Blind and asked whether there were three places going.

'Yes, we do have guaranteed places, but each runner must commit to raising £1,500 for the charity,' they told me.

'No problem,' I breezed, not really giving it much thought, and Joe, Roy and I signed on the dotted line. We were in.

Then the serious training began. I had been suffering with my breathing, as my lung capacity wasn't up to much after all the years of inactivity – oh, and smoking and drinking, of course. I enjoyed a smoke, and I used my habit as a sneaky way of concealing my blindness. When I was out walking in the street, I was always terrified of colliding with people coming the other way, as I couldn't see them. I found that if I lit a fag, the minute I could hear the voices of people coming towards me, I could feign dropping my lit cigarette and having to stop and light a new one. This would give me plenty of time for the people to pass, avoiding an embarrassing collision. I dread to think how much I spent on cigarettes and matches, but a gargantuan smoking habit was easier to admit to than blindness, I found.

It was Grace who eventually persuaded me to give up smoking, when she was only a little girl. Her friend's dad had died from cancer and poor Grace had been alarmed and astonished. She had learnt, from reading the warnings on my cigarette packets, that smoking caused cancer and that was that – she didn't want to experience the same. I realised how important it was to her. What could I do? She was right, of course, so I duly gave up.

Grace didn't stop at smoking, though.

'Dad, I've heard that drinking also gives you cancer,' she said, once. But there was no way I could honour that one.

'A drop of beer in moderation is absolutely fine,' I told her, decisively.

That would be one step too far.

CHAPTER 6

Once we started to throw in a few 20 milers, the training started to click into place. This running malarkey was beginning to make sense again. The hills didn't feel quite so steep, and my legs could take the strain. I was enjoying it!

At the turn of the year, we could feel the marathon on the horizon. I applied my salesperson tactics into getting the funds in, and Deb and I set up a couple of fundraising nights with tribute bands, too, so the £1,500 target seemed doable. We were excited; it was happening.

So when April 2002 dawned, our loyal – and incredulous – families made their arrangements to follow us down to see us on the start line. On the Friday night, we took the Tube to register and get our numbers at the expo, and I just hadn't anticipated the atmosphere, nor the sheer volume of people taking part. We were queuing for our numbers, queuing to sign and show identity, queuing to receive our chips that we would attach to our trainers to record our times, queuing for our goody bags. Then, once we had processed our way through all of that, there were the stalls and stands selling the latest gear or energy drinks, the talks with famous marathon runners, the giveaways. And despite all of this noise and commotion, the incessant brushing of bodies, it hadn't really dawned on me that I would be taking part – not really.

Game plan? We didn't have one as such – just keep going. Roy and Joe planned to take it in turns to guide me. Though neither had done it before our training sessions had begun in earnest, all three of us soon realised that it was a skill, an art form. We had learnt together that there were times when we needed to run wrist-to-wrist, and there were times where I could be given a longer rein to do as I pleased. And all that talking while you're running – unless you've got good lung capacity and stamina, you haven't a chance. It was understandable that Roy and Joe wanted to share the load. After all, 26 miles when you hadn't run for 30 years or so would be challenging enough.

On the morning, we were up at 6am. The Underground was free for runners and it was packed with nervous chatter and shivering bodies. We made our way across London to our particular start at Blackheath, one of thousands with my white stick and bag tucked under my arm. We spoke with everyone we bumped into or passed; everyone wanted to know our stories: why were we doing it? Was it our first one? Who were we raising money for? We were offered water, Lucozade, cups of tea; we were ushered out of our trackies and into our kit, our bags placed on the relevant buses for transportation to the finish. Roy and Joe pinned my number on. Our numbers tallied with the time we expected to finish, and corresponded with the pens in which we were corralled. We'd guessed at four and a half hours, though it sounded like an enormously long time to be running.

I still didn't feel nervous as such, but the occasion had quietened me as I listened to the thousands of voices around me. I'll always remember the five Cockney lads standing in front of me.

'I don't know if I can do this,' one said. There was no machismo: he was terrified, and his voice wobbled and wavered. You could hear the nausea bubbling in his throat.

'Listen,' one of his friends said, nearby. 'We said we'd do this for him, and we will. You will; we all will.'

To me, that summed it up. They, as a group, believed they could pull their mate through, in the name and memory of another friend.

The horn went and for seconds – two, three, maybe five – I felt alarmed. But then my ambition, my belief – yes, my ego – told me to pull myself together. We could do this. We began to walk, as it would take another five minutes before we could cross the start line, and then we kicked into gear. The hairs stood up on the back of my neck. Excitement hardened into concentration and we snapped into a jog, Joe guiding me for the first few miles.

CHAPTER 6

After the first five miles, I swapped to Roy but when Roy came to give me back at the ten-mile mark, Joe was nowhere to be seen. We didn't know if he was in front or behind, but we'd completely lost him. Poor Roy was stuck with me for the rest of the marathon.

It was such an experience. I didn't have much chance to think or worry, as my senses were distracted constantly. The conversation and laughter continued between the runners for much of the course; music – live and recorded – blared from street corners and platforms. I could smell barbecues and beer, I drank water and energy drinks as they were shoved into my hands. Roy was doing a great job of simultaneously watching me and the bodies in front. We kept going, and finished in four hours 16 minutes. We were delighted to have finished, but to have beaten our four and a half hours guestimate was even better. Though my legs were aching, my head was pounding, my mouth was dry, I loved it, in a purely sadistic way. I decided, there and then, that I would do it next year, too.

We found Joe and were comparing notes when a woman approached us.

'Oh, hello gentlemen,' she said. 'I'm from Sky and I'm looking for some English runners who have completed the race.'

Roy piped up instantly. 'Well, we've completed it, we're English and not only that, he's blind!' he said, nudging me in the ribs.

She whipped out the microphone, beckoned over her camera crew and before I could worry about the sweat on my brow, I was being interrogated.

'What's it like to run the marathon blind?' she said.

I had to smile.

'Well, I started the marathon blind; I finished it blind and knackered,' I replied.

It went out on national television.

Back home, a few weeks later, we held our final fundraising night and began counting up the donations. The three of us together had raised in excess of £10,000. Guide Dogs for the Blind saw me as part of their running team, which was fantastic. Peter Emmett, head of events and fundraising, became a good friend. As the charity had a confirmed 100 places in each marathon, Peter and his colleagues guaranteed me a spot and I was grateful that I had reason to keep up the training.

After our first successful London Marathon, Joe and I decided to try a few other half-marathons, one being the Watford half. The day was murky and down south we were surprised to find more snow than we had, but the race was still on. We set off, heading into the countryside from the town. The roads were damp with smatterings of snow at the edges, but the air was crisp. It was good running weather, and we felt like we were doing quite well, more than halfway up the field.

Along one country lane, Joe told me that he could see a raised cattle grid in the distance. As we neared the obstacle, he explained that it would be tricky to tackle: firstly, a 12-inch step, followed by a grille, rounded off by two concrete posts, six feet apart.

Things happened so quickly. Joe told me when to step but catching one of the concrete posts sent me colliding into him. As 13st hit 15st, we bounced off in opposite directions. I fell, gambolled over twice then struggled to my feet, finding the running cord had snapped but my hat was still on my head. I had kept hold of my water bottle, too, but where was Joe?

He hadn't fared any better, flying through the air and landing in a pool of water, winded. He gathered up the remaining running cord, pushed it into my hand and told me to run.

We didn't think about what we looked like, but Pat, Joe's wife, couldn't control her laughter at the finish. The other runners were coming in with mud-spattered legs, while we were apparently black from head to toe, wet and streaked with blood.

'It could only happen to you two!' she laughed.

CHAPTER 6

Joe's watch was later returned after being found submerged in a puddle. He was delighted it still worked, and we decided that it was an omen to keep running.

After all, I was hooked. From 2002 I did 12 consecutive London Marathons.

The second one, in 2003, was just Joe and I, but it proved a really tough one for him. Joe picked up a foot injury at around the eight-mile mark but persevered, telling me he didn't want to let me down. How he did it, I'll never know, but when we went to the first aid tent at the finish line, his foot was apparently black. Despite his Black Country determination, he never really came back after that, so that's when I teamed up with Mac. My 2003 London was also memorable for another reason – my third and final daughter, Dannie, was born soon afterwards.

The running bug had returned. As part of my training, I'd do the Great North Run, the Great South Run, the Manchester 10k, and I'd do it all for Guide Dogs. Deb's Uncle Peter Anderton would generously chauffeur us to each and every one, often accompanied by Auntie Mavis's famous lemon cake for the finish.

Each time, of course, I wanted to raise more money, and I began to wonder how I could encourage people to part with that extra couple of bob. I began to plan for bigger, better fundraising stints, which, somehow, caught the attention of Buckingham Palace and Deb and I were invited to a Christmas reception at the Palace in 2004 as a thank-you for our dedication to fundraising. Of course, it didn't run smoothly: mid-conversation, I felt a body brush past me as if they were stumbling. 'What's that?' I called out, instinctively groping outwards with my hands. I caught a small hand in mine. Deb broke off her conversation hurriedly.

'Your Majesty!'

I had only grabbed the hand of the Queen. Deb later relayed the scene back to me as one of her most embarrassing moments.

'Did you really have to say, "*what*'s that?" *Who*'s that would have been better!'

It was at the Palace that Deb and I met for the first time Geoff Hill, a West Midlands entrepreneur well known for his electrical appliances business. We have stayed in touch ever since, and support each other in our charitable endeavours.

The Palace's recognition was just the push we needed, and we planned a series of events for the 75th anniversary of Guide Dogs for the Blind in 2006. One of these events was a charity cricket match, featuring Dave English's Bunbury XI. Dave English's achievements are incredible: most would think that a fruitful career in the music industry, managing the likes of the Bee Gees and Eric Clapton, is enough to write home about, but Dave, cricket-mad, set up the Bunbury Club which supports aspiring young cricketers and, with its senior team, raises millions of pounds each year for a range of different charities.

That year, I also ran the London and New York marathons, the Great North Run, organised a ladies' night and a sponsored, blindfolded Go Ape assault course. Though the events raised lots of money for the charity, I still hadn't found that big splash. What could I do *differently*?

It was June 2006 when I was in my workshop, listening to national radio. There was a piece on Ranulph Fiennes and how, in 2003, he had become the first person in the world to complete seven marathons in seven consecutive days on all seven continents, and he gave a short interview to the presenter. I listened quietly.

'You know what, Sir Ranulph,' I thought as the feature came to an end, 'you've become the first *able-bodied* person to complete seven marathons in seven consecutive days on seven continents. Could I be the first blind, disabled person to do it? That would certainly get a few extra bob on the sponsor sheets.'

I strode into the house.

'Deb,' I said. 'I've just heard Ranulph Fiennes on the radio and he did seven marathons in seven consecutive days on seven continents.' She knew why I'd brought it up.

'You're off your tree, you are,' she said. But she didn't do anything to dissuade me.

It had begun; it was as simple as that.

Guide Dogs for the Blind were more than happy that I would be carrying out this feat for their cause, but they didn't come on board officially at first. I wondered if it was because they thought it was too ambitious, that it couldn't be done. It was a slightly bigger step than the events I had been doing, after all.

I ran my idea past Dave English. He didn't recoil – he just thought it would do as I wanted: raise a shedload of cash for a cause I believed in. He put me on to Costcutters, as the chair at the time was also a big supporter of English's Bunbury team. To my delight, not only did Costcutters come on board as the main sponsor, but they organised a consortium of their own suppliers and customers, companies like Lucozade and PG Tips, for further support.

With the main sponsor confirmed, the wind was in my sails. Now it was time to tackle the route. Honestly? I didn't know where to begin. I decided to get in touch with the man himself. I typed up a letter and Deb popped it in the post. I've still got it, saved on my computer. It read:

Dear Sir Ranulph

I write in the hope you can help and advise me. I've listened to many of your exploits over the years and I admire you for your sense of adventure. Unfortunately, being blind put paid to many of my ambitions – joining the army and seeing the world – although I still enjoy life and have many tales to tell.

Having a guide dog has encouraged me over the years, and as a way of thanking [Guide Dogs for the

Blind] for how they have changed my life, to raise awareness and funds for them, I completed my fifth consecutive London Marathon, in a PB of three hours 30 minutes.

I'm always looking for a fresh challenge. I have a couple of events in mind; firstly, running from John O'Groats to Land's End, but one of the stumbling blocks at present is to find someone who can give me the time to run as a guide, as it will take a few weeks.

But one challenge I would really love to attempt is seven marathons on seven continents, in seven days. It would be fantastic to follow in your footsteps and be the first blind person to run it.

So hence my reason for writing: would you or your running partner give me any advice, help or assistance in the planning of this challenge? I'm sure, as you are reading this letter, your advice would be to say 'forget it', but I do hope you will consider giving me some help.

Thanking you in anticipation.

Kind regards,

Dave Heeley

Six weeks later I called Ranulph at the pre-arranged time we had agreed and listened to him talk about the challenge he had undertaken. I was enthralled.

'You'll get some PR for this, Dave,' he said, as he imparted his advice. 'If I can help in any way, I will.' With regards to the route, he told me, 'There's only seven continents, so there's only seven places you can go,' and I used that as my mantra: we would find a way. We remained in contact through e-mail over the next couple of years.

However, I couldn't just copy Sir Ranulph's locations: his last marathon had been New York and I was adamant that my last marathon, my seventh and final, would be the London Marathon in the April. That meant I pretty much had to design my route across the seven continents in the opposite direction to Sir Ranulph.

As it often has since, serendipity played a part in proceedings. I was invited to talk at the University of Winchester by lecturer Katie Bull, after she had heard me on the radio. Just after the gig, I told her about what I had up my sleeve and that I had roughly plotted my route round the world, choosing the towns and cities on each continent where Mac and I would run each marathon. She was immediately fascinated – did I know one of her close friends worked for a worldwide travel consultancy? No, I didn't, I told her, but I was glad she had said. I desperately needed someone with insider knowledge, to tell me what to avoid, which airlines were reliable, how to join the dots in the more remote places.

A week later, the phone rang. It was Victoria Cheeseman, Katie's friend.

'Dave,' she said after all the necessary introductions, 'this is stupid!'

'Why?' I asked her. It didn't sound stupid to me, just hard work. 'I just need to know about scheduled flights.'

'Well, there's only one scheduled flight that gets you into the Falklands, for example, and that's on a Saturday, so we're going to have to find you a private jet...' She might have thought it was stupid, but I could tell she was hooked. She was already on the case. I had that stomach-lurch of excitement.

The phone call was brief, but she promised to do what she could. Next thing I knew, she was back on the phone: not only had she the full support of the company she worked for, but she had the route confirmed.

'We'll start off in the Falklands, then Chile. We're then going to go to LA; from LA, we'll go on to Australasia. Then Cairo, then South Africa, maybe Cape Town or Johannesburg, I haven't decided which yet, then back to England.'

Easy. We started with Victoria's plan and began to work up the detail, but it had to remain figurative. We were talking about two years down the line, so there was no way we could book flights and confirm schedules. As soon as she got something down on paper and the schedules were released, it had to change. For example, to get between Cairo and Jo'Burg, as the route was at one point, suddenly it became two planes which would have scuppered the timings and costs. Then getting back to England from South Africa on a particular day became a problem, when the airlines released the fact that there wouldn't be a direct flight and we had to have a stopover via Athens, or somewhere. One of the Kenyan states that we had on the list as a possible destination was soon struck off when a violent uprising swarmed across the country.

It became like a game of chess, a dance between us and the locations which saw us moving two steps forward, only to then move one step back. Victoria was a diamond, though, her knowledge was invaluable. She kept researching, making phone calls and studying schedules, even when it seemed impossible.

Over a period of two years, the route changed in the region of six times, with constant small tweaks here and there. But I was ably supported by Victoria, and others. Deb was on the challenge with me, pretty much full-time, but the events co-ordinator at Guide Dogs, a young enthusiastic lad called Davy Newell, was also right behind me. With a challenge like this I knew I would need a number of guide runners on hand. When I decided I would do the challenge, I spent six months of quiet planning, just between myself and Deb, working out the feasibility of the routes, mentally putting together a team before I even mentioned it to Malcolm, Mac, my main guide runner at the time. We were on a train in London together when I popped the question.

'Listen, Mac, I'm coming up with a plan: I've got a new challenge,' and I told him about the seven marathons. He went quiet for a bit and then took a breath to speak.

'Are you completely stupid?'

'Well, I might be, but if Ranulph Fiennes can do it, I'm sure I can do it. I'm asking you the question before I ask anybody else: do you want to do it? Do you want to be my guide?'

'Yeah, okay, if you think we can do it.'

'Well,' I said, clearing my throat. 'I don't *know* we can do it, but anything's possible.'

'Right, okay, I'm in,' he said, with the simplicity of RSVPing to a party.

However, it wasn't so simple with Guide Dogs. Partway through all the planning, representatives from the charity came to see Deb and I at home. They told us that they were looking at ways to reduce costs and had considered not having Mac as my guide runner. What did I think? Well, I was dumbstruck.

The charity knew that there would be others in attendance fulfilling other jobs – so Phil Glasgow as our physio, or Davy Newell as a kind of project manager from the charity side – that were capable, confident runners. They thought it would be more cost-efficient if they could take it in turns to guide me. I wasn't sure how to answer. After all, I'm sure Phil and Davy would be great as a back-up, perfect to parachute in if there was a hitch, but they weren't the ones I had been running with on and off for years.

Thankfully, Deb, always eloquent in times of need, jumped in. She knew exactly what I was thinking. She explained that Mac and I were already a team, that we were friends who had taken time over the years to understand each other's running styles so Mac could support my needs. Phil was based in Northern Ireland, Davy in Cumbria, so it wouldn't be possible to put in the amount of training together that we required. And it wasn't a case of someone who could run alongside me: it needed to be someone that could feel as I did, that was experiencing the same searing muscles, pounding head and dry mouth. Alternating marathons was out of the question: my guide runner and I needed to be as one. Mac knew me, and I knew Mac.

Deb was not only persuasive, she was right, and the charity could see it, too. Thankfully, they agreed: Mac would be my main guide runner, with Phil or Davy primed to step in if a problem occurred. Davy at Guide Dogs introduced us to world-renowned physiotherapist Dr Philip Glasgow, head of sports medicine at the Sports Institute Northern Ireland, and wow, what a man he is. As soon as he heard of the challenge, he was in and vowed to come with us around the world as our physio.

It turned out that I was quite the specimen for Phil Glasgow and his team back at the Sports Institute. I suppose being 50, blind, a relatively new runner in the grand scheme of things and attempting such a feat was enough to turn their heads, and we were invited over to the Institute for a couple of training camps.

There, Phil, the head of performance science, Declan Gamble, and David Lasini, head of strength and conditioning, put us through tests and trials to see how we were doing and to understand how we would need to improve for the event itself. It was Declan that gave me a little computer to wear on my arm that would monitor everything I would do, from breathing and lung capacity, to sugar and glucose levels. Apparently, they had never met anyone less flexible than me and I was given a series of daily exercises to improve. I took to them with urgency and by the next time I met them, I could already bend and touch the box I had previously been so far from touching.

During the completion of the obligatory medical forms, I was invited to tell them how much I drank per week. On confessing to Declan I had in the region of 20 pints, he seemed astonished and told me that I needed to reduce my alcohol consumption to 15 pints a week, much less if I could. It was a good job, then, that I hadn't told him the truth: that it was closer to 50 pints a week. Once I arrived back from training camp, I discussed the matter with Deb.

'What are you going to do?' she asked.

I told her that there was nothing else for it – I would go teetotal for the duration of the training. She then knew how serious I was.

The team was keen to impress upon us the dangers of our challenge, or the things that could go wrong physically, as a result of jet lag, running in extreme conditions, dehydration, sleep deprivation and glycogen depletion, or lack of carbs as we know it. So the Institute got to work on us: Phil devised us a physical training programme, and Dr Sharon Madigan put together a nutrition plan while Des Jennings worked on our mental skills.

It was a first for them, too.

'I can put together a training programme for you, Dave, for a marathon. You can either run it fast, or you can run it slowly, and the training programme would reflect that. But I have never been asked to co-ordinate a training programme for seven marathons on the bounce!' Phil said.

So we decided it would be a collaborative effort. He would schedule six-weekly training plans and at the end of each period of six weeks, we would respond with our own thoughts and feelings about how it went. I've kept all the training plans and they're pretty full-on affairs. Here's an extract from one as an example:

	Wednesday 17 October	Thursday 18	Friday 19	Saturday 20	Sunday 21
AM	Flexibility • Hamstrings, • IT bands • Calves • Hip flexors • Glutes	Strength and Proprioception	Flexibility	16 Miles (HR 136-145)	10 Miles (HR 152-160)
PM1	10 Miles Steady (HR 136-152)	Cross-trainer: 15min, Level 14/20, Random profile, HR <150BPM, 15min, Level 16/20, HR 164-171, 20min, Level 12/20, HR 136-152	10 Miles (HR 150-160)	Pool Recovery Session: Gentle 20min swim	7 Miles (HR 136-145)

	Monday 22	Tuesday 23	Wednesday 24	Thursday 25	Friday 26	Saturday 27	Sunday 28
AM	8 Miles: Miles 1-2, HR 136-152 Miles 3-6, HR 164-171 Miles 7-8, HR 136-152	Aqua jogging: 10Min steady (HR ~140) 20 x 30s on/off- work at max during 30s on 5Min steady Width x 6 x 4sets: 20s rest between widths, 90s rest between sets	Exercise Bike: 15Min steady RPM 70-80, 20 x 1min on/off (on= 90-100RPM, Level 14/20; off= 60-70RPM, Level 6/20)	Cross-trainer: 15min, Level 14/20, Random profile, HR <150BPM, 15min, Level 16/20, HR 164-171, 20min, Level 12/20, HR 136-152	Flexibility	16 Miles (HR 145-155)	10 Miles (HR 152-160)
PM1	Strength and Proprioception	Flexibility	Massage if possible	Strength and Proprioception	10 Miles (HR 150-160)	Pool Recovery Session: Gentle 20min swim	7 Miles (HR 136-145)
PM2	Cross-trainer: 60 Min Random profile, Level 12/20, Speed >14Km/h, HR 140-150		10 Miles Steady (HR 136-152)				

	Monday 29	Tuesday 30	Wednesday 31	Thursday 1 November	Friday 2	Saturday 3	Sunday 4
AM	10Miles Steady (HR 136-152)	REST DAY: Recovery Pool Session	Exercise Bike: 15Min steady RPM 70-80, 20 x 1min on/off (on= 90-100RPM, Level 14/20; off= 60-70RPM, Level 6/20)	Cross-trainer: 15min, Level 14/20, Random profile, HR <150BPM, 15min, Level 16/20, HR 164-171, 20min, Level 12/20, 136-152	Strength and Proprioception	18 Miles Easy (HR 136-145)	12 Miles Steady (HR 152-160)
PM1	Flexibility	Massage	Strength and Proprioception	Flexibility	12 Miles Steady (HR 145-155)	Pool Recovery Session: Gentle 20min swim	8 Miles Easy (HR 136-145)
PM2	Cross-trainer: 60Min, Random profile, Level 14/20, Speed >14Km/h		12 Miles Steady (HR 136-152)	10 Min steady warmup, 3Mile Tempo (HR 164-171), 10 Min easy cool-down		Flexibility	

	Monday 5	Tuesday 6	Wednesday 7	Thursday 8	Friday 9	Saturday 10	Sunday 11
AM	REST DAY: Flexibility	Aqua jogging: 10Min steady (HR ~140) 20 x 30s on/off- work at max during 30s on 5Min steady Width x 6 x 4sets: 20s rest between widths, 90s rest between sets	Strength and Proprioception	Cross-trainer: 15min, Level 14/20, Random profile, HR <150BPM, 15min, Level 16/20, HR 164-171, 20min, Level 12/20, HR 136-152	Strength and Proprioception	18 Miles (HR 136-145)	12 Miles (HR 152-160)
PM1	Massage	Flexibility	14 Miles Steady (HR 136-152)	Flexibility	10 Miles Miles 1-3, HR 136-152 Miles 4-6, HR 164-171 Miles 7-10, HR 136-152	Pool Recovery Session: Gentle 20min swim	7 Miles (HR 136-145)
PM2		12 Miles Steady (HR 140-152)		5 Miles Race Pace (i.e. as fast as possible)			

CHAPTER 6

Despite the unknown, the training programme was perfect; absolutely spot on in every way. We felt blessed to have Phil and the team's involvement – in fact, I'd go so far as to say that we couldn't have done it without them. It felt tailored, bespoke, and it pushed us but so incrementally that it didn't feel like we couldn't do it. For example, I was experiencing knee pain, even back then, so Phil and the team had me doing specific knee strengthening exercises every single day:

Decline squats:
- Stand on 30 degree slope, toes pointing down slope
- Slowly lower with affected side
- Raise with unaffected side
- 3x15reps x 2 per day

while Mac's weak Achilles was treated through daily rehabilitation, too:

Eccentric Training:
- Stand with heel dropped off edge of step
- Slowly lower as far as possible on affected side
- Raise to starting position using unaffected side
- Repeat 3x15reps x 2 per day

Mac and I felt empowered – the training programme proved to us that we could do it!

Still, the team was keen to illustrate the risks we would take and the pressures the challenge would wreak across our bodies. The Sports Institute's Physiological Report cited that:

'This demanding endurance challenge had previously been completed by Sir Randolph Fiennes [sic] and his partner. Although, Dave and his running guide, Malcolm Carr (Mac), would experience similar physical and psychological stress as the previous travellers, this challenge was considered unique and much more difficult due to Dave's visual impairment and the extra demands that this placed on the two runners and indeed the team.'

We had our work cut out. It took a good couple of years to get to the point of having the main sponsor on board, the travel expert sounding everything out, and the fitness regime under way. Then, in early 2007, just a year before showdown, Guide Dogs for the Blind, satisfied that the event was most definitely going ahead, decided to back it officially. But this actually proved tricky: though it was great to get their official support, meaning the charity would plug it across all their channels and put their own resources behind it, it also meant that we would be subject to their risk assessments, health and safety protocols, and financial agreements.

And we unearthed a few clashes.

Just weeks before the challenge was due to start, I was sorely tempted to take it away from the charity and revert back to how it had been initially: me and my amazing team of helpers and supporters. It had become a case of handling everything with kid gloves and I had to put my foot down. Such was the nature of the challenge, there would be some risk involved, and I was prepared to take it.

But it wasn't just health and safety issues, which I could understand. It went right down to procurement. Charities, like many organisations in the public and third sectors, have their certified list of suppliers and we had to become party to this, too, meaning that our shirts and literature were supposed to be manufactured by Guide Dogs-approved companies. What the shirts looked like also proved a problem.

My running shirt had, of course, Blind Dave emblazoned across it. After all, it's my name, my moniker, my company's name. But Guide Dogs for the Blind didn't like it. The charity thought it wasn't sensitive to the issue, that it was stigmatising me for my condition.

CHAPTER 6

'But that's my name!' I told them, exasperated. 'If I call myself Blind Dave, surely that's up to me?' Dozens of shirts had already been printed up, too, of course.

'It might upset people,' the charity told me.

'Well, if people are upset by the words "blind" or "Blind Dave", that's their problem,' I replied firmly. There was no room for manoeuvre on this one. I told them that if they printed alternative t-shirts, I wouldn't wear them. After some to-ing and fro-ing, they relented. 'Okay, Blind Dave,' they said wearily.

I had been going to wear my Blind Dave t-shirt anyway. Still, that case was closed.

Only for a new one to open immediately. To me and my pals, my trusty guide was known as 'Mad Mac'. Pretty fitting, really. I'm not sure there would be many others out there willing to accompany me on what we were about to do. But this time Guide Dogs wouldn't budge. The negative publicity from any other charity's outrage would be too much to bear, and Guide Dogs weren't going to take the chance. Fine, fine, we said, and removed the 'Mad' from his shirt.

Then there was the contract. The charity had asked that I signed a contract with them, now that I was a participant in an official Guide Dogs event. It seemed an offer harmless enough, but when the contract arrived, it stipulated that any articles, any TV and radio, any photos would be copyright Guide Dogs; and not just during the event, but for the subsequent 12 months, too.

To be honest, I was offended. I had lived and breathed Guide Dogs for years: speaking, fundraising, event organising, running. I didn't know where this challenge would take me, what sort of doors would open. And, of course, I was doing it in the name of the charity. I didn't want to be bound by copyright rules – if it made sense to host images and text on my website, as I thought it would, if I wanted to get in touch with the many journalists and broadcasters I had come to know, then I wanted to go ahead. This was a job for Deb.

It was during one of my stints at the Sports Institute that Deb called.

'Remember that contract?' she asked. She was being funny, of course; I hadn't spoken about much else since it had arrived. 'Well, it's all sorted now.' I imagined the twinkle in her eye.

'Oh?'

'Yep, we haven't agreed to anything,' she replied.

'Now how did I guess you'd say that?' I smiled. She's a good one, Deb.

As was to be expected, I suppose, travel became a real headache. Guide Dogs would only use one particular travel company, based in Solihull, and it became the charity's obligation to book the flights. Week in, week out, I found myself hassling the charity.

'Have the flights been booked?'

'We're sorting it, Dave.'

Always, 'we're sorting it'. But it didn't feel like it, and I was beginning to get impatient. This was a couple of years of work; we could not afford – mentally, physically, financially – for the challenge to fall flat on its face due to issues with travel.

One day, I was told that they were sorting it.

'No, I want to know what the problem is,' I said firmly.

After some hesitation, I was told that the travel company was experiencing difficulty with the flight to the Falklands. I was puzzled, having passed on Victoria's recommendation that we get a private jet due to the scheduling issues. The charity was insistent that this wouldn't work, and that their travel company was doing all it could.

'Please,' I asked, 'will you ring Victoria? She has researched it, she knows her stuff.'

This went on for another week by which time we noticed that the seats were beginning to fill up on all the other flights we needed to take.

Victoria called in a panic. 'Dave? What's happening? These flights are filling up!'

CHAPTER 6

Finally, Guide Dogs spoke to Victoria direct. Sue, from Guide Dogs, called to apologise.

'I've fully come to realise that the company we've been working with haven't done this kind of thing before,' she said, 'so we're taking all the necessary steps we can to make Victoria's company the named supplier this time.'

As soon as I put the phone down, I jumped for joy! We were on! With Victoria on the cards it was all things go. Victoria's knowledge and dedication to the challenge proved invaluable. She even slept in her office throughout the duration of the challenge to ensure everything went to plan!

Guide Dogs also employed a logistics company to do a full recce of the run. At first, I wasn't sure of the necessity to do this: after all, I'd been putting together a list of contacts, from accommodation providers to marathon organisers, for the past four years. But David Carter, an ex-major, was commissioned to go round the world, following our route, in ten days, just to test flights and connections, locations of this and proximities to that.

'It was a nightmare,' he said, on his return, sighing. 'Dashing from one flight to the next, no sleep.' The tone of his voice said it all.

I had to run seven marathons in between!

Then our contact at Costcutters, Angela Barber, went down poorly for six weeks and her cover wasn't up to speed on the project, meaning things started to fall behind. Thankfully, our Angela made a full recovery and returned to smooth things over.

It started to take shape, and the chatter began to accelerate. This brought new sponsorship with it, so North Face supplied our kit, Bentley our travel to and from the airport, Lucozade our energy drinks and, pleasingly, West Bromwich Albion started plugging it in every which way they could.

We began to tell everyone. It was time to make it official.

But with the explanation of the challenge came the questions.

'Can you do it, Dave?' they would ask, with, I imagined, eyes wide and eyebrows held high. It did sound ambitious.

'I don't know,' I had to answer. After all, even if you're fit enough, even if you do all the training, what if you miss a plane? What if you stumble over a pothole and twist your ankle?

Ranulph Fiennes was supported in his Sevens challenge by a colleague named Mike Stroud, a doctor and senior lecturer in Southampton and an expert in endurance challenges and their impact on the body. He had previously accompanied Sir Ranulph in his polar expeditions. I got in touch with him, explaining that I intended to follow in his footsteps and he wrote back, wishing me luck and enclosing a copy of his book, *Survival Of The Fittest*. Deb read the book to me over a week or so, and the section describing his and Sir Ranulph's seven marathons challenge made for daunting reading.

'Dave, this challenge nearly killed Sir Ranulph! Are you sure you want to go ahead with this?'

All I could say was that whatever happened to Sir Ranulph wouldn't necessarily happen to me.

Mac borrowed the book next, and returned to training perhaps less excitable than he had been previously. His swagger was lost.

'Are we going to be all right?' he asked. He had obviously been dwelling on it.

'Let's just put the training in and see,' I said. 'There's nothing stopping us.'

Having Guide Dogs for the Blind on board officially brought massive benefits, too. The charity's PR team began to ramp up the media work in the run-up to the event. They even made their then PR officer, Nicky Wright, available and seconded her to us. I also told Eric MacInnes, the then senior reporter for Central News, about the challenge plan and asked him what the likelihood of coverage would be. He had taken a liking to me and had covered my endeavours a few times, and seemed enthused about the challenge. He promised to do all he could to secure coverage, by lobbying ITV. At first it didn't look hopeful: it wasn't cheap, transporting journalists and cameramen around the world to document a local lunatic attempting something he had no idea whether he could achieve.

But Eric persisted, and eventually succeeded by promising to make all his content available to all news crews that wanted it, syndicating footage and text constantly from wherever he and the team were in the world. It was a fantastic idea, and one I hoped would generate even more coverage than anticipated.

The challenge was on.

7

HOW do you look back on a challenge such as the Sevens and put it into words? How do you describe to people who have perhaps never run a marathon what it feels like to run seven, in seven consecutive days, thousands of miles apart? As soon as one event finishes, the mind distorts the memory – if a runner had a terrible marathon, but made a better-than-expected time, for example, it might be remembered as not so bad after all. If a runner is fatigued or experiencing pains or illness, completing the marathon at all is a miracle. And when all you're doing for seven days is running, eating, and climbing in and out of ice baths, how do you distinguish between marathons without the landmarks or visual memories on which sighted people rely? Sounds, smells, stories?

I kept a diary on my Dictaphone during the course of the challenge. I hoped I would be able to recount, at the end of each day, what had happened: how I felt, how we had performed, the landscapes Mac had described to me. I wanted something I could listen back to in years to come, and play back to Deb and the girls when I arrived home. And when we flew out for training, before the start of the challenge, it started off so well. My diary entries covered what was going on each day, though it was mostly the same routine of pool exercises, team meetings, physio, a nervous anticipation building as the days went on.

CHAPTER 7

Once the marathons got under way, though, it was so fast-paced, getting from one place to another, one airport to the next, that I wasn't able to keep up the diary. Though I could account for every day, much of the resulting diary was recounted in the past, a good day or so after the action had happened. And listening back, it surprises me how matter-of-fact I am: I rarely mention tiredness, and nervousness is barely touched upon at all. It's quite a factual diary; I talk about where we were, where we were going, what I was told, what times events took place, and I think that was a subconscious thing to keep me going. I didn't realise at the time, but I think this was a coping mechanism. If I had dwelled on and remembered every blister, or pain in my legs, or every time I'd asked Mac if he could see the summit of the hill, then I doubt I would have made it through. I've used this diary to aid me in recounting the adventure below.

The day it all kicked off was Sunday 30 March 2008. From 10.30am it was utter mayhem, the phone ringing off the hook and the front door barely closing. I had interview after interview, from the local papers to talkSPORT. The BBC and Central television crews turned up, their kit and vehicles at one point blocking off the road. Friends and family gathered at our house to wish Mac and I well. There were hugs, kisses and plenty of tears. They saw us off in the Flying Spur that Bentley had kindly loaned us for the occasion. It only had six miles on the clock and our driver, Claire Pettis, indulged us in a little ride around the block so we could wave out of the windows like royalty.

The rest of the team – Davy, Phil, Sue, Nicky – met us at the airport and between us we began to sort the mountain of North Face gear we had been donated. Of course, there were nerves flickering, but it was certainly more exciting than stressful – until Air France told us that five of our bags were too heavy and we were required to pay a surcharge of £112 per bag! Infuriating! And the next hurdle? Our plane to Charles de Gaulle – where we would change for Rio – was delayed by 20 minutes, which made the time for us to get off one plane and on to the other one very, very tight.

However, after much clock-watching and gritted teeth, we landed and were on our way to board the Jumbo 747 to Rio where we met Eric and the TV crew and David Gagen, the boss of David Carter who had been forced to pull out after injuring his back. Rio – and more specifically the exclusive Copacabana Palace, right on Copacabana Beach – would be our home for the best part of the following week, allowing us time to acclimatise and warm up, gradually. We had a gentle daily routine of massage and stretches, acupuncture, pool exercises and jogs, under the scrutiny of Phil, supplemented by a little bit of sightseeing – the Corcovado, or the famous Christ the Redeemer statue, and the Maracanã stadium – and fantastic meals, with plates piled high of what Phil deemed 'safe' food, like pasta and meat. Seafood, salads and tap water were out, as we couldn't determine how our bodies would react to the local water supply.

Saturday 5 April took us to the Falklands on a private jet, a Lear 55. Phil described to me exactly what it looked like inside: 'Inside there are seven seats, four in the middle, so you're sitting opposite me, and on the other side, Mac's sitting opposite David, and Nicky's behind Mac. Kevin and Eric are sitting up at the front, side by side. It's all very well finished off with wood panelling and gold gilt finishing round all the knobs and on the seats, leather interior as well. Very plush.' It sounded pretty impressive.

However, two pieces of bad news filtered through: that the Albion lost 1-0 at Wembley in the FA Cup semi-final against Portsmouth, and the Argentinians would not allow us to cross their airspace unless we landed at an Argentinian airport first. No aeroplane since the Falklands War had crossed that contentious zone without landing in Argentina first, and it took David Gagen's excellent diplomacy – on the phone to the

Foreign Office and to the Falklands governor's office – to get us on our way again. After landing and refuelling, radioing and persuading, we sang 'Don't Cry For Me Argentina' and tried not to think about the impact a similar delay would have on the journey back – it could mean the difference between making the next marathon in time, or failing the whole shebang.

In the Falklands, the weather couldn't have been more different. It was cold and raining. Travelling to our destination of Port Stanley, Mac told me that the surrounding road signs warned of minefields. We didn't see any penguins, sadly, but we did meet some of the army and RAF personnel at a reception at The Brasserie, a really rather swanky hotel. A corporal, Chris, told us he and seven others would be joining us in the run the following evening, along with Hugh Marsden, three times winner of the Falklands Marathon. We retired to bed in the barracks known as Hillside Camp in a cosy room of four: Mac, Phil, David and I. Mac baggsied the bed next to the radiator but soon found it wasn't working anyway.

Sunday 6 April 2008

The morning wasn't too early: a 7.45am start. But the freezing showers left a lot to be desired. David went on a recce for something a bit more comfortable and a female chef from the army took pity on us and allowed us to take a shower in her living quarters.

Following breakfast, we decided to make the most of it and go for a spot of sightseeing. Surf Bay didn't reveal any penguins either, but a town tour uncovered some really interesting facts about the place. We met the governor and his wife at their house, posing for photographs on their lawn, and visited a memorial to all those who had died during the conflict alongside the totem pole where the military lads pin the name of their UK home town with how many miles it is away. We found it to be a very moving place on the whole, a kind of sombre feeling hung over it.

At the lunch reception, it became apparent how word about us and our daft challenge had got around. Amidst a great spread, I was told that at the start of our first marathon, a Tornado would fly by and a 21-gun salute would send us on our way. We swapped shirts and signed memorabilia for a whole host of different people who had gathered at the lunch and then the manager of Standard Chartered presented Mac and I with a Falklands medal. I beamed from ear to ear – what a gift!

We spent the afternoon at Mount Pleasant, the wind dropping and the sun shining. I took the time to give Deb a call before she and the kids gathered with everyone else at The Hawthorns to give us our countdown, and tried to get as much liquid inside me as possible. It was a strange feeling, a build-up to the unexpected on the other side of the world.

Outward flights:

1. First leg: 5 April day time departure from Rio-Galeão Tom Jobim International Airport, Brazil, to Montevideo Carrasco International Airport, Uruguay, where there was a delay of two hours. Flight time 2.8 hours.

2. Second leg: 5 April day time departure from Montevideo Carrasco International Airport, Uruguay to Ezeiza International Airport, Buenos Aires, Argentina. Flight time 30 minutes.

3. Third leg: 5 April night time departure from Ezeiza International Airport, Buenos Aires, Argentina, to Mount Pleasant Military Airport, Falkland Islands. Flight time 2.9 hours, of which the last 30 minutes was actual instrument time.

Returning flights:

1. First leg: 6 April night time departure from Mount Pleasant Military Airport, Falkland Islands, to Aeroporto Internacional de Porto Alegre, Salgado

Filho, Brazil. Flight time 3.5 hours, of which 3 hours were flown at night. The last 30 minutes was day time.

2. Second leg: 7 April day time departure from Aeroporto Internacional de Porto Alegre, Salgado Filho, Brazil, to Santos Dumont, Rio de Janeiro, Brazil. Flight time 2.1 hours, of which 0.4 was actual instrument time. The weather was awful on arrival.

3. Third leg: 7 April day time departure from Santos Dumont, Rio de Janeiro, Brazil, to São Paulo–Guarulhos International Airport, São Paulo, Brazil. Flight time 1 hour.

Monday 7 April 2008

Mac and I were ready on the start line at 7.40pm local time, which was 11.40pm back at home. The idea was that we would link up with friends and family having a New Year's Eve-style party – a party to which I wasn't invited! – at The Hawthorns, to count us down to midnight and set us off.

But technology failed us and we simply couldn't get a signal. We never did hear that countdown.

Somehow that set me off thinking that it was a bad omen. Up until then, I'd told myself I could do it, providing no accidents or transport malfunctions occurred. But now I felt a little unsure.

Even though I'd known about the gun salute, Mac and I still jumped over the moon when we heard it – even Phil Glasgow found it difficult to stay on his bike! I was told that, once we got under way, the Tornado flew over us and as it became level, the pilot did a manoeuvre and shot up vertically. Apparently the afterburn was a sight to behold!

It was quite the start to our little challenge. The night proved perfect in terms of running conditions. There was very little wind and it was certainly cold – bobbing between -2 and

0 – but there was no rain, other than a few sprinkles here and there. Amazing really, when the previous days had seen wind and rain lashing down. It was just a cracking run for our first.

And just as we kicked off, Steve Dent and his partner came rushing down the hill in their van, handed me a mobile phone and told me they had finally got a line to Deb. Although it was a bit crackly, I managed to speak to her as we were doing the first mile. It was absolutely fantastic to gauge the response from the room at Albion. It sounded so much fun. I was even a bit jealous! And that settled my nerves. There was no bad omen; we could do this.

The MoD continued to support us round the course, cheering us on and joining in to boost our morale. They were absolutely brilliant, with their lead car out front and the fire engine directly behind to give us some light as there were so few streetlights along the course. The MoD had even rallied round to put down sheets of plywood so we had kinder surfaces to run on than some of the rockier intersections. Simon Almond, PTI for the RAF, had been instrumental in much of the Falklands side of the organisation and he joined us on the run, along with Hugh. Mac continued with his usual commentary and apparently we ran past MPA, Mount Pleasant Airport, heading down towards the coast, where HMS *Clyde* gave us a nod of approval with a big sounding of the horn, then back into the camp for the last 13 miles.

Our course took us past a Phantom and a missile set-up, past British headquarters and the signals, or 'Sneaky Beakies', as they are called, and amazingly, we also had the chance to run along the runway at Mount Pleasant – something that nobody else has ever done. That was Simon's doing, too. A coachload of squaddies appeared at the 20-mile mark, 60 of them, in full battle dress, with bergens and rifles strapped to their backs. They ran two miles of the course with us which was absolutely incredible! Other people chipped in for the odd few miles, here and there. It really was an electric atmosphere, especially when we ran back into the barracks to rapturous applause from the audience waiting for us. We completed the first marathon in **four hours and 14 minutes**. It was pretty good going, considering we were looking for about four and a half.

After all the handshakes, and photographs, and ITV filming, we were whisked off to the new squaddie blocks for the dreaded ice bath, followed by a nice hot shower and food. Then, sadly, it was time to leave – no rest for the wicked. The Lear was waiting, the captain was – I wouldn't say flapping, but he had his flight plan arranged. If we didn't take off within the next five minutes, he was going to have to reissue another flight plan which would obviously delay us. Up and away we went, heading back to Rio, in what felt like a heartbeat.

Forget the luxury of private jets: our flight back to Porto Alegre, the stopping-off point we should have made on the way over, was cramped and uncomfortable. There was food and kit strewn all over the place and Phil took to massaging us with our feet resting on boxes and bags. I had a seat that couldn't recline so I experienced real discomfort as my muscles tried to relax and I tried to sleep. That Lear became known as 'The Golden Toilet' by the time we had finished with it, such was its untidy state.

At Porto Alegre Airport, we fulfilled our immigration duties, meaning we could save time at our destination of Santos Dumont, the second major airport serving Rio. We landed at Santos Dumont at 9am on the Monday morning, 7 April. Then it was a frantic dash in the cars to Copacabana, ready for the start of the Rio leg.

We arrived at the Copacabana and, in my haste, I threw my clothes off in the foyer. The concierge began to complain, telling me there were too many people around to change in public, but too late – it was off, and probably not a pretty sight. And it proved to set the scene for the subsequent marathon. We would not have the support and morale-boosting atmosphere in Rio as we had in the Falklands. It was an altogether different kettle of fish: a lonely run for the pair of us and as individuals. After doing the first one, only eight hours prior, our legs had no recovery time, our bodies were still aching from lack of sleep. We were numb.

The run took us along that familiar Copacabana promenade and up to Ipanema. From there, we made our way to Lake Lagoa: three laps of the lake, back to Ipanema, back down the promenade, where we finished right outside the front doors of the world famous hotel.

Phil and Davy were on the bikes, giving us the relevant supplements and drinks, but it felt lonely and isolated. Mac, who usually described landscapes and scenery in detail, barely uttered a word. I rabbited at times, but mostly the silence bore down on us to focus and concentrate. The five miles from Ipanema to Copacabana saw us rely on our mental capabilities to pull us through – our bodies alone wouldn't have done it. It was such an effort to keep going. Phil and Davy could feel the pain and pressure, too, and began to shout at us, to urge us on. It wasn't pleasant; it was desperation.

In the last four miles, Davy bawled at us relentlessly, 'Left to the finish, right to another four miles to get the mileage in.' It grated, and I gritted my teeth with no thoughts. I had to keep going.

Eventually, we came through and we finished in **four hours and 45 minutes**. Mac collapsed at the finish line, crying. It was tears of both pain and pleasure, and I joined him. I sobbed even when the cameras were thrust at me and I had to think of something magnanimous to say.

Mac told me later that he had been ready to throw the towel in. Though it was so soon into the challenge, it already felt like a lifetime. It was too much; he couldn't do more. But he had looked across at me and had seen my determination.

We felt broken and dejected. Phil and the Sports Institute team took us into a room in the hotel and told us to buck up our ideas. At first I thought they were out of order, and both Mac and I retaliated, until I realised that this was part of it – to provoke us into fighting mode. We needed to feel fired up and ready. I knew the others looked shocked at the fiery exchange of words, but it was needed.

Our ice baths were ready and waiting for us back at the Copacabana hotel, courtesy of the wonderful hotel proprietor, Annie Phillips. As I showered, Davy banged at my door to hurry me as the PR needed to get under way. It was something I didn't appreciate – I understood all too well our tight turnaround, and I told him what I thought. It wasn't elegant. Eric wanted to capture the moment on camera and asked us to re-enact it, to highlight the mounting pressures of the challenge, but I flatly refused. We hadn't time, anyway.

Annie laid on a buffet in the boardroom and presented me with a Brazilian bandana and I felt terrible that we couldn't stay longer to show our thanks. We gave her a bunch of flowers and left with painful bodies and sore, sensitive egos.

Back at Santos Dumont, the Lear was waiting to take us on our scheduled short hop: about 20 minutes to São Paulo. The rain teemed down and soon, from the cracks and grumbles outside, I realised we were in the midst of a thunderstorm, the Lear lurching and dropping. It was frightening, but it didn't stop me needing the loo so I stumbled my way to the toilet at the back of the plane. The others found it hilarious – they all thought we were about to die, while I was desperate for the toilet! We made an abrupt landing, with me still on the toilet. It wasn't until we got to the airport that we found out we had been given the ultimatum: either land then, or the airport would close due to the awful weather conditions. Luck was on our side.

At São Paulo, when we took stock and got ready to board the flight up to LA, I found there was a wheelchair waiting for me. Apparently that's how disabled people are transported in the airport so I laughed and told everyone that I wouldn't be saying no – after all, my legs could do with a rest. My chauffeur, a chap from the airport, wheeled me right to the front of the queue, too. All eight of us got to the front of the queue, baggage checked in, within 45 minutes. Not bad, eh? The wheelchair came out again when we had an unscheduled stop in Lima, in Peru, and I was wheelchaired through to bypass everybody. Being disabled sometimes does have its advantages, it seems!

Tuesday 8 April 2008

We landed at LA International Airport at around 7.30 in the morning and a Mercedes took us to the Rose Bowl in Pasadena, where a crowd of kind people had already gathered. The Braille Institute, co-partners with Guide Dogs in the US, had done us proud: marquees, a stage, a band, so many supporters. I felt myself perk up at the reception. The Rose Bowl itself had opened up all its facilities for us to use, while a press conference saw me ushered on to the stage to thank everybody and explain what on earth we were doing. The Mayor of Pasadena followed me and the Braille Institute presented me with a proclamation which was absolutely fantastic. Keith Nye, a Tipton Harriers runner, would you believe, had flown in from the UK to LA to come and accompany us on the LA leg. It was fantastic to think he'd put himself out just to come and support us. We were hoping to meet up with Keith again on Sunday at the London Marathon when he was actually becoming a guide runner himself and taking a blind lad around the course.

The marathon got under way at 11am, with the mayor sending us on our way. The course consisted of laps of the Rose Bowl, 3.1 miles each. After the loneliness of the Rio leg, we were delighted at the support here. The hype machine had worked a treat and around 30 runners joined us, having heard about the challenge through the press. Many of the runners were from the Elvis Presley Running Association – it seems there's an Elvis Association for every occasion! Some of our kind supporters completed laps with us, dipping in and out, like Ken, a retired FBI agent, and the chief of the fire brigade, whose faithful team followed in the fire engine. One lad called Andy did the whole marathon with us. Even so early in the challenge it became difficult to remember names, such was the level of support. Well-wishers shouted mantras of support out of car windows as we passed. The momentum was growing.

After the eighth lap, and one shorter one in the grounds of the stadium, we heard the band strike up and we powered through the finishing tape – only to find that we were a few yards short. Frenzied shouting from the team encouraged us to carry on so Mac guided us around the perimeter of the car park before running back over the finish line to satisfy the sat navs. We finished the LA leg in **four hours and 35 minutes**, well on our schedule of five hours each. The supporters, strangers gathered for pure altruistic reasons, gave us rapturous, deafening applause.

We were accustomed to the drill at the finish: the dreaded ice bath, of course, but this time we had a bit more of a relaxed schedule. The Rose Bowl had allowed us to use the stadium's aqua centre and outdoor swimming pool and though we were assured it was 16 degrees, I found it chilly when the wind blew. It was certainly more of a cool-down that I anticipated. Phil took the time to work out the knots in our legs, and then, feeling a little more human, we could sort out our kit and repack – in the haste to get between marathons, our gear had been thrown together in whichever way it had fitted.

But the best thing to the day? I tore my way through cheese and onion sandwiches and chocolate Dunkin' Doughnuts. In fact, whoever bought them made a mistake putting them near me – my arm was in and out of that bag of doughnuts like an elephant's trunk. Now that was a reward.

Thursday 10 April 2008

Though we boarded a plane on Tuesday 8 April, we landed on Thursday 10 April. I carried two watches with me on the challenge: one local time and one GMT. Peter, an Australian member of the flight team, told me that we had taken off at 11pm and we had been flying for three hours so that made it 2am on Thursday. Thursday? What happened to Wednesday? I joked. It had got lost somewhere, in the mists of time. I will not forget that the big man in the sky owes me that forgotten Wednesday!

We arrived in Sydney around 6.30am, and to our surprise, there were Guide Dogs officials waiting for us, speeding up the whole airport process: fast-tracking us through immigration, passport control, and in the baggage area literally within ten minutes. It was during this time that we learnt that the chief executive of Guide Dogs Sydney actually knew West Brom well, having worked opposite The Hawthorns years before. You find us West Brom lot everywhere! In the few minutes where we waited for baggage to come through, I gave Deb a ring. It was wonderful to hear her voice, though she sounded almost as tired as Mac and I – the phone hadn't stopped ringing, and even Grace had pitched in to answer calls.

Though it had been a speedy process through the airport, the getaway we had envisioned didn't quite come off – on our final count, we realised we were a couple of bags short. The carousel wasn't forthcoming. But the airport staff were incredible, racing down to the plane hold to see if they could see them. They could, and the bags were duly sent up. After 40 to 45 minutes in total, we were whisked off to Centennial Park, for the Sydney leg.

On opening the car door to Centennial Park, I knew we were somewhere exotic: the sounds of the birds were unlike anything I'd ever heard. 'There's parakeets here,' Jenny, one of the drivers, told me. 'And cockatoos and macaws. They're just flying around freely.' And we were in the centre of Sydney! I imagined the splashes of colour against the pale blue sky.

Our reception in LA had been fantastic – but perhaps here it was even better. We felt like the challenge was snowballing. People seemed to know all about us, even before we'd opened our mouths. Film crews from all over Australia were there to greet us, radio presenters keen to get a sound bite. An American chap from Pennsylvania, in Sydney on a fortnight's holiday to celebrate his wife's retirement, had heard about the challenge on the radio and came down in his running shoes to join us. A young lady named Lisa, who was training for a marathon in four months and had never run further than a half-marathon, told us she would do a few laps to help in her training – and she ended up doing the whole thing!

Around the halfway mark, a TV reporter called Barbara ran alongside us in her heels. 'What was your experience of the Falklands? How are you coping with jet lag?' All sensible questions that I hoped I answered well – until her closing question. 'What's with the "Blind Dave" across your vest?' she asked innocently. I doubted she'd been given much of a brief back at the studio.

'Well, my name's Dave and… I'm blind!'

Her silence gave it away – she'd had no idea.

Finally, we were serenaded over the line with 'Waltzing Matilda'. We'd completed the marathon in **four hours and 40 minutes**. After the interviews and photographs, the dreaded ice bath was waiting for us at the aquatics centre. We had been given the option to use an indoor swimming pool for some gentle stretches and this time I was promised it was heated – but it very definitely wasn't. I didn't know which was worse: the ice bath, or the pool! But it did the trick, as slowly the legs started coming back to life.

However, rest would be different in Sydney; we had actual down time. We were taken to the Sydney Harbour Bridge and guided across, in front of television crews and print journalists. Mac gave me an interesting commentary on what he could see: the Sydney Opera House; the fact that we were probably about 150 to 200 yards above the road; that there was a ferry coming in. We had time to eat and sink into a sofa at a Holiday Inn before the time came to leave, with the Emirates flight to Dubai next on our incredible journey. Things actually began to feel a little more jovial, despite the extreme fatigue. I had felt nothing like it. Though we continually ate and drank, my body didn't feel like mine: it was heavy and light at the same time, I felt pains and aches that I couldn't pinpoint on my anatomy, and I felt like I could dissolve into tears or hysterical laughter at any moment.

Friday 11 April 2008

During our flight to Dubai, I found that my picture of Deb and the girls, hung on the gold chain around my neck, had broken somehow. The flight attendants seemed to notice my dismay and came over to help, eventually fixing it with a wedged cocktail stick. We were so well looked after, and the flight staff were genuinely interested in our challenge, asking questions and wishing us luck.

The hospitality continued as we landed in Dubai. People from the charity, Foresight, were already waiting for us at the airport. I counted my lucky stars – we had been treated like kings at every juncture. All the organisations that had helped us with logistics, or to get the word out, in their home countries had been so happy to help, so pleased to see us.

A fully branded Mercedes transported us to Safa Park where a quick press conference got under way, before we dressed in the public toilets in the park – which were incredibly pleasing to the nose. Most unlike public toilets as we know them in the UK! Phil performed some last-minute miracle physio and the ITV crew did some filming. In keeping with the trend, there was quite a crowd gathered already – 100 or so runners ready to support us, despite it being 7.30am and already 25 degrees.

The marathon, our fifth leg, began at 8am.

The course was around the exterior of Safa Park and underfoot it was fabulous, just like a running track. It was purpose-made for runners and cyclists. But it was also quite a funny experience. Being a Friday and the start of the weekend, locals were coming to the park with their families, setting up barbecues and whatnot, and I am told that we attracted some curious expressions. Slowly, they seemed to find out what we were doing – that this was just part of an around-the-world marathon challenge – and the support they gave us was unbelievable: applause, some shouting in Arabic! It was great!

The course itself was two and a half miles, so we did around 12 laps. On the one side of the course, it was well shaded so, although hot, we weren't in the direct sun. But the other side we nicknamed Death Valley because the sun was directly on us – 25 degrees and hotting up, getting hotter still.

By lap eight, it was starting to show. Our batteries were beginning to drain. In the sun itself, when it was about midday and we were coming up to the latter stages of it, we hit the heights of 39 degrees. It was particularly cruel when the lap counter board came up to show that we had three to go – when it actually transpired the officials had got it wrong and there were, in fact, four.

Still runners joined us, the nutcases. Why they wanted to run in desert conditions was beyond me, but I was incredibly grateful – it just kept us going, one-two, one-two.

Physio Phil had taken to reciting a poem by Robert William Service, called 'The Quitter', at the 25-mile point during each marathon to give us a little bit of strength. It always did the trick.

The Quitter

When you're lost in the Wild, and you're scared as a
    child,
And Death looks you bang in the eye,
And you're sore as a boil, it's according to Hoyle
To cock your revolver and . . . die.
But the Code of a Man says: "Fight all you can,"
And self-dissolution is barred.
In hunger and woe, oh, it's easy to blow...
It's the hell-served-for-breakfast that's hard.

"You're sick of the game!" Well, now that's a shame.
You're young and you're brave and you're bright.
"You've had a raw deal!" I know – but don't squeal,
Buck up, do your damnedest, and fight.
It's the plugging away that will win you the day,
So don't be a piker, old pard!
Just draw on your grit, it's so easy to quit.
It's the keeping-your-chin-up that's hard.

It's easy to cry that you're beaten – and die;
It's easy to crawfish and crawl;
But to fight and to fight when hope's out of sight –
Why that's the best game of them all!
And though you come out of each gruelling bout,
All broken and battered and scarred,
Just have one more try – it's dead easy to die,
It's the keeping-on-living that's hard.

We knew when we had turned into the last 400 metres. The crowds had gathered and the runners – now grown to around 150, so I was told – were jubilant. It was an incredible, incredible finish, possibly the best yet; an emotional finish, as it always is if you've put your body through something that bit extra. Hot, sweaty strangers hugged me or slapped my back. Mac and I clung to each other with grins pasted to our faces. We had finished in **four hours and 55 minutes.** Foresight made a surprise presentation of certificates, which was very kind of them, but the bus – air-conditioned, I might add – was ready to take us to the hotel for the ice baths. And this was a different kind of ice bath: Jacuzzi-style. The TV crew laughed like sadists when they captured that on film.

Once we were fed, showered and dressed, the early afternoon flight to Tunisia beckoned. It was goodbye to Dubai, and our flight would wend its way towards Tunis, Tunisia, and the penultimate leg. But do you know the most exciting thing? That we were actually – actually! – getting a bed for a few hours that night, at the hotel. Everybody soon converged on my room for a get-together, but it wasn't the quiet, calm gathering we hoped for – poor old Eric MacInnes managed to break the glass coffee table to smithereens. And do you know what? He blamed it on me! The crafty sod told reception, 'You know the blind chap? He's had a little problem with the glass table in his room and broken it.' Still, I couldn't have cared less – I had the opportunity to put my back in a proper bed and close my eyes for almost three hours.

I think I slept. I was up again at three in the morning.

Saturday 12 April 2008

5am local time, Tunis.

Up, dressed in kit.

Africa might be renowned for its warmth but this morning was a little cool. Fatigue, pure exhaustion, inevitably played a part in our feeling chilly. Our bodies didn't know what time or day it was. Though we were pumping ourselves with sustenance, our bodies couldn't get enough, and our bodies didn't know when – or if – they would next be rested. No wonder they couldn't keep any heat in. We were all over the place.

After breakfast, we retired to our borrowed ambulance, our vehicle to the start of the penultimate marathon. It was an unusual mode of transport, a pre-war job: there was an old bed in the back and some uncomfortable seats.

The journey wasn't exactly luxurious either. We travelled about an hour and 20 minutes until we arrived at a little village. As we creaked out of the ambulance, our stiff limbs tasting the air, we created a bit of a stir: camera crew, bicycles that had to be taped up because they were falling apart, and us two runners standing in the middle of the road, ready to go. The villagers were scratching their heads as if to say, 'What on earth is going on?' And could you believe it? Right opposite our starting line was a bike shop! Phil and Davy took the opportunity to buy new inner tubes – serendipitous, and the kind of omen I clung to.

We kicked off at 7am. Though it started cool, by two miles we had to stop to take off leggings and tops because we had got a sweat on. At three miles, we picked up a police escort; a police car to the front, I'm told, and a van to the rear. It was lucky, as this part of the course took us along the main Tunis road, from Bani Khallad heading east towards Korba, where the traffic had picked up. In fact, it was a little bit hair-raising to be honest, with Davy and Phil on the bikes on our outside, to the middle of the road, trying to shelter us from these 40-foot juggernauts powering towards us. Then suddenly I was told that in the middle of the road, causing a traffic jam that must have gone back for miles, Tunisian TV had turned up.

Unbeknownst to Mac and I until later in the day, the rest of the team had a discussion over the radio and it was decided that they would look for a slightly different route because the main road was getting to be so busy that it was dangerous. So, for health and safety reasons, an alternative route was found, and a mile up the road, we took a left, on to a quieter country road. We ran through a herd of sheep, a first for this trip, and after about five kilometres, we came into what I was told resembled a little village, a few houses dotted about in the lemon groves and strawberry fields. The village yielded a loop of about two and a half kilometres among the lemon groves and we decided to stick on it, to avoid the main road.

It was mind-numbing – the same old landmarks, the continuous fields. Thankfully, the police in front and behind, and a curious audience of farmers and people working the fields, provided Mac with something to talk about and keep up morale. The workers made their way to the edges of the field to take a look at us and, if they were curious during the first lap, by lap seven, they were shouting their support. If we had done another lap, I think we would have been invited to lunch!

CHAPTER 7

The local mayor and the chief of police appeared, clamouring for a photo call en route, but there was no way we could stop. Timings only afforded us the smallest of toilet stops anyway, but my right leg, the very bottom of my calf, was troubling me greatly. It was agony. Each time I restarted after a short stop the pain was almost unbearable. Phil reassured me that it would subside – or I could always stop for good, of course.

So on we went, round and round and round. And unfortunately, there are toilet stops and there are toilet stops.

'Bush?' the team said.

'I think I need more than a bush,' I replied, frankly.

Phil decided to explain the situation to the farmer, in his basic French. But the farmer point blank refused for me to go in the field. The policeman clocked what was going on and he just simply ordered the farmer – that's it – in that field, do what you've got to do.

As I squatted, a strange fear crept out of nowhere. There I was, alone in a field in Africa, camouflaged by trees, my metallic sweat no doubt a beacon to anything with a strong sense of smell. What animals were lurking nearby? I shuddered with the thought and hurried, listening to the rest of the team arguing over who would bring me the paper.

Things were a little easier after that, so to speak. We did the seventh lap of the route around the lemon groves and we took a left off on to another little road taking us up towards the coast, or so Mac explained. And believe you me, it was up. It went up for about three or four miles. I pleaded with Mac, asking him, 'Can you see the top?'

He said, 'Dave, no, I can't, if I'm honest. I don't want to tell you that, but I honestly can't.'

There was a headwind blowing towards us, too, and with my calf bleating with pain, I am sure they were four of the longest miles I've ever run in my life.

It was such an arduous slog that we decided that if the hill continued, after the subsequent two miles, then we would alter the course and turn back downhill to give us a bit of help. But as it happened, the summit arrived within those two miles; we hit another village, called Tazirkah, and it levelled. Mac described the view of the sea and the coastline, the cane fields that stretched out before us. We were certainly ready for the end. It was hard, hard work.

The police understood we were nearing our finish. The cars came screaming past us, sirens blaring and Mac informed me that they screeched into the middle of the road at a t-junction, stopping the traffic in both directions. We had 60 yards up to the finish. I don't know where the energy came from – perhaps we felt like we were being watched by the stopped traffic – but suddenly we found ourselves sprinting, overtaking the police car. What a joyous occasion that was! Legs, feet, everything hurting, but the thing was: we'd done it. We jumped up and down like two silly school kids. **Four hours and 44 minutes.**

And we knew that now the Tunis leg, the sixth leg, was completed, the real, gruelling, unforgiving hard work had been done.

The last leg would be the London Marathon, coming up the following day.

As far as we were concerned, London was our carnival.

London would be so, so sweet.

Though our respective language skills were rudimentary, both sets of TV crews seemed to work out what they needed and we obliged – even though, really all we wanted to do was collapse in a heap. The local ambassador turned up with his Union Jack and invited us to run a couple of 100 yards up and down the road for his film crew and photographers. Did he know what he was putting our legs through? But we did it. And we smiled.

And like every time, we had to hightail it out of town. We had about an hour and a half journey back in our ambulance and the atmosphere in the back was just magic. We knew we had done the challenge; we knew that the start line of London was just hours away and the celebrations began. The pain wreaking our bodies was pure, but the laughter outweighed it, somehow.

We got to the hotel eventually. The ice baths were ready, but having been situated around the hotel pool, the ice had melted so it was not freezing cold. The swimming pool, for relaxation and warm-down, was very much welcome.

However, it materialised that the pool attendants were not very happy with us leaving our kit on the side of the pool. There were even less happy when Phil and David emptied the ice bath over the side of the pool, though they thought they were helping. In punishment, we were forbidden any towels. There was nothing for it: we just had to put our kit back on and walk through the hotel foyer, in the lift and up to our rooms, completely soaking wet.

After showers and food, we were back down at the vehicles, ready for the airport. It was as simple and as quick as that.

We were on our way home to London, and the Tower Hotel.

Sunday 13 April 2008

Somehow, it felt easier getting up at 6am on the last morning. I pinned on my number very proudly: 777, a prior arrangement with the marathon team. At breakfast we met up with all the others, getting our passes for the buses and strolling out of the hotel like we owned the place. Eric and his team filmed on the bus. Phil worked his physio skills but it was certainly becoming more painful each time. He strapped up my troublesome calf but what the hell, I thought, it would soon be over. What was a bit of pain if we could complete the challenge? I had an interview with Jonathan Edwards and then we made our way back to the VIP tent – yes, we were VIPs for the day! – and to the start line.

My good friend, Garry Wells, chose that opportune moment to pop up out of nowhere and read three letters to me: one from each of my girls. The adrenalin turned to pure emotion and I burst into tears. This would be an emotional marathon, that was for sure.

At 9.45am on 13 April we began the last leg of our seven marathons in seven days on seven continents.

It was absolutely fabulous. We were given thank-yous, well-dones, and good-lucks; you name it, every sentiment people could find to put their tongues to. We kicked off. We had Davy, Phil and Garth behind us, and Garry and Sue were running with us, part of the way. They were feeding us the bottles. They did a fantastic job, the team, all to be commended, the whole team pulled together, it was incredible.

Unfortunately, straight away, Mac experienced stomach trouble. It began to bother him, then dogged him all the way round. He started to worry that he was going to let me down. I told him to shut-up-put-up; it was a run and he was going to do it and it didn't matter what time we were going to do. We would finish together (and if he kept on, I was going to slap him!). He reported, after his frequent toilet stops, that he had begun to pass blood.

Other friends, such as Karl Moore, Phil Calcott and Paul Cole, followed us round the rest of the marathon: some competing themselves, others chasing along from the sidelines. We heard David Lasini, head of strength and conditioning at the Sports Institute Northern Ireland, on two or three occasions, calling out to us and egging us on. It was just an incredible atmosphere, electric.

But, no two ways about it, we were tired. We did enjoy it, but the rain came, the wind came, it got cold and our bodies shook with it. But what the hell, we were going to do it regardless. We all pulled. Phil read us our poem, and at 25 miles, we knew we had done it. To turn into Birdcage Walk and down The Mall, I knew that family, friends – everybody – were in the stands on the right-hand side and I can just remember the shouting, the screaming, the applause. It was just an absolutely incredible finish.

We crossed the line and I don't care – the emotion came, the tears came, it was pain, it was joy, it was absolutely everything. Me and Mac hugged, we hugged Phil, we hugged Garth. I turned to Eric and remember saying, 'Eric! We did it! We bloody well did it!' This time we had broken our five-hour rule, as it had taken us **five hours and 20 minutes**, but we told ourselves that was more to do with the interviews and photo opportunities than anything else. We didn't care, anyway – we'd bloody well done it!

I am the first and only blind person in this world to have run seven marathons in seven days on seven continents. And Mac is the third person in this world. What a club for us to join!

But poor old Mac didn't have time to celebrate: he was escorted to the St John's tent for rehydration. I was taken to the press area, back to the Guide Dogs station and it was just a fabulous response: friends, family, everybody was there. Applause and thanks, it was just incredible. It was an occasion I will never ever, ever forget in my life – yet it was also a blur in some respects. I know I said a few words and at the point I was talking about Mac, he happened to walk into the room to rapturous applause.

And the moment that I heard Deb and the kids was unlike anything else. We all wept, grabbing on to each other with joy and relief.

The rest of the day, following the marathon, is also a bit of a blur. I'm trying to remember who I spoke to, trying to remember what I said, trying to remember who was there, trying to remember how we got back. I just don't know. One thing I won't forget: the ice cream with the flake, complete with hundreds and thousands, that I had ordered before the challenge was handed to me without a word. It tasted like heaven.

I do remember that when I got back to the hotel, somebody bought me a pint. And after six months, it took me about an hour and a half to drink it. But anyway! That was the end to one hell of a challenge.

FROM LIGHT TO DARK

* * * * *

Though we were tired, though we were shattered, the adrenalin still buzzed through us, and I managed to get up at half-past five on the Monday after the London Marathon, despite only getting to bed at 1am. Those few hours of sleep were incredible, but more important was an interview with CNN at half-past six. It was the first of many – I left the hotel at six in the morning, and I wasn't back with Deb and the kids that evening until 8pm, following rounds of TV, press and radio interviews. Deb couldn't relax either. As well as amusing the kids, she had to fetch her mother, Broomstick, from the hospital, who had fallen on marathon day and broken her arm and fractured her shoulder. She knew it was bad, but she'd kept quiet until she had seen me cross the tapes. Then she and my mom went to the hospital afterwards, all matter of fact. I couldn't believe it.

For me, it was a case of trying to put the previous seven days into words. It was a difficult thing to do, especially when I was still sleep-deprived and hadn't had a moment to myself to digest the whole thing.

There was one funny moment, of course. I had already been to the BBC for an interview with the World Service, but afterwards, when I thought the coast was clear, I arranged to meet Deb and the kids at the Disney Store in Oxford Street. Unexpectedly, I had a phone call on my mobile. It was Radio Four saying that they would also like an interview. Oh blimey. 'Can you find a quiet spot?' they asked. They didn't realise I was in the perpetual throng of Oxford Street.

Thankfully the manager of the Disney Store saw our dilemma and allowed us to do a pre-record for Radio Four in the storeroom. How good is that?

On Wednesday 16 April we were finally due to make our way home. But it wasn't without fanfare. The West Midlands newspaper, the *Express and Star,* met us at Euston station and travelled back with us to Sandwell, documenting the journey with photographs and interviews. And as I stepped off the train at Sandwell and Dudley station, I was greeted by the most triumphant, unexpected sound – clapping and cheering by the crowd that had gathered there. The most noise seemed to be generated by the singers and dancers from my old school, George Salter's. Steve Muxworthy, one of the kind chaps at Guide Dogs, had, along with the council, organised the happiest, noisiest welcome home reception on the platform. Lorraine Astle, my hero's widow, and Bomber Brown stepped forward to present me with one of my now most treasured possessions, an Albion scarf that only comes out on very special occasions, while the mayor handed us the biggest glass vase I had ever held. We were then jostled on to an open-top bus for our very own parade! The bus took us right across West Brom, to cheering crowds along the high street, at the girls' school and our other local haunts. Mac and I couldn't believe our luck – what a reception! What a way to finish! We couldn't stop grinning.

But there was one particular moment that really made it all worthwhile. A group of blind students from Queen Alexandra College were also part of the welcome home contingent, and I heard one turn to his friend and say, 'Well, if he can do this, what can I do?'

That wonder made me burst with pride.

ON RETURNING from the seven marathons, I didn't have the chance to close the door to the outside world and breathe a collective sigh of relief with my family. The immediate days following my return were taken up with press: television and radio interviews, discussions with newspaper journalists for features, phone-ins with the people who had supported us along the way. It was almost as exhausting as the challenge itself, but it was also exhilarating and important, too. We had done it, and the media realised our achievement. As long as our names were still in the media, the fundraising would continue, and that was the crucial thing.

Eric and his crew had been filming and documenting throughout the duration of the trip, with regular updates back to the UK and content made available to other news crews around the world as planned. But when he got home, he didn't stop: he did a piece for the Sunday bulletins on the Sunday, and when he arrived back in Birmingham on the Monday, his priority was a big piece for the six o'clock news on the Monday night, a review of the week and all the celebrations afterwards. He also featured in the studio, too, describing his experiences to his news crew colleagues. He spent the remainder of the week putting together *Marathon Man*, a documentary that was later shown on ITV. Deb and the girls enjoyed the subsequent DVD that plopped through the letterbox. It didn't sound real to me as I listened in – a proper documentary with yours truly at the epicentre! The girls hooted in delight at their old dad yelling as yet another bucket of ice was poured over him, and revelled in seeing themselves on screen at the finish line, all three of them sobbing, Deb finding it difficult to keep a poker face. Even Eric and Mac were crying – we had the footage to prove it!

Then the team from Sports Institute Northern Ireland got in touch with their report following all their measurements, questionnaires and calculations, and it made for fascinating reading.

Firstly, the team had monitored exactly how far we had run:

> 'One hundred and 83.4 miles, travelling more than 35,000 miles, through 24 different time zones and exercising in extreme climates, ranging from cold in Antarctica to hot in Asia and Africa (range from 6 – 35°C).'

Apparently I hadn't been in the ideal condition when I first arrived at the Institute:

> 'Dave initially presented in a de-conditioned state, was slightly overweight, and reported sub-optimal nutritional practices'

– which is a pleasant way of saying I drank too much – and the report follows our progress as the fat melted away, the fatigue increased, and sleep was a thing of the distant past. In fact,

> 'On average, between the marathons, there was a total of four hours 14 minutes lying down of which three hours and 20 minutes involved sleep. Between the marathons in [the Falklands] and London, a total of only 20 hours of sleep were achieved!'

The report compared each marathon in terms of our performance and our physical and mental wellbeing. It was no surprise that Rio and Tunis, with its unexpected twists and turns, were the most trying, and the effects were plainly written across our bodies. And it was interesting what a difference the climate made. We released the most energy in Dubai, the hottest marathon, and the least in the Falklands, the coldest, while the highest levels of fatigue and psychological torment were after Rio, the marathon before which we had the least amount of rest. The report praised our team's efforts in between each marathon, too, stating:

> 'The physical recovery strategy implemented between the marathons, involving nutrition, fluid, ice baths, massage, pool recovery, stretching and sleep was very effective in reducing fatigue post-exercise and facilitating preparation for the next marathon.'

Marathon One			Environment						Flight Schedule					Marathon			Preparation	
Continent	Country	City (Time Zone - GMT)	Temperature (°C)		Humidity (%)		Weather	Time (hours:mins)					Time (hours:mins)			Sleep	Appetite
			Pre	Post	Pre	Post	Cond. (wind speed mph)	Flight Duration	Arrival	Depart	In Country	Start	Finish	Total	Great / Ok / Poor	
Antartica	Falkand Islands	Stanley (-4)	9.5	6.4	76	75	Cold & dry (wind 7.8 max, 5 av)	05:30	02:30	05:40	36:00	00:01	04:15	04:14	Ok	Great

Physical								Psychological						Recovery	
Muscle Condition		Body Mass (kg)		Hydration (USG)		Energy Expenditure (kcal)		Fatigue (0 = None / 5 = Extremely)				Mood State		Rest (h:min)	
Pre	Post	Pre	Post	Pre	Post	Marathon	Recovery	Pre	Post	Pre	Post	Pre	Post	Lying Down	Sleep
Great	Poor	75.6	74.6	1.004	1.015	3280	1103	0	2	0	2	Great	Great	00:00	01:00

Marathon Two			Environment						Flight Schedule					Marathon			Preparation	
Continent	Country	City (Time Zone - GMT)	Temperature (°C)		Humidity (%)		Weather	Time (hours:mins)					Time (hours:mins)			Sleep	Appetite
			Pre	Post	Pre	Post	Cond. (wind speed mph)	Flight Duration	Arrival	Depart	In Country	Start	Finish	Total	Great / Ok / Poor	
South America	Brazil	Rio (-4)	22.0	28.0	90	90	Hot & humid	05:30	13:00	20:20	09:00	13:38	18:23	4:45	Poor	Ok

Physical								Psychological						Recovery	
Muscle Condition		Body Mass (kg)		Hydration (USG)		Energy Expenditure (kcal)		Fatigue (0 = None / 5 = Extremely)				Mood State		Rest (h:min)	
Pre	Post	Pre	Post	Pre	Post	Marathon	Recovery	Pre	Post	Pre	Post	Pre	Post	Lying Down	Sleep
Ok	Poor	74.8	73.6	1.009	1.005	4306	2881	0	4	2	4	Ok	Poor	05:00	03:30

Marathon Three			Environment						Flight Schedule					Marathon			Preparation	
Continent	Country	City (Time Zone - GMT)	Temperature (°C)		Humidity (%)		Weather	Time (hours:mins)					Time (hours:mins)			Sleep	Appetite
			Pre	Post	Pre	Post	Cond. (wind speed mph)	Flight Duration	Arrival	Depart	In Country	Start	Finish	Total	Great / Ok / Poor	
North America	USA	L.A. (-8)	23.5	28.3	36	33	Warm & dry (wind 2.4)	14:30*	15:15	06:30	15:15	19:00	23:35	4:35	Ok	Great

		Physical											Psychological		Recovery	
Muscle Condition		Body Mass (kg)		Hydration (USG)		Energy Expenditure (kcal)		Fatigue (0 = None / 5 = Extremely)				Mood State		Rest (h:min)	
Pre	Post	Pre	Post	Pre	Post	Marathon	Recovery	Pre	Post	Pre	Post	Pre	Post	Lying Down	Sleep
Ok	Ok	74.8	74.9	1.003	1.006	4121	3170	0	2	1	2	Great	Great	07:28	04:45

Marathon Four			Environment							Flight Schedule				Marathon			Preparation	
Continent	Country	City (Time Zone - GMT)	Temperature (°C)		Humidity (%)		Weather	Time (hours:mins)					Time (hours:mins)			Sleep	Appetite
			Pre	Post	Pre	Post	Cond. (wind speed mph)	Flight Duration	Arrival	Depart	In Country		Start	Finish	Total	Great / Ok / Poor	
Australasia	Australia	Sydney (+10)	19.4	24.2	45	52	Hot & dry	13:35	20:05	11:10	15:05		23:20	04:00	4:40	Great	Great

		Physical											Psychological		Recovery	
Muscle Condition		Body Mass (kg)		Hydration (USG)		Energy Expenditure (kcal)		Fatigue (0 = None / 5 = Extremely)				Mood State		Rest (h:min)	
Pre	Post	Pre	Post	Pre	Post	Marathon	Recovery	Pre	Post	Pre	Post	Pre	Post	Lying Down	Sleep
Ok	Ok	75.6	76.6	1.005	1.006	4197	3706	1	2	0	1	Great	Great	04:21	03:35

Marathon Five			Environment							Flight Schedule				Marathon			Preparation	
Continent	Country	City (Time Zone - GMT)	Temperature (°C)		Humidity (%)		Weather	Time (hours:mins)					Time (hours:mins)			Sleep	Appetite
			Pre	Post	Pre	Post	Cond. (wind speed mph)	Flight Duration	Arrival	Depart	In Country		Start	Finish	Total	Great / Ok / Poor	
Asia	UAE	Dubai (+4)	26.0	36	71	66	Hot & dry (wind 1.2)	15:35	02:45	14:10	11:25		05:15	10:10	4:55	Great	Great

		Physical											Psychological		Recovery	
Muscle Condition		Body Mass (kg)		Hydration (USG)		Energy Expenditure (kcal)		Fatigue (0 = None / 5 = Extremely)				Mood State		Rest (h:min)	
Pre	Post	Pre	Post	Pre	Post	Marathon	Recovery	Pre	Post	Pre	Post	Pre	Post	Lying Down	Sleep
Ok	Ok	75.6	75.3	1.001	1.008	4549	3120	2	3	0	2	Great	Ok	03:38	02:35

Marathon Six			Environment							Flight Schedule				Marathon			Preparation	
Continent	Country	City (Time Zone - GMT)	Temperature (°C)		Humidity (%)		Weather	Time (hours:mins)					Time (hours:mins)			Sleep	Appetite
			Pre	Post	Pre	Post	Cond. (wind speed mph)	Flight Duration	Arrival	Depart	In Country		Start	Finish	Total	Great / Ok / Poor	
Africa	Tunisa	Tunis (+1)	16.3	22.0	54	60	Warm (windy 8.4)	06:05	20:05	16:35	20:30		07:00	11:40	4:40	Ok	Great

		Physical											Psychological		Recovery	
Muscle Condition		Body Mass (kg)		Hydration (USG)		Energy Expenditure (kcal)		Fatigue (0 = None / 5 = Extremely)				Mood State		Rest (h:min)	
Pre	Post	Pre	Post	Pre	Post	Marathon	Recovery	Pre	Post	Pre	Post	Pre	Post	Lying Down	Sleep
Ok	Poor	76.4	76.2	1.012	1.008	4210	1974	2	4	1	2	Ok	Poor	04:55	04:33

Marathon Seven			Environment					Flight Schedule				Marathon			Preparation	
Continent	Country	City (Time Zone - GMT)	Temperature (°C)		Humidity (%)		Weather	Time (hours:mins)				Time (hours:mins)			Sleep	Appetite
			Pre	Post	Pre	Post	Cond. (wind speed mph)	Flight Duration	Arrival	Depart	In Country	Start	Finish	Total	Great / Ok / Poor	
Europe	UK	London	7.0	12.0			Heavy showers, cold spells	02:55	20:00			09:45	15:05	5:20	Ok	Great

Physical								Psychological						Recovery	
Muscle Condition		Body Mass (kg)		Hydration (USG)		Energy Expenditure (kcal)		Fatigue (0 = None / 5 = Extremely)				Mood State		Rest (h:min)	
Pre	Post	Pre	Post	Pre	Post	Marathon	Recovery	Pre	Post	Pre	Post	Pre	Post	Lying Down	Sleep
Ok	Ok					4312		2	4	1	2	Great	Great		

But, after the event, once the furore had finally died down, I presumed life would go back to normal.

However, I can't really say that life was ever the same again.

Firstly, the challenge had fundamentally changed my life. Giving up drinking, and instead channelling my efforts into training, had proved to me exactly how important family values are. The challenge strengthened my dedication to my family, with drink loosening its grip on my daily life.

Secondly, an award came my way, completely unexpectedly. On Sunday 7 December, Mac and I were invited to the BBC Midlands Sports Awards at the National Motorcycle Museum near Solihull where we were presented with the Special Achievement Award in recognition of the challenge. I was bowled over – here we were, being presented with an award, alongside real, professional sportsmen and women.

The challenge also had a massive impact on Guide Dogs for the Blind, too. It prompted an enormous increase – 600% – in the number of enquiries to run for Guide Dogs in the London Marathon and awareness levels of the challenge were extremely high. We received positive coverage on *News at 10*, *Channel 4 News*, CNN, *Channel 5 News*, BBC News 24, Sky Sports, *This Morning*, *Eye Witness News USA*, Channel 12 and 7 Australia, features in *The Independent* and *The Telegraph* as well as coverage in *The Times*, *The Guardian*, *The Daily Mail*, *The*

Mirror, The Daily Express, and *The Sun*. The charity reported back that official analysis of the media coverage showed that the equivalent publicity value of the campaign amounted to over £5m and that the total circulation figure was 132,000,517.

And the amount the challenge raised? We announced £375,000 at the time, but, unbelievably, the figure continued to grow. Guide Dogs actually told us that the true figure would never be known, such was its lasting legacy.

It demonstrated to me the power of the challenge: that an ordinary bloke could do something, raise a few pounds, and actually influence something, or make a difference.

It got me thinking.

What would be next? That was the question I was being asked at every turn: at the Albion, at the shops, at the doctor's, by neighbours, by relatives, by the press.

A year on from the challenge, an e-mail to Eric demonstrates that I'm already thinking about challenge two:

> From: Dave Heeley
> To: Eric MacInnes
> Subject: GL Blind Dave
> Date: Sun, 5 Apr 2009 20:24:17 +0100
>
> Hi Eric, hope you are sober! Well, would you believe it? 12 months today it was just starting and now we're celebrating the first anniversary!
> Speak soon and keep up the training – you could be a part of the next one! Dave

> From: Eric MacInnes
> To: Dave Heeley
> Sent: Monday, April 06, 2009 5:41 AM
> Subject: RE: GL Blind Dave
>
> Morning, Dave. I'll never forget it. What a journey. And it was a pleasure being with you and Mac and Phil and Davy and Kev and the other guys.

Unforgettables: you in a wheelchair at Lima Airport, you going to the bog in the Lear while we were landing in a thunderstorm, me getting lost out of Australia, the ambulance drive out of Tunis and dodging the suburban traffic, and you and Mac bringing it home in London on day seven.

Funny thing, I'm just sitting here at my desk in Abu Dhabi and the picture of us all standing next to the Lear has just flashed randomly on my digital photo frame. When is the next one??? Count me in. Enjoy The London.

Eck

Then came the offer of speaking. I had done one or two talks in the past, always on behalf of Guide Dogs, to explain the charity's work and illustrate its value. I suppose I was an informal ambassador to the charity, able to speak about their work from a beneficiary's point of view. Schools and community groups were the main recipients.

But this time people wanted to hear me talk about the trials and tribulations of the seven marathons challenge: every blister in training, every panicked moment when I or Deb thought I couldn't do it, every blip in the training schedule or flight logistics. It was flattering to be asked, I couldn't deny it, but more excitedly, it gave me another opportunity to extend the reach of the challenge, another chance to up the total.

Now it's how I make my living. I give talks to big corporations, such as Virgin and Barclays, to schools and universities, community groups such as the Women's Institute and Rotary. I'll give a talk specifically on my running habits for a runners' club or how I became accustomed to a guide dog for a church group. And I absolutely love it: it's the people I meet and the questions I'm asked. The questions from school kids are by far the best.

Like 'How do you put your socks on?'

To which I'll answer: 'Erm… how do you put on yours?'

Wasn't I angelic? I remember my first pair of glasses well

Me and my glasses meeting a giant Sooty in Blackpool

West Bromwich Schools Secondary Athletics Association

Standard Certificate

Name *David Healey*

Event *1st. Year Boys 1500 metres*

Time/Distance *5min. 13.9 secs.*

Date *14th. May 1970.*

Hon. Sec.

My name might be spelt wrong, but it was definitely me that won the 1500 metres!

I always got on well with Gran and Grandad Clee

I was straight out of school and into work, rocking the long hair look, too

Heeley's was my baby. And look at those glasses!
Copyright: Birmingham Mail

I spent a lot of time in my office and even Grace liked to visit!

I'd always dreamt of driving a tank like my dad

Being blind didn't prevent me from being a hands-on dad

Nobody knew about our Gretna Green elopement… apart from bridesmaid, Carla!

Dave English wasn't too impressed with my cricketing skills ahead of the Bunbury charity match Copyright: Express & Star

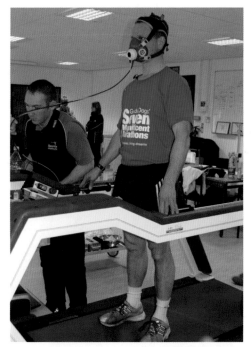

Being put through my paces at The Sports Institute Northern Ireland with Declan Gamble at the controls

Me at Heathrow in a promo shot for the challenge

And we're off! The Seven Marathons challenge started with an amazing ten-gun salute

The pain at the finish of the Dubai marathon is evident on our faces

Hi Dad!

Well done so far pop's! Really really uber proud! Just the one to do now. which yes I know, it's easy for me to say but you know what I mean!

Looking forward to seeing you in a wee while.

Much love and an I.O.U. hug

Gracie x

The girls have a tradition of writing to me before each challenge, and their letters are read to me at the beginning. It's always an emotional moment

Finishing the final marathon, London, was something else

I'm so lucky to make my living from speaking about my experiences Copyright: The PGS Team

The start of the Top To Toe at John O'Groats (left to right: Dave Dourass, Steve Dugmore, Rosemary Rhodes, Dave Long, Garry Wells, Blind Dave, Steve Dourass)

As fast as a cheetah and as graceful as an eagle? I had a lot to live up to on the Top To Toe!

Day five was an emotional one. I broke down when the girls turned up to surprise me Copyright: Benedict Wilkins

Mom's always been supportive of my daft endeavours

On the road for the final marathon (left to right: Mike Hopkins, Dave Sinar, Dave Long, Steve Dugmore, Blind Dave, Tony Ellis, Karl Moore, Rosemary hanging out of the vehicle)

A champagne shower to celebrate the finish (left to right: Karl Moore, Dave Dourass, Steve Dourass, Blind Dave, Mike Hopkins, Dave Long, Garry Wells, Steve Dugmore, Dave Sinar)

A lap of honour at The Hawthorns: the stuff dreams are made of! (left to right: Karl Moore, Blind Dave, Dave Long) Copyright: Albion Foundation

Dr Dingle: what an honour! Copyright: Wolverhampton University

Not many people can say they can drive their sheep down the High Street in West Bromwich, you know Copyright: Phil Hill

It was a proud moment, carrying the Olympic Torch Copyright: John Workman, Black Country Bugle

On the pitch with Adrian Chiles and Tony 'Bomber' Brown to be appointed Ambassador for The Albion Foundation Copyright: Albion Foundation

*Duggie's a great tandem partner
– I enjoy making his legs work!*
Copyright: Benedict Wilkins

*We were the only ones to catch a glimpse of the famous
Eddy Merckx statue* Copyright: Andy Lamb

Dad,
You are an insperational man, who makes peoples dreams come true. As well as having all your other achieuments, There is one that is always in my heart. and that achieument is that you are always louing me, and I hope you never give that up. Good Luck in the Saharah desert dad and when you are feeling its tough Just think of you family that might motivate you even more.

I love you
Daddy
With all my ♡ HEART
Love
From Dannie xxxx
P.S: Bring me back Some
sand!

*Who knew that a towel
rail could be an emergency
substitute for tandem
handlebars?*

*You can see why my
girls' letters make my
eyes wet!*

I finally managed to catch up with Sir Ranulph Fiennes after years of email and phone correspondence

Rosemary and Tony expertly guiding me across the sands MDS2015©WAA/ CIMBALY

The terrain in the desert was surprisingly varied MDS2015©WAA/ CIMBALY

We did it! Marathon des Sables 2015 in the bag MDS2015©WAA/ CIMBALY

Cooking in the desert was an experience, to say the least!

'How do you brush your teeth?'

'With a toothbrush and toothpaste. How about you?'

There's certainly no grey areas with kids – it's black or it's white. And in schools I'm always second best. It's the dog they want to talk to, not me.

Though I've given talks everywhere – at the end of my street, at Cheltenham Racecourse, St James's Palace, in London, Dublin, in Spain, Dubai, the US – I still get nervous. It's not necessarily nerves about the act of speaking per se, as I speak about my challenges so frequently that they are just as vivid to me as they were when I undertook them. I speak from the heart, and when that's my mantra, it feels like little can go wrong. But I do fear my clumsiness getting the better of me: will I trip up the steps to the stage? Will I drop the microphone? Once I get the audience laughing, I feel like I'm on the home straight – it's just when they're silent that I begin to worry.

The problem I'm having now, several years into my speaking career, is weighing up the challenges, and giving accurate reflections of my achievements. For example, many of my audiences still want to hear about the seven marathons – that's often the reason I'm booked in the first place – but in my mind, it was the Top To Toe challenge which took the greatest toll. I often want to give an account of the more recent undertakings, too, to make sure the talk is bang up to date, but there is a danger of dilution when I'm limited to a 45-minute engagement. Friends have suggested that I talk about the seven marathons for the rest of my life, but I'm not sure I can do that. I'm often wondering *what's next?* so surely my listeners are thinking the same.

* * * * *

But back to the latter half of 2008 and 2009.

I was hungry for another challenge.

And the first presented itself through the radio again. In hindsight, perhaps Deb wishes I wasn't such an avid radio listener, given the trouble it's got me into. But this time, it was something closer to home.

The first Birmingham half-marathon, or the Great Birmingham Run, as it is now, began in 2008, and by 2009, it attracted a great buzz of publicity as it became affiliated with the World Half Marathon Championships. Phil Upton, then a presenter on BBC Radio WM, mentioned that the station would be using the race to lead the charge in a new campaign: fundraising for the Birmingham Children's Hospital's new kidney unit, which would replace the crumbly old buildings that young kidney patients had to visit as part of their regular treatment.

My ears pricked up, and I wondered if I could help. It was a cause that interested me threefold: of course, I had children and I naturally sympathised as a parent; it was a hospital which served the whole of the Midlands; and my dad, shortly before he died, had a kidney removed in a bid to tackle the cancer that was attacking his body. I rang the station and offered my support, and the station was delighted. We formed Team Blind Dave and when the race rolled around, in October 2009, we had 30–40 runners. The campaign was fantastic, with the station organising all kinds of fundraising events including the 'Big Sit Still', a sponsorship challenge where thousands of school kids had to endure sitting still in solidarity with children undergoing dialysis.

When the Kidney Kids Appeal came to a close, over £1.5m had been raised and we were fortunate enough to be shown round the shell of the facility. It was fantastic to be invited back to the launch of the new, state-of-the-art department when it was all completed, early in 2010.

Since the Sevens, I had formed a list of ambitions in my mind. These were the 'big ones', the races that many a runner dreams of: the Marathon des Sables; the Comrades Marathon; John O'Groats to Land's End. It was the latter I shuffled to the top of the list.

But it needed to be different in some way, enough for people to reach into their pockets. We pored over the record books. Challengers had walked and run the well-trodden route; they had ridden motorbikes and bicycles, driven classic cars and tractors. All kinds of modes of transport had been used, all kinds of feats attempted. But we soon saw that nobody had yet made a combination run *and* cycle, with marathons as a key feature.

That would be it.

Deciding for which charity I would attempt this next challenge was much easier. My dad, Deb's dad, our good friend Mick Edmonds, and Carla the guide dog had all died from cancer, and we knew many other friends and relatives who had been affected. We learnt through our friend Steve Dourass, then the regional fundraiser for Macmillan Cancer Support, that it is estimated that half of the entire UK population will be diagnosed with cancer during their lifetime. And there was further evidence to support our choice: 2011, the year we hoped to host the challenge, would be the centenary anniversary of the charity. We also discovered that Douglas Macmillan, the charity's founder, was born on 10 August 1884 and as I was planning on doing the challenge in August anyway, due to the likelihood of kinder weather, that set the start date. I had already done seven marathons, so how about ten marathons? Ten marathons, ten days, representing ten decades for a centenary, kicked off on 10 August. Easy.

We put it to Steve at Macmillan who reported back that the charity was overjoyed. We decided to stay as a third party, though, rather than take it in-house. From our experience with the Sevens, it proved that when the big charity needed to knock on some big doors, its clout meant it could do, and when we wanted to use a little – shall we say 'sympathy' – as a third party, then Blind Dave could do so, too.

It was set. Unlike the Sevens, there would be no official challenge organiser, no logistics officer or route planner.

We would co-ordinate the whole thing, from start to finish, putting together the team, planning the route, booking the accommodation, informing the police, co-ordinating the PR – oh, and training and fundraising. I am lucky to have such an enthusiastic wife as Deb. Steve, his partner Tracy and brother Dave also joined us.

As soon as circumstances allowed, we took ourselves up to John O'Groats. This was something we couldn't leave to lines and scales on maps: this was something we had to live ourselves, albeit in the family car with the kids in the back. As Deb drove us from one point to the next, the girls became the eyes in the back of the car, jotting down notes for us to remember as I reiterated the same on the Dictaphone, taken from Deb's running commentary. We recorded the mileage and the useful landmarks: 'on the left is a layby', 'a set of public toilets at this crossroads', 'a café is coming up on the right', 'a public telephone just before the turning', and so on. It was a case of measuring out each marathon, each 26.2 miles, then deciphering the best cycle route towards a bed for the night and a suitable marathon starting point in the morning.

We nipped in and out of hotels, hostels, guesthouses and bunkhouses, recording names and numbers, mentioning the challenge to gauge initial reactions. We ate more petrol station snacks than can surely be recommended, we peed behind more bushes than I would care to mention, but it seemed like progress.

It took us two days to get to Gretna, but we had to make a stop there, so we could show the girls where their mom and dad got married. We stayed at the hotel again, just one night, but by then, Steve, Dave and Tracy had to return home for work.

At Penrith, we came across two cyclists, a father and son team, Jerry and Joe Williams, attempting John O'Groats to Land's End.

'We live in Cornwall,' they told us, 'we'll help you with the route down there.' Sure enough, once they had recovered from their successful attempt, they sent us up their maps, plus hints and tips for accommodation and eateries. Local knowledge was particularly helpful when it came to back roads and as-the-crow-flies moments: Google Maps and A-Zs can be as accurate as they like, but there's nothing that beats someone telling us, 'No, what you want to do there is…' We were delighted with our serendipitous find, and we kept in touch with Jerry and Joe throughout the preparation for the challenge.

The next day, we continued as we had been: measuring out each 26.2 miles, logging the amenities along the way, tipping off the pubs, cafés, hotels and restaurants, right down the length of the country. And there were some lucky coincidences to be had along the way, too, which made us feel positive about the whole thing. For example, we had taken the A38 – the country's longest two-digit A road – to Gloucester and the tip of Bristol towards Bridgwater. Richard Harris, Deb's cousin, is a regular at the Lime Kiln pub in Bridgwater that he'd brought us to many a time, and that particular set of 26.2 miles took us almost to its door.

Once we arrived home, we surprised ourselves. We had expected to come home and collapse in a weary heap, daunted by the prospect of doing it all again through our own steam rather than by car. We fully expected to chide ourselves for our outrageous ambitions and spend the resulting few days in crisis talks, 'Could we really do this?'

But we didn't. Arriving back home was lovely, of course, but we couldn't wait to turn what we had seen into a real concrete plan, a route drawn up and cemented with coloured blobs on maps and reservations for hotel rooms. We spent the next few days sitting at our house phone, calling every hotel and guesthouse and pub and café and confirming the conversations we had made on the fly. Some even waived their fees for us, or offered discounts, seemingly inspired by our chutzpah and keen to help us amplify our fundraising. The then assistant chief constable of West Midlands Police, Garry Forsyth, told us he would speak to the forces that we would encounter during our trip to ask them to keep an eye on us. Suddenly our plans, our home-based hunkering over maps and itineraries, seemed very real.

> John O'Groats
> Drumnadrochit
> Loch Lomond
> Lockerbie
> Lancaster
> Stoke
> West Bromwich/Birmingham
> Weston-super-Mare
> Okehampton
> Truro
> Land's End.

Next we secured the support of Team Blind Dave. With the intensity of the challenge – ten marathons over ten days – I felt I possibly needed more than one guide runner, and I did have a few niggling fears about the cycling: of course, not all marathon runners are capable cyclists, and vice versa, so I couldn't necessarily rely on the guides wanting to cycle. And who was I kidding? I hadn't been on a bike for 35 years! I hadn't even ridden a tandem seriously before.

After the Sevens, Mac had decided to retire from marathons and take up cycling. I didn't blame him. Two other regular guide runners, my good pals Dave Long and Karl Moore, were still up for it, with Karl doing the London with me each year. During a run, I tentatively put it to them.

'I'm thinking of doing another challenge,' I said, clearing my throat.

Thinking? If only they knew! The whole route was planned out and stuck to the notice board at home.

'Right...?' they answered. What madcap plan did I have this time?

They almost seemed relieved when I told them.

'Dave, put my name down for the ten marathons,' Longy said, confidently.

'I'll run the ten marathons and cycle as well,' Karl responded.

Steve Dourass knew an excellent, keen cyclist who he thought would make a welcome addition to the team. He set me up a meeting with him: Mike Hopkins, the principal of South Birmingham College.

Sitting in his office, I carefully went through each detail about the challenge that we had confirmed so far: the dates, the charity, the route, the support. It was just the sticky question of a tandem.

'Tandems are notorious!' Mike said.

'Would you take me out on a tandem?' I asked him. There was no point beating about the bush.

'Yes, I'll try it out,' he said.

'Fancy the Top To Toe?' I couldn't help myself.

'Go on then,' he answered, as though I had just enticed him into the pub for a pint on a school night.

Mike then volunteered his friend, Dave Sinar, himself recently recovered from cancer, as the second tandem cyclist, and wondered how the wider college could come on board.

'Leave it with me,' he said. I imagined him tapping his temples as his brain whirred.

And true to his word, he came back to me with a plan: his colleague, Andy Williams, head of transport at the college, would help us with support vehicles, while a group of media students would document the event, assisting Macmillan with media enquiries en route.

Deb was infected with asking outright, too. We had known physiotherapist Rosemary Rhodes since a speaking engagement in Dubai, just after the Sevens, when she had shown the kids how to massage dad's pesky calves with a rolling pin. A runner herself, she knew the impact of marathons on knees and muscles and minds. 'They'll need a physio with them, I would have thought,' Deb suggested.

'Oh yes, definitely,' Rosemary replied. 'I'd love to do it.'
For Rosie, the challenge didn't sound so crazy a feat – she's
surrounded by endurance runners and long-distance athletes
who seemingly spend all their time working out what mad
thing to try next. She seemed rather blasé about the whole idea,
and that pleased me. Rosemary could bring some perspective
to proceedings.

Deb and I were also invited to the 2011 Mayor's Ball and
found ourselves sitting at a table with Steve Dugmore, the then
chief superintendent. Immediately, good old Deb dived in.
'Oh you like cycling? Why don't you come along?' He was
retiring that year, he had time to do it, it didn't matter that he
hadn't ridden a tandem before... the sweet-talking paid off.
He was in. It wasn't long before Duggie and I were clocking
up 50 miles, 100 miles, regularly on a tandem kindly donated
by Dawes Cycles.

Many of our friends and relatives wanted to get involved,
even if they weren't runners or cyclists, and we had numerous
offers of help and support, all of which were greatfully
received. Garry Wells, though a runner himself, felt that ten
marathons was just too much. Instead, he volunteered to lead
the pack on a motorbike, clearing the way for the runners
and cyclists, and warning other motorists of our advance.
Other friends and friends of friends volunteered their services
through spreading the word in their local areas, and taking
our maps and tweaking the route to better suit the terrain or
to avoid congestion hotspots. We were signposted to people
that could help us in their official posts, too, such as the folks
at Volkswagen that lent us the support vehicles including
what came to be christened 'The Mommies' Bus', the people
carrier containing wives, girlfriends, partners and kids, with
Deb at the wheel, keen to follow and support the team in the
challenge. Jim Kelly at the council arranged the metaphorical
and literal green lights, while the lovely Liz Mabley, since sadly
passed away, sorted the risk assessments and health and safety

concerns through Sandwell Council. She became a good friend to the challenge and to us. She had a laugh like the charge of a herd of elephants!

When Steve Dourass started to rev up the hype machine, we couldn't believe our luck. He is well connected, that man. Through Macmillan, he harnessed community fundraising teams across the country to support us, raising both money and awareness that we would be passing through, and he controlled all the Macmillan PR, encouraging local and national television stations and newspapers to follow our story. We backed it up with our own contacts. It was looking pretty formidable.

Naturally, I wanted my beloved Albion to get behind us and through the contacts I'd built during the Sevens, it seemed that the club would do everything they could. When Steve announced he had good contacts at the Blues and Villa, too, it got us thinking. Could we get all the local football clubs involved somehow? Then we settled on it: we would appeal for fans of the West Midlands football clubs to join us on the Birmingham marathon leg, which we planned to start in Victoria Square in the city centre. It worked, and a fantastic article about the challenge and our appeal for additional runners went out in the *Birmingham Mail* around Easter time.

We received enthusiastic correspondence from runners keen to run the Birmingham leg with us, all representing the football clubs in the area and each raising a significant sum in the process. In the end, five runners from each club joined us, including: Larry Parkes, a Villa fan, unofficial supplier of Fruit and Nut and dad of my co-writer, Sophie; Gareth Stubbs, Derek McDonagh and Chris Sprules, fellow Baggies fans; Tim Andrews, the Blue Nose; and Tony Meehan, who decided to do the whole thing dressed as Loopy Leprechaun!

Then there was the training. Little by little, we increased our running, running more frequently and for longer. Then we had to fit in cycling, too, getting to grips with the quirks and frustrations of a tandem.

9

AND, OF course, after all that preparation, those months of thinking about those ten days in August 2011, they arrived.

Like I had with the Sevens, I knew that I needed to record the challenge somehow. I wasn't sure how much time I'd get to do it – after all, most of my days would be taken up with cycling and running, and any remaining time I had, I suspected I would want to spend in bed – but keeping a diary would allow me that chance to relive it, to savour it, to remind myself of the people we met along the way, the laughter we had, the inevitable moments of disaster... The Sevens had passed in the blink of an eye: all that planning, preparation, training, then the challenge itself. Done. I knew this would be the same.

I did manage to keep my diary and add to it most days during the challenge. Rosemary Rhodes also recorded her experiences in a diary, while Garry Wells wrote a daily update on Facebook, which helped us enormously in getting the word out about the challenge and keeping our supporters up to date with our progress. He also wrote a poem he christened the 'Ode To Toe', highlighting some of the more memorable moments of the challenge in his wry, humorous fashion. It was fantastic when they offered their thoughts up to me afterwards to give me a rounded picture.

CHAPTER 9

So here's my account of the Top To Toe, a flavour of the hardest, most challenging test I've yet endured, that took us from John O'Groats to Land's End in ten days – what we encountered, the pain we suffered and the sense of camaraderie that will stay with me forever.

Wednesday 10 August 2011

I started the day sitting alone in the support vehicle at 3.45am. The rest of the team was busy getting everything ready. I was very much alone in my thoughts, wondering if I'd done enough training, whether I really could do this. Was I truly fit enough? I was already missing Deb and the girls. But before I could get too lost in my thoughts, Garry Wells burst into the support vehicle. I could picture him standing there in his bike leathers, crash helmet to boot, eager to get going and guide us safely down the country. But he wasn't here to chivvy me on. He opened three letters, one from each of my girls, and began to read. They wished me all the luck in the world. With fear, adrenalin and excitement hurtling round my body, I began to cry.

'Come on mate, let's do this!' Garry slapped me on the back.

It was cold and windy. I was told that John O'Groats seemed desolate in these early hours, but the team was bubbling, the start line erected and ready. I was delighted that a local also joined us. Well, a local originally from West Bromwich – Ray from JOG, as I call him. He moved up this way some years ago, got to hear of the challenge and now, with his classic Morris Minor, was joining us through the first marathon.

I was one lucky guy, in the company of such good friends. Dave Long, one of my guide runners, and I were preparing to run, supported by three lads on cycles who would supply us with drinks whenever we needed them: Steve Dugmore, affectionately known as Duggie, who had been a tremendous training partner on the tandem, putting in many hundreds of miles; Mike Hopkins, the tandem captain and experienced cyclist, principal of South Birmingham College; and Dave Sinar, another experienced cyclist and the reserve tandem captain. His knowledge over the coming days was to be invaluable. Another runner, Karl Moore, was initially meant to be starting with us, too, but now he hoped to meet us further along the route. His mom had been recently diagnosed with cancer. It made our commitment to Macmillan even more relevant and worthwhile.

Everyone shook hands, 'good luck' the phrase of the moment, Longy and I strapped wrist-to-wrist. A non-functioning wristwatch sat on the other, its face exchanged for a family photo with its interior holding something very special and very secret. Around my neck I had a unique diamond-encrusted pendant that would later be auctioned for the charity.

Then we waited. 4am – and the start.

Garry kicked the motorbike into life and on the stroke of 4am, our music for the challenge, Phil Collins's 'Tell Everybody I'm On My Way' burst out into the cold morning air, and we were on our way! In the quiet of the night I let rip the first 'Oggy Oggy Oggy!'

Once the first mile was under our belts, Longy informed me that we were just passing the John O'Groats Guest House where we had stayed the past couple of days. I roared another Oggy Oggy Oggy! for Alistair and Sheena, the owners and great hosts. To my surprise Longy reined me in, telling me I was going too fast! Coming from him, this was rich – he's well known as the speed merchant.

Longy was doing a great job guiding, as always, continually chatting to me. He was keen to let me know that at that particular moment in time, we were all in the same boat: it was only the lights from the support vehicle which allowed him to see, otherwise darkness enveloped us all. As the previous two days had been very wet, we were delighted to find that the weather this morning was kind. As we clocked the first ten miles or so, the sun rose and Longy could describe the scenery:

fields as far as the eye could see, heather, hills, the occasional building with mist framing it all. It sounded beautiful.

The miles crept on and surprisingly not much traffic came our way. The road seemed very straight but undulating. I was grateful to Longy's vivid descriptions of the places we were passing. One of the stranger sights we passed was a garden in Wick, all dressed up with a wonderful flower arrangement celebrating Macmillan Cancer Support. I couldn't believe it when Longy described it to me; the coincidence! It made me feel like luck was on our side; that we were being looked out for.

Even in the first four hours of the challenge, folks along the way were shouting words of encouragement. We could soon smell the finish, having broken the back of the first marathon. I heard Garry come roaring back to us on his motorbike and then one of the lads shouted, 'A mile and a half to go!' It was then the adrenalin took over, the legs and arms pumped, we hit a slight hill and then a right turn. I remember Longy telling me he could see the finish line, I heard our song playing, and with arms aloft, we crossed the finish line. The shouts rang round, everyone was full of excitement, but marathon number one was now completed and, to my surprise, in a time of **four hours and three minutes**! Body and mind seemed still in good shape. I was relieved.

Our finish line was at the community centre at the Hill O' Many Stanes. Two days prior we had visited it in preparation. When the centre had been described to me, I was told it was grey, desolate, a bit like a bunker from the last war. But today it was simply an amazing Aladdin's cave of support, with Margaret Sinclair, a local farmer's wife, along with her granddaughter, Lynn, who had been up since five in the morning, baking and getting the place ready to support us. They hugged me, a total stranger, and I sensed the kindness; it was very special, such a welcome.

Our stay here was short-lived; we had a few rounds of photos, interviews, jam sandwiches, freshly baked cake, a coffee, and then our Rosemary Rhodes – physiotherapist supreme – made herself known. No more time for PR, she was insistent: running kit off, cycling kit on, on the bike, it's time to go. And with both Longy and now Rosemary sorting me out, there was no arguing!

We were rather reluctant to go, given our wonderful reception. Once we'd given Margaret a huge thank-you, Garry's bike roared into action. Steve and Dave Dourass assumed their places. For the first time of many, I cocked my leg over the tandem. Almost simultaneously, the rain began and the temperature dropped.

We now had well over 100 miles to cycle on to Drumnadrochit, with Andy Williams, a driver from South Birmingham College, pulling the caravan, which acted as our sanctuary while cycling. It was 30 miles until our food stop, but the ride to Drumnadrochit was horrendous. It took us up hill and down dale, and that's an understatement. We experienced the worst ever rainfall recorded in August in Scotland since records began, and the temperature plummeted. It didn't feel like summer. We just couldn't get enough layers on. At one point I had on two jackets and two pairs of gloves with rubber gloves inside them, but still my feet and hands were soaked and very cold. Wind hit us sidewards. I had never experienced weather like it, and certainly not at this time of the year. It made us very glum, silent, as the rain and wind whipped and taunted us.

At one point, one of the media team, Sean, a reasonable cyclist I'm told, decided to get on his bike and try and ride the first leg. At the first 30-mile stop, he was shivering so much he simply had to stop. To add to the mayhem, the lads expressed that at times they struggled to see much more than me as the rain was making visibility dangerous. But we had to crack on.

Though our marathons were non-stop, we would pause periodically during the cycle, for food mainly. The caravan was always a welcome sight – or in my case, music to my ears! With the relentless rain and aching muscles it was simply heaven to get off the bike for a spell, grab food and warmth. Always the phrase 'Come on, let's go' came too soon.

On leaving the Hill O' Many Stanes we passed through so many places: some I can remember, like one mother of a hill, Berrie Dale, where I found out later, young Ray from JOG, 68 years old, was perched on the side of the hill in the rain taking photos of us coming up that hill. I bet we looked a picture, collectively gurning up! We then moved on to Helmsdale, past Dunrobin Castle, through Golspie, over Dornoch Firth. At this point we were over halfway, but it was still rain, rain and more rain. We were soaked through, muscles aching but still pumping. We rode on to Invergordon, Dingwall, Beauly.

Coming out of Beauly, I remembered from our first recce that Deb had commented on a very steep hill with an extremely sharp left bend at the bottom. 'One to watch out for,' she had said. 'At speed, coming down that hill, that turn could have serious consequences.' I mentioned it to the lads and they were pleased I had remembered it as it proved quite a tight turn, even for a bike!

At 8.30pm the Loch Ness Backpackers Hostel, Drumna-drochit, was a very welcome sight. I don't know quite what the team was expecting in terms of accommodation as there were a few grumblings about the outside showers and basic rooms. I wasn't bothered. I mean, after kicking off at four in the morning – earlier! – running 26.2 miles, cycling a further 110 miles, over 16 hours on either foot or in the saddle, riding through driving rain and intense cold on the back of a tandem, not being able to lift out of the saddle, leg muscles screaming for rest, arms, back and shoulders stiff, my bum red raw, soaked to the bone, tired, hungry… all I wanted was food, a clean bed and a pillow for my head! Wendy was yet another great host, putting hot food on for us.

Five of us bunked together: Duggie, Rosemary, Garry, Longy and myself. A sign read, so I'm told, 'Keep the heater clear', but there were more clothes on that little heater than you would find in a Chinese laundry! Rosemary, bless her, sorted out our collective aches and pains and she was, by far, last to hit the sack. The first day was over – only nine left! Lights went out at midnight.

Thursday 11 August 2011

I don't think I even had time to dream. An alarm went off, all five of us roused, then one timid voice said, 'Sorry chaps.' It turned out that Duggie had left his alarm on from the previous night and it was actually only 3am! But to his surprise – and he'll never get away with it again – when we all heard it was only 3am, we all sighed with relief. Someone said, 'Oh yes, two hours left!' and it was like winning the lottery.

But 5am did come, and our feet wearily hit the floor. Rosemary gave my legs a gentle massage, Longy thrust a breakfast bar in one of my hands and a drink in the other; then it seemed only seconds later and Garry stood in the doorway and announced ten minutes to the off. I asked Rosemary what the weather was like, begging her to tell me it was dry. I didn't think I could face the weather we had experienced yesterday. But she told me it was overcast and I instantly felt a little more optimistic.

Garry also gathered us all together for a talk. There had been a little incident the previous day with a heavy goods vehicle coming up Berrie Dale. It could have ended tragically and would have been avoided if people had listened to him. In the excitement of getting the challenge under way, the direction and guidance had been a case of too many cooks. As far as I was concerned, it was Garry who was in charge. I told Garry that all I wanted to do was run and cycle and hopefully complete this challenge. We all agreed that Garry would do all the directing and guiding, and if there were any problems with negotiating traffic, he would be the person to sort it. From then, things went so much more smoothly.

CHAPTER 9

At 6am, Garry's motorbike growled into life and Longy and I stood at the start of the second marathon. Our tune played and we were off, on our way to Loch Lomond. It was certainly a fresh morning, I could feel the mist in the air but no rain – yet! We ran out of the Loch Ness Backpackers Hostel up and alongside of Loch Ness, passing Urquhart Castle, following the A82 all the way down to the bottom of Loch Ness. For an A road, it was a single lane and it wasn't too busy at this time in the morning but Garry still kept out in front, checking for any hazards. The three lads, Duggie, Mike and Dave Sinar, were once again cycling alongside offering any support we needed, while Steve and Dave Dourass, along with Rosemary, were bringing up the rear in the support car, passing us nutrition out of the window. The traffic that passed us was mostly courteous. I think it was mainly due to the signage on the car explaining what we were doing.

I was feeling pretty good considering the exploits of the previous day: my legs felt quite fresh, though I had to admit that my undercarriage was very sore; the combination of yesterday's rain and soaked saddle had chafed me raw! Considering the loch was flat, the road alongside was certainly very up and down; extremely hilly. It was also uneven, so I found myself running on a camber, my left foot seemingly three or four inches higher than the right, but still we ploughed on. After time, though, this really took its toll on my muscles, particularly my ITB, which is, as Rosemary told me, a thick chunk of tissue from the hip, along the thigh to the knee. It worried me, this pain, as I hadn't felt something as sharp and as continual as this before. Rosie assured me she would keep her beady eye on it, and taped it up as soon as she was given the opportunity. It was one of the hardest marathon courses I can remember running. I'm very surprised that we didn't come across mountain goats!

Longy found it difficult to adhere to his usual continuous commentary of what was going on around us as there wasn't really much to see: the mist covered most of the loch, there were plenty of trees around the perimeter and that was about it. 'Oh, plus 20-odd miles of road in front of us.' Delightful.

Occasionally Longy told me to smile as the lads from the college took photos or footage of us. They were media students from South Birmingham College and Mike had sponsored them for the challenge. Great work experience, we thought, and hopefully we'd get some great photos for keepsakes.

We got to the bottom of Loch Ness and it seemed so surreal, running the length of such a famous loch and not catching sight or sound of that monster! Our next mental landmark would be Fort Augustus at around 18 miles, meaning we had broken the back of marathon number two. We came upon a narrow bridge with a very tight turn immediately after it. Perched across the bridge, as we approached, was a rather large lorry, desperately trying to manoeuvre the turn. A few cars were also in the queue, so Longy decided it was much safer for us to stay in the convoy of vehicles; the pack of us running down the side of the lorry would be too dangerous. So for a few minutes we were caught up in a traffic jam on foot! Oh, how the legs welcomed the rest!

Surprisingly the day began to warm up, and at our last push, our legs were starting to feel the run. The hills had certainly taken their toll, but we were heading for the finish line at Invergarry. From the original recce, I remembered a petrol station at Invergarry with a bus stop right next door and a café area just slightly further on. When Longy said that he could see the petrol station, it was music to my ears. We ran into the car park of the café, the finish line waiting patiently and our music playing, lots of people shouting, arms aloft and legs relieved. Number two had been completed in a time of **four hours and 27 minutes**.

It was there we were met by Michelle Malone, a young native of the Black Country who had recently moved up to Inverness. She, along with her mom, plus her two lads, Joseph and Zac, had been trying all morning to find us. I had met Michelle some years ago when she had come to a talk I was doing. Her eldest lad, Joseph, then only seven, had just been diagnosed with Retinitis Pigmentosa. She was so upset, with good reason, thinking her young son's life was over, but after we had a good chat and she listened to my talk, taking in all the crazy things this blind man did, she realised that there could be a life for Joseph after all. Sadly, around two weeks later, Michelle had contacted us to tell us that her youngest son, Zac, had also been diagnosed with the same complaint. She stays so positive, though, and we have remained good friends.

Why is it that last mile you run takes forever but rest time goes in a flash? Rosemary and Longy were on my back again; running kit off, cycling kit on. Rosemary got to work on my legs, sitting under the table, as I ate my lunch. There was little time to think, let alone to relax. As soon as I took my seat on the tandem… Christ, my bum had become a bag of razor blades, cutting and nipping into me.

We were now heading towards Fort William, with our final destination, Loch Lomond, some 100 miles down the road. Our entourage was on its way yet again, Andy heading off for our first 30-mile stop, the monster on the motorbike up ahead, the support vehicle bringing up the rear and the sighs of relief from Duggie, Mike and Dave Sinar, pleased to get their legs turning at a sensible speed. While supporting us on the marathon, they travelled along at a snail's pace, putting pressure on their legs, arms and hands, with the cold setting in. As my legs turned, I enjoyed the relief of the lactic acid flowing out from the run – though I wished the bag of razor blades I was sitting on would disappear.

The sun was still shining which was a bonus, and we sailed through Fort William, passing Ben Nevis, and then we hit Glen Coe. Did I know I was on Glen Coe? My legs started shouting; I didn't need anyone to tell me where we were.

Mike dropped the gear ratio down, heads and shoulders leaning forward, hands and arms pulling on the handlebars to give leverage. With our teeth firmly gritted, our legs got into a pace, the pedals turned and we got ourselves mentally prepared for a long, hard climb. We kept going up and up and up, each and every one of us shouting out encouragement to the others and still we climbed. Though the sun was being kind to us, the headwind wasn't. At one point Garry tried to position his motorbike in front of us to act as a windbreak, but old Glen Coe was now too steep and he just couldn't go slow enough to help. We had to battle on regardless, the pedals going round as quickly as the road went up. It was over two hours of solid pedalling up, hearts pumping and calf muscles hardening.

Anyone who has ridden a tandem knows it's so difficult to get out of the saddle, especially when going uphill, as both parties have to pedal in harmony or off you come. But one positive in this instance was the concentration and the continual pressure on the legs took my mind off that bag of razor blades I was sitting on; well, at least until we reached the top. Then I could put some more cream on. Dave Sinar gave me hope. Coming alongside me, he said, 'Dave, I think the car in front is actually levelling out; we might be nearly at the top!' But the hope left as soon as it came and as we rounded a curve in the road, Dave sighed, 'Sorry Dave, it's going up again!'

We pedalled on. Someone mentioned a sign on the roadside which read 'Blind Summit'. I had to smile as it was right: I couldn't see the top, either! After what felt like an age, I was told we were 1,142 feet above sea level and finally at the top. Once we actually came to a halt and put our feet to the floor, we could breathe a sigh of relief: we had, at last, conquered Glen Coe.

We had a drink break and the lads began to describe the views to me. From their descriptions, it was breathtaking. Waterfalls and hills for miles… even ski lifts. I said that it was a pity the ski lifts hadn't run along the road, as they could have given us a pull.

With a mountain road up, there has to be a mountain road down – and, oh boy, did we go! We stood up on our pedals, alternating the legs for rest and giving our bums respite from the saddles. We sailed down the other side, freewheeling, touching over 45 miles per hour. Thank God that Mike was controlling the bike like an expert! It was amazing how quickly we came down the mountainside, when the climb up had taken so long. Although the rest was fantastic, we soon hit the flat, passing rather quickly through Tyndrum. Pedalling resumed.

'Why did you go through those red lights?' someone shouted from behind. I realised the tandem was in front. What red lights? I wondered. The rest of the party caught up. 'Is everything all right?'

I leant forward. 'Mike?'

He quietly confessed that although he had seen the red lights, there was nothing he could do about it. The tandem's brakes had packed in. We had been hurtling down a mountainside without any brakes. We couldn't stop until the road had levelled out. The thought of it still haunts me. What if…?

Thankfully, the brakes were soon fixed, and Mike vowed to keep a watchful eye on them. We headed on to Loch Lomond and Tarbet. There were no more Glen Coe-type hills, but the road ahead was certainly not flat; let's say there were a few juicy inclines. We came across Loch Lomond with some 15 miles or so to go, and the roads were very twisty, tree-covered and generally quiet. After a quick stop for nature, we pushed on as the night was drawing in. On this quiet road, there was a set of traffic lights and yes, they were on red. We made sure we stopped this time.

Maybe five miles from Tarbet, I made a casual statement, 'Well, it seems we've left all the hills behind!' Of course, I soon wished that I'd kept my big mouth shut. Out of nowhere there suddenly appeared a short, but very steep hill. Soon, though, we entered Tarbet. I mentioned that during a conversation I'd had with someone at the hotel, the Arrochar Hotel, our resting place for the night, was only up a slight hill for half a mile from where we currently were. But it was poor Duggie who read me the road sign, 'Arrochar three miles'. I shut up and pedalled. It was now getting on for 9pm and at that moment, no one was in the mood.

We rode into the Arrochar car park and through the finish line with our signature tune blaring away, though we were too exhausted for great gestures of joy. The shouts and clapping rang out nonetheless from our band of loyal supporters, the other guests at the hotel who had come out to see what this merry band of men were doing. We were all very tired, hungry and, boy, was I glad to get off that saddle. Contrary to how we felt, the hotel seemed full of life and as soon as we walked in, we heard a Tom Jones tribute singer. Our very first port of call was the dinner table. The hotel manager was superb and had purposely stayed on late to make sure we had hot food waiting for us. I didn't hear anyone moaning about the accommodation that night, either! Certainly no outside showers: three-star and comfort.

That night, I shared a room with Garry. With my legs aching, bum red raw, needing a shower and my bed, I had to smile at Garry – the first thing he moaned about was a dirty cup! Well, I guess that put everything into perspective.

Rosemary came up around midnight and was once again my salvation, massaging my legs. She certainly found the spot, and on this challenge, she was worth her weight in gold. I think the long days and short nights surprised her: the amount of treatment she had to give in such a short time, to so many people, was challenge enough. I had sleep for a paltry five hours before I had to get up and do it all over again!

Friday 12 August 2011
Five in the morning already! In came Rosemary to give me a light leg massage, followed by Longy with a breakfast bar and a drink. But I also had another companion this morning: a very sore knee. It seemed like only seconds later and there we were,

standing under the start line, ready to run marathon number three. Longy and I had company this morning for the start, Jo Sinar, Dave's better half, who had donned her trainers and would be running a few miles with us.

On leaving the Arrochar Hotel, we learnt that the loch it sits beside is Loch Long, and, strangely enough, the Loch adjacent to the café we had dined in during the previous day's activities was Loch Garry! Blimey, I said, all the lads are having lochs named after them. Mind, a loch, they say, is always in need of a monster, so what that says about those two…

Just like the previous day, we followed the loch down its length. Our song piped out and we took to the A82 in the pouring rain. My knee was giving me some serious grief. Rosemary told me that if I could run through the pain barrier, I would find it would ease once the muscles around the knee warmed up. Trusting her judgement, I ran on. And of course she was right: after around four miles, the pain started to subside and I was actually running normally again.

It was nice to have Jo running along with us; different conversation helps the miles go past quicker. She ran with us for about six miles and it was a good job she did as I lost Longy for a few minutes. It appeared something hadn't agreed with him at breakfast, but he was soon back and chirpy. We pulled over at eight miles, close to Inverbeg, as Radio WM rang for a quick interview to see how we were getting on. The station had actually intended to ring us from the beginning of the challenge, but they told us that their coverage had been taken up with the riots back at home.

Pulling up in a lay-by, I got to sit in the support car for the first time since John O'Groats. It was then I found out Steve Dourass had been chomping on my Fruit and Nut bars. I began to think it was a serious mistake, leaving so many boxes in the car with him!

And would you believe it? While sitting in the car and chatting on the phone to Radio WM, the rain actually stopped.

But – no exaggeration – as soon as I put my feet out on to the road, it started again! And so did the pain in my knee!

Then I realised that day three would be a trying day, grinding the third marathon out. With the rain certainly dampening spirits and my knee pain relentless, it was going to be a long, hard 26.2 miles. Rosemary decided to pull on her trainers and run a few miles with us, boosting morale and giving us a change of scenery.

Once we left Loch Lomond behind, it was back to Longy and myself as the sole runners. I did feel for the lads on the bikes as it must have been so uncomfortable, riding so slowly. We ran past Balloch on a dual carriageway, but Garry assured us that the local police force was keeping a watchful eye on us. With the support vehicle, plastered with signage, at the rear, it was truly amazing the support we were getting from both pedestrians and road users alike. After running so many miles on the road, you soon know the toot of support and the toot of anger, thankfully the latter being very rare.

We passed by a place called Renton, and a road adjacent to the dual carriageway was declared the safer option – until it inched further and further off course. It had been worth a try but it backfired, meaning we had to get back on the dual carriageway.

Once we were back on course, my legs actually beginning to really hurt, I concentrated my mind on the road ahead. We were now only five miles or so from the finish line at the West Park Hotel. The lads on the bikes were now really egging us on; it was island after island, incline after incline. Longy and I didn't talk; it was just left foot, right foot.

Then Garry came alongside me and told me that the hotel was at the 27-mile mark, rather than 26 because we had gone slightly off-course, and he asked if I'd prefer to stop at the official marathon end or carry on. The answer I gave him is unprintable, but we kept going. Finally, Longy said he could see the finish line. Our music came on and where I got the strength from I'll never know, but I picked up the pace. Longy cursed me, but the finish line was so, so sweet. Marathon number three was completed in **four hours and 30 minutes**.

More photos, interviews, and then we had a chance to sit and rest, replenishing our bodies with sandwiches and coffee. The West Park Hotel hospitality was superb, and after a mere ten minutes of rest, it was off to a hotel room to get changed. The soft bed was so inviting, and I was so tired, but I told myself not to even sit down – I wouldn't have woken for a week! All pride had gone: it was now just a case of getting my running kit off as quick as I could so poor Rosemary could put Germolene on my open sores. In fact, it had taken a bit of persuasion to get me to show Rosemary my open sores because the sores in question were on my undercarriage.

'Dave,' Longy had said after his inspection, in which he sharply inhaled his breath through his teeth in sympathy, 'you're going to have to let Rosie look at this, as she's the only one who knows what to do.' She was professional and matter of fact, telling me how to clean and treat the area. But I later found out Deb had called, asking what was wrong, and the two of them, Deb and Rosie, had discussed the state of my undercarriage over the phone.

I wasn't looking forward to that saddle and now poor old Longy was nursing an injured Achilles heel, another legacy of Loch Ness and that cursed uneven track.

As we said goodbye to the West Park Hotel, we also said goodbye for a short while to the support vehicles and to Garry. We were heading on the bikes to the River Clyde. Our intention was for us on the bikes to follow the river and canals, cutting out the centre of Glasgow and meeting up some 15 miles downriver at The Carmyle Heron.

But even the best-laid plans go wrong.

We found ourselves right in the heart of Glasgow, smack-bang where we didn't want to be. We rode around the city centre for quite a while, trying to pick up signs for the river path, but to no avail. We found a local to stop and ask directions. First we were directed one way, and after a couple of miles' riding, we grew suspicious and asked again – only to be instructed to go back the way we had just come. Backwards, forwards... I was getting giddy. To make matters worse, Duggie had encountered a couple of problems: his cycling shoe had split and his stomach wasn't feeling too grand.

Everyone we asked seemed to point us in different directions so we came to the conclusion that it was our English accents; they simply didn't like us much. We later found out that the annual bagpiping championships were taking place that weekend and so most of the people we spoke to probably weren't even locals. The back and forth meant that we had lost significant time and both Garry and Steve rang us to find out where we were. Trouble was, we didn't know ourselves! They were parked up in Hamilton, 13 miles or so from Glasgow city centre, and I promised that I would ring as soon as we had our bearings.

It was Duggie who clocked the two policemen. We explained our plight and the best they could do was direct us towards Hamilton. After about ten minutes of riding, a sign for Hamilton was seen. Being on the back of the tandem, at least I could use the phone so I rang Garry and Steve to tell them we were now on our way, along the A122. Minutes later, the lads told me it was actually the A123, so I had to ring again. As soon as I hung up, I was told it was the A124. I dutifully rang again to let Garry know, but then minds were changed again and it was back to the A122. I gave up ringing and just hoped! We were all so relieved when we heard the sound of a motorbike – it was Garry! We had to crack on as we had lost almost two hours. The finish line was still a long way off.

After our last encounter with Garry, we had certainly put some effort into pedalling: the razor blades were back, my legs were hurting, but the focus was getting to the caravan. No one mentioned any places we passed so I can only guess that all eyes were on Garry and where he was directing us. The only incident that I can recall is that someone passed us and, for whatever reason, shouted some obscenities from an open window. Next a can of beer sailed towards us, narrowly missing Mike. I don't know what the problem was – perhaps they were Wolves fans and had read of my allegiances?

On reaching the caravan, I decided to stand outside. I didn't want to get too comfortable in case I was tempted not to move again, especially as my knee was still bothering me. I managed to burn both lips and the inside of my mouth with a particularly hot cup of coffee, and, by now, poor Duggie was feeling so terrible that he had to retire to the support car for the rest of the day. We were going to pieces.

We told ourselves that the ride from here was going to be particularly hard. We had time we needed to catch and it was beginning to get dark. We estimated we wouldn't get to Moffat until 10pm. Then, just what we wanted: rain. And then the hills kicked in! The serious hills came with only 15 miles or so to go but the rain became torrential. As we began to climb again, the road rising up sharply above us, Mike shouted back to say that visibility was terrible – the only lights were those of the support vehicle and an occasional glimpse of Garry's rear light. We climbed up and up and up. It felt as though old Glen Coe had taken a 100-mile walk to join us again. From what I could glean, there was not much of a view from up there anyway. Someone mentioned a signpost that read 'Beattock Summit, 1058 feet above sea level'. It wasn't quite Glen Coe, but it wasn't far off. Then we started to descend, and one of the group spotted a sign that told it was only six miles to Moffat. We howled with delight! Mike told me that streetlights were visible, and then came our music… then sanctuary. Clapping hands, cheers and a finish line all on the car park of the Moffat House Hotel.

Wet and tired, we still had to pose for photos. I did a couple of interviews, as the lads and lasses of the college media team deserved a moment or two. They were doing a great job. Food followed, then bed.

Rosemary, Longy and I roomed together that night. Rosemary said it was far easier to treat us both at once, instead of roaming from room to room. She could sort out my bum, so to speak, plus my legs and knee, that evening, then in the morning have more time to tape them up. She could also work her magic on Longy's heel which was beginning to worry us, especially as Karl, guide runner number two, hadn't joined us yet. An injury to my only guide runner wouldn't have been good.

Rosemary made me smile: she took a shower and told me she was standing stark naked in front of me, feeling very uncomfortable. 'Dave, I do hope you're really blind!' she said.

I closed my eyes out of courtesy.

Saturday 13 August 2011

All I thought, as I opened my eyes wearily, was how everything seemed to hurt: legs, knee, bum, and, most recently afflicted, my mouth. Rosemary gave me a gentle massage, then taped my knee up with some special tape she had. Longy, bless him, was there as always with his breakfast bar and drink. Then, just like a bad penny, Garry turned up to give the good news: it was time to go. Marathon four.

We had a slightly later start time this morning, getting on for 6.15am. A chap from the Moffat newspaper took a few photos and then we were off again. It was raining, but only lightly; nothing like last night, thankfully. Both Longy and I were limping this morning, while Duggie was holed up in the support car, as he'd been so ill during the night. Not good news. Dave Sinar and Mike, now on the bikes, were also complaining of sore bums. What a motley crew we were.

After about five miles, I felt my knee easing into the pace. The rain stayed with us for another three, until the eight-mile mark, and then Radio WM rang. I thought that I'd run and give the interview today, rather than stopping; I didn't want to give my knee any encouragement to seize up. I secretly thought it also might sound a little more dramatic, too.

It was now I realised how the whole team was beginning to feel the tiredness, especially after yesterday: a heavy day that certainly took its toll. But although weary, the camaraderie was growing between us all, the banter was non-stop which was great as it kept smiles on faces, and the jokes and obscenities kept flying between us. We could happily see that the team was building as one; each and every one of us egging each other on, and it was a fantastic atmosphere.

Today, the course was ideal: a few inclines, but on the whole, relatively flat and pretty straight. It was, under normal circumstances, the kind of course where you would hope to do a personal best. But in this more unusual moment, these old legs were feeling every step. Jo and Rosemary joined us for a few miles, with silly conversation helping the miles pass by.

It was always nice to hear the 20-mile mark announced: it meant the finish was looming. Then a car came towards us and there was lots of shouting, the horn beeping manically. Someone shouted, 'It's Karl!'

What a great surprise! Instantly morale was boosted. His mom had been operated on and after a string of complications, had been finally allowed home. She was on the mend, and Karl was satisfied. Kindly dropped off by Karl's good friend, Martin, along with Martin's wife and young son, Connor, it was only minutes later he was taking the cord and guiding. We were all so pleased to hear about his mom, and overjoyed he could join us. The team was now complete and what a lift it gave us all.

Our entourage had suddenly grown over the last few miles. Garry was still at the helm, but us runners were now joined by Connor. There were the two lads on the bikes, the support car with Steve 'munching' Dourass at the wheel, followed now by Martin and his wife. We ran through the finish line seemingly in the middle of nowhere, an area called Newton, and the time certainly reflected our tired legs: **four hours and 51 minutes**.

Karl's arrival made the finish even more special – what a great buzz! Karl wanted to catch up on all the gossip and goings-on, and Martin and his family were asking all sorts of questions, but catching up would have to be done over the next few days – as we had the small matter of a bike ride to Lancaster. Just before we pulled away, I had a quick call from Deb, always glad to hear her voice. She laughed about Karl's surprise appearance, a well-kept secret, she had said. I asked if she had any others in store and she replied, 'Who, me? No! I'll see you on Monday at the Spread Eagle,' and we said our goodbyes.

Our team of cyclists was expanding, too. Mike and I were still on the tandem, then there was Dave Sinar, Karl, Martin, Sean making another appearance and Duggie was back, too! We were under way and with fresh faces came fresh banter. We passed through Gretna Green with a big smile on my face, happy memories racing back of when Deb and I eloped there to get married.

We were fast approaching the border and just before the 'Welcome to England' sign, our rear brakes failed again, so after a very big cheer, we put our feet down in good old England to fix the brakes. Everyone had a go at trying to sort them out, leaning their respective bikes against the nearby fence. When one of the lads turned around, it was brought to our attention that a hungry horse had taken a chunk out of the rubber on the handlebars belonging to one of the bikes. Laughing, we all moved off – but then the chain came off the tandem. Not the best start to the border crossing!

But we instantly felt better, arriving into England. The weather actually played the game for once. The sun shone and we got up a good head of steam. Oh, how a bit of warmth on the body makes a difference! There were smiles all round. We passed through Carlisle, and Garry found a slightly shorter route that saved us some time, always a bonus. We passed through Penrith, with a very welcome caravan stop just a few miles on. With the team expanded and Birmingham now not so far away, it felt like we were finally progressing. Rosemary said that she feels she never has to visit Scotland ever again, given the unwelcome reception it gave us.

On the road out of Penrith, I heard someone shout from a passing car coming the other way. They had yelled 'Blind Dave!' in greeting, and it was most definitely a Geordie accent. Hmmm… could it be Jim and Laraine Knot, our guide dog puppy walker friends who we had met through the Great North Run? Lo and behold, it was! As we stopped at the caravan, they pulled up behind us. Although the couple knew our challenge was under way, they had just been to visit a specialist vet in Kendal and had, by pure chance, spotted Garry's motorbike brandishing its Top To Toe stickers. What a coincidence, being on this road at the same time! Sadly, we only had time for a quick chat; they wished us luck and off we went.

We pushed on; our ETA in Lancaster was about 9pm, eating late again, so we didn't want to lose any more time if we could help it. We went up and over Shap Summit. I thought we'd left all the mountains behind in Scotland, but I was wrong; the hills in Cumbria were cruel. With already tired legs and bodies, Christ, was it hard work. We touched the tip of Kendal and then followed the A6 all the way to Lancaster.

When I was told we had entered Lancaster, I was delighted – but then Duggie had to disappoint me. 'Dave, this is just the outskirts, we've got about another ten miles to go yet.' My heart sank, and almost instantly, the razor blades came back with a vengeance and my legs screamed to stop. Those ten miles turned out to be a very, very long way. As we approached the centre, the stop–start of negotiating cities became a nightmare, and a very painful one! At that point, I just wanted to get off, to leave my saddle. But soon, we found the students' accommodation where we were staying overnight. Hilariously, as we rode on to the campus, there was one last challenge: we hit a little ramp. This little ramp certainly made us work very hard; it was short, sharp and, I reckon, almost vertical! Was I so very glad to get off that saddle? You bet!

We finally sat down to eat at 10pm, and despite the latter half of the day's slog, the ambience was wonderful. Everyone began talking at the same time, over each other, desperate, for Karl's sake, to relive the last four days.

But the first hurdle was done: Scotland. With its hills and valleys, terrible weather now behind us, this, our first night back in England, was something to celebrate. We were all comparing our war wounds, as almost all of us had an ache or pain of some description. Tiredness was definitely the biggest killer. But still we felt the thrill of the challenge; we knew that the team working as a single entity would see us through. Oh, what it would be to get up and also go to bed in the same day, we groaned, turning the lights out at another 12.30am.

Sunday 14 August 2011

I was woken rather rudely this morning. My watch told me it was 3am, but it wasn't time to get up quite yet. Instead, my knee was throbbing like a good 'un! As we were in individual rooms, I hadn't a clue where anyone else was to ask for a painkiller so tried to doze off again. Five o'clock came eventually, and Rosemary massaged and taped the troublesome knee. Tired was an understatement, but I knew that to get up and running would take my mind off the pain.

It was a quiet Sunday morning in Lancaster, and we were all pretty subdued due to collective fatigue. But at 6.15am, marathon number five commenced.

Now there were the three of us running, and with Karl's arrival, his humour spiced up proceedings somewhat. It's always silly chatter that helps the miles disappear more quickly. Our destination today was Preston; more specifically, the Railway pub in a little village called Euxton, Chorley way. The roads seemed quiet and, thankfully, there were no serious hills. But it became one of *those* runs: hard, one foot in front of the other. The way I was feeling, I just wanted it out of the way. My knee settled around five miles into it, but Dave's heel was still hurting. He seemed to be having fun regardless, running along with a Macmillan collection bucket. The weather was with us, sunny and warm, and Jo and Rosemary joined us at times, but today I was very pleased when that 20-mile mark was announced.

Feeling tired – exhausted, even – but with only a couple of miles to go, I upped the pace. Again, I didn't know where the energy came from and we crossed the finish line in **four hours and 47 minutes**. But this was one finish I will never, ever forget: through all the shouting and enthusiastic cheers as we passed through, two simple words reduced me to my knees, then to tears! 'Hello, Daddy.'

To my total surprise – yes, Deb had done it yet again! – my two youngest daughters were waiting at the finish, followed only seconds later by Deb. I actually burst into tears with joy, relief, exhaustion… words failed me, but it was the injection of energy that I needed. In fact, I strongly believe it affected the whole team. I learned afterwards that Garry's visor stayed down for a long minute as he had a secret little sob when his wife and son also appeared. Longy was rumoured to have hidden his face, too, while Duggie didn't remove his sunglasses. Suddenly, all these grown men and women were in floods! I hugged Deb and the girls, the best prize of all. The love I felt at that moment in time reassured me that I could do it.

With a smile like the Cheshire cat, my tiredness was soon forgotten, The Railway was perfect, and with Deb and my two youngest to share this moment, what more did I want? But there they were again, Rosie and Longy, rounding us up and telling us it was nearly time to go.

We climbed on to the bikes and were sent off in style. As we headed towards Wigan, Garry told us we weren't far from passing his house. My legs felt stronger now and we followed the A49 towards Warrington.

The next milestone would be Haydock Island, a very busy place that would require some careful negotiating, but Garry had help in the form of his mate, a policeman who patrolled this patch. Moving at a rapid rate of knots, I suddenly heard a commotion up ahead: screeching tyres accompanied by the smell of burning rubber. Dave Sinar came alongside me and excitedly explained what he could see.

'Dave,' he babbled, 'I can't believe what I'm seeing! There's one! No, two! Three! Four or five squad cars complete with blues and twos!'

The rest of the group was chattering excitedly and I could hear the busy junction up ahead, the familiar whirr of lots of exhausts and tyres on the road. But then, the noise just disappeared. Was it an accident? I wasn't really sure what was going on, but I kept on going. Mike then explained, 'This is like royalty. The police have blocked it all off for us!' A police car blocked off each exit from the junction, and we suddenly couldn't hear the noise of a single engine. In fact, at this infamously busy intersection, I could actually hear birds singing! Absolutely fantastic!

The novelty spurred our legs into action and we seemed to flow gracefully towards Warrington, Mike negotiating heavy traffic with ease by weaving in and out. We soon passed Warrington and after a few miles more, we found our caravan parked up in a pub car park. The lads relived the Haydock junction and we all gave Garry a massive thank-you for sorting it out. What an honour! Even the razor blades had been forgotten, temporarily.

With the weather continuing to be fair, we travelled through Knutsford and estimated that it was 20 miles to Stoke – before disaster struck. Mike and I were travelling quite quickly uphill, as the lead bike, when we heard frantic shouts of, 'Bike down!' We stopped and Mike surveyed the scene. Karl had hit something in the road and had been thrown up into the air. When we pitched round, I was told he was lying on his bike in the middle of the road and we automatically began to panic. But Rosemary was out of the support car in a flash and checked him over, tending to his cuts and grazes. He was shaken, but otherwise all right and soon got back on the bike. We all knew he'd continue and he did, although the mood was a little subdued as we rode the remaining miles to the hotel and the night's resting place, the Moat House in the Stoke suburb, Etruria.

The reception we got at the hotel was fantastic. There were so many to welcome us in now that we were getting closer to home. And tonight we hit the big time: the penthouse suite! I shared the biggest room we had experienced to date with Garry, Karl and Longy and then we decided to take an ice bath. That terrifying cold sent me daft and I started talking away to myself, but I could instantly feel the aches and pains disappear. Then the hot shower, oh yes! I later heard some screaming from Longy, and found out that he'd only managed to dip his foot into the bath – what a wuss! Karl braved the water next, and I'm told his bruising came out bright and bold. Afterwards, we limped downstairs to tea like wounded soldiers, returning to bed just before midnight.

Monday 15 August 2011

Why don't holidays come round as quickly as this 5am alarm, I wondered, as it interrupted my dreamless sleep. The moans and groans that came from our room this morning were brilliant; we were like four old men sleeping rough. Rosemary came in quite chirpy though, saying, 'Morning boys, how are we today?' Our moans said it all.

The three walking wounded stood on the start line. Though Karl was not in Scotland with us, his accident yesterday made him feel just as tired and battered. Longy had cut the back out of his trainers to ease his Achilles, so with my knee, Longy's heel and the left side of Karl, we were a great advert for fitness! But we were all smiling. We were joined this morning by a couple of pals, Paul Cole and Keith Nye, to support us on this leg.

At 6am we started marathon number six, heading towards West Brom and home turf.

Over the past couple of days we had had a few hiccoughs with the tandem, so this morning, while running, we had arranged for the bike to be taken to Fred Williams' Cycles in Wolverhampton who promised to give it a quick service. Along with Dawes Cycles, Fred's had been a tremendous help throughout the challenge.

We hit the A34 and would follow this to the finish line at the Spread Eagle pub, Gaily Island, just outside of Wolverhampton. This would be where our families and friends would also be waiting. The mood was good, the weather and traffic kind to us. Karl was stiff and sore. 'People will say "look at that blind bloke, leading the cripple",' he joked. Dave seemed to be running okay, my knee started slow but loosened up after five miles or so, so it seemed a pretty good morning all round.

There were a few smiles on the way, in particular when I had to stop for nature. Over the past couple of days, when stopping for any reason, my knee had begun to seize so I had taken to jogging on the spot to keep it moving. However, trying to wee while jogging on the spot – and then having Rosemary rubbing my knee at the same time – must have looked pretty strange. The remarks have been… different! But it works – though there are certain elements poor Rosemary has to avoid!

Speaking of Rosemary, she joined us around ten miles out; always with that smiling voice, 'How are my boys doing?' Then to distract us from the pounding miles she tends to enlighten us with some very interesting facts. Today's was a classic, 'Do you know how you castrate a bull?' Before we could answer, she then went into detail – how my eyes watered!

Our happy little band made its way past Stafford, through Penkridge, the miles being eaten up, and before long, the finish line was within five miles. As we got closer, Jo and Rosemary re-joined us and we slowly picked up the pace.

With about half a mile to run, I'm told the finish line in sight, we were also joined by Jo and Dave's son, 'Ben 10', as we called him. He came alongside on his bike and the pace went up again as a wonderful tingling feeling descended. Our song started up – I'd never get tired of that one! – and we all ran or rode in a tight bunch through the finish on the Spread Eagle car park. It was the most amazing noise that day: family, friends, passers-by, TV, radio, the newspapers. We weren't quite at West Brom, but what a hell of a welcome back to the Midlands and the Black Country. Marathon number six completed in **four hours and 46 minutes.**

For the first 20 minutes after we had finished the marathon it was question after question, photos, interviews, radio, TV, more photos; it was amazing the PR coverage we were getting, absolutely fantastic for the charity. I did a live interview with Radio WM and their morning presenter, Phil Upton, who would later join us on the cycle ride to West Brom. The atmosphere was electric, all the team were buzzing as questions and laughter were fired their way. Karl's war wounds were being admired, too. It was so good to be back on home turf, to hear familiar accents again and voices I recognised, with West Brom still to come!

But before long, the dynamic duo, Rosemary and Longy, were back on my case again and I said goodbye to the Spread Eagle and its fantastic team of staff. Our entourage had swelled tremendously this time, with friends joining us on their bikes and even another tandem, expertly navigated by Mark Green and Lee Woodhall. Our route took us through Bilston, Wednesbury, and then West Bromwich offered us a nice incline up to the town. We popped our heads into a couple of places which had supported us: the YMCA, where my eldest daughter, Grace, worked and she came over to shower me with tears; Stokes Opticians who had sponsored the cycling glasses; even the police played their part, briefly closing the High Street as we made our way to Dartmouth Park. I couldn't believe the crowds in the park as we pulled in, all cheering and queuing to slap me on the back.

The police then gave us an escort up to The Hawthorns, the home of my beloved West Bromwich Albion, and once again the support there was fantastic. We were met by the Mayor of Sandwell, Councillor Joyce Underhill, and the Albion had also put on hospitality and it was great to spend some time at the ground. Throughout the challenge, and even during the build-up, the club had shown me, as a fan, fantastic support.

From the Baggies' ground we rode to Birmingham city centre, the Lord Mayor offering the team refreshment in the Town Hall and the Mayors' Parlour, a fitting end to a great day.

The ride today was quite short in comparison to the other days, but it gave us – well, the legs, anyway – a well-earned rest. The razor blades got no better, though! We actually arrived at the Copthorne Hotel for around 7pm. Would this be the early night we had dreamt of? Of course the answer was no! We still weren't in bed until well after midnight – but what would you expect after arriving on home turf?

Tuesday 16 August 2011

If an alarm was a cockerel, I'd have shot it by now; another 5am! Still, I couldn't believe at 5.45am how Birmingham's Victoria Square could be bouncing and full of people in support. The start line erected, Baggie Bird, the Albion mascot, was ready to send us off, among the many loyal supporters who had gathered together to cheer us on. We had additional runners with us today, supporters of our local football teams. Other staff and students from South Birmingham College had also come along for this extra special marathon, so in total, there were around 25 runners. An old guide runner of mine, Mac, also joined us today. After 2008's challenge, it was very fitting he joined us on marathon number seven.

CHAPTER 9

My old mate, Jim Kelly, then head of international and local events at Birmingham City Council, had arranged – somehow – for us to have all the traffic lights on green as we passed through. Also following us was a large vehicle which is more often used on the motorway, those lorries with a big arrow on the back with the warning 'slow moving traffic' – that was us! For this leg, our convoy had grown substantially: Garry in front, all us runners, support car with music, caravan and now a big truck! I wonder if we got on the radio, reporting us as congestion.

Our entourage moved off from Victoria Square at 6am, marathon number seven under way, with the loudest Oggy Oggy Oggy, all 25 voices helping! Heading down the A38 Bristol Road out of Birmingham, the start was once again painful for me, my knee taking time to warm up, around seven sore miles. Karl's body was aching and then there was Longy's heel, too, but we had to crack on. Radio WM wanted an earlier interview today, so we took it on the run on Bristol Road – no stopping this time!

Our route was the A38 all the way to the finish line at the Raven Pub in Worcester, passing by Longbridge, Bromsgrove, and Droitwich. The traffic was once again very courteous though there was one slight hiccough just after Bromsgrove – apparently we had caused a four-mile tailback, so we took a quick break for nature to allow them to pass. By now, I was quite used to my antics when I needed a wee – jog on the spot, a quick knee rub – but of course, the other runners had never seen anything like it before. That gave them all a good laugh!

It might have been the familiar location or the excellent loyal support boosting morale, but marathon number seven was a great run. The course wasn't without its hills; it made us puff a few times, but the general mood from everyone was fantastic, all in good humour and good voice. As the miles clocked up, the majority of us managed to stick together, with just a few falling behind, but they finished. At one point, I was running with one of the chaps who told me he lived locally. Going up one rather nice hill he said, 'Last one now, Dave, all flat from here!' If the remaining miles were what he called flat, I wouldn't like to see what he called a hill!

With the 20-mile point announced, the excitement began to grow. The majority of us runners were still together and the pace didn't falter, even over those last miles of flat hills! The finish line and the announcement of the first sight of the Raven – like the first to see the sea on a trip to the coast – made us pick up the pace as well as the volume of our voices. We crossed the finish line of marathon number seven in **four hours and 41 minutes**, on to a car park full of amazing support and noise.

I was getting quite used to the TV, radio, newspapers and magazines. John Workman, from the *Black Country Bugle*, was present, telling me he had followed us all morning, taking snaps at every opportunity. There was even a representative from Nova who presented me with the number 1,000 for the 2011 Birmingham Half Marathon – more running, then! Fantastic! Interview after interview, photos, photos and more photos, then food. The Raven had done us proud; like all the other venues, the hospitality was second to none, lovely hot food. Then it was on to the bikes.

We left The Raven to fantastic applause. After yesterday's low mileage on the bikes, we were back to the heavy miles again today, heading for Weston-super-Mare, albeit the outskirts. We were also joined by a couple of extra cyclists today, Gareth Stubbs and Tim Andrews, managing director of Hollywood Monster, who had supplied us with the portable start and finish line, along with all the magnetic signs for the vehicles. The weather was great; it's always good to feel a little sun on your back, helps to keep spirits up. We were heading for Gloucester and Police HQ, but en route we had been asked to pop into a little shopping area in Worcester to visit a portable cancer awareness unit. With Macmillan's name emblazoned all over our chests and our equipment, we felt it fitting to show willing and offer support – if only for a fleeting few minutes.

Just outside Worcestershire, the police met us on cycles and motorbikes to escort us and help keep the traffic moving. The police cyclists were part of the police triathlon team and they guided us all the way to their HQ. With these experts sitting to our front, we motored along at a rapid rate of knots. It was great to get the legs moving, really ridding my legs of the lactic acid from the run, but I still hoped that the razor blades on my saddle would disappear. It was agony.

The hospitality at Gloucester Police HQ was superb; not only had they arranged the motorbike escort, but as a unit they had been very active in fundraising, presenting a cheque to us for Macmillan to the tune of £500! Also joining us at HQ were Deb and my girls, Georgie-Lee and Dannie. They were travelling in a vehicle with Alison, Garry's wife, and their son, Adam; Laura, Longy's wife and their son, Charlie – Laura also being around eight months pregnant! The Mommies' Bus continued to follow us on our route, shouting encouragement out of the window.

At the Worcestershire border, and after thanking the police for their escort, Garry took the helm once again. We didn't want to ride through Bristol city centre, as it would have been chaos, so Garry plotted his way around the outskirts, down a few country lanes. Though in theory it added a few miles, it was much safer and with the wheels always turning, would prove much quicker, too. We were now well on the way to our next overnight stop, New Ditch Farm. It was going to be yet another late night.

My backside, at this point, was unbearable; it was all I could think about. I mentioned to Mike that I thought it was because he was in a low gear making our legs turn quickly and making me bounce in the saddle more than was necessary. He found a higher gear and it helped, my legs powering rather than spinning which meant I moved around less. Although the razor blades weren't going anywhere – they would stay for the remainder of the challenge, I could tell – it did ease a little. Still, we reached New Ditch Farm, passing through the finish line with a fantastic reception.

Being so late again, it was a quick hello to Penny and her husband, then off down the road to the Fox and Goose for tea. They had been very good holding back the kitchen staff so we could be fed, like guests of honour. We also met up with Jerry Williams and his son Joe, who we had met on our original recce and had given us many wonderful pointers, and David Crosby, the South West area representative for Macmillan. They would run the next marathon leg with us.

Garry and I roomed together again and it was funny in the morning to hear Rosemary say that I had fallen asleep halfway through my massage. Garry had also fallen asleep in the bed next to me, still clutching his laptop to record the day's events, so she simply finished my massage, turned out the lights and left us to it.

Wednesday 17 August 2011

Today was a special day: mine and Deb's sixth wedding anniversary, and I was looking forward to grabbing her at the finish! But before I could think about that, it was another 6am start and another case of heaving three battered bodies, Karl, Longy, me, to the starting line. But at least this morning my mouth felt a lot better which was one less thing to dwell on. Garry powered the bike up, our music blasted away and we ran out on to the A38 headed for Bridgwater and our next stop, the Lime Kiln.

The first few miles or so were hard work, but then, saying that, so were the next 20. Surprisingly, my knee warmed up much quicker, but as we ran downhill, I found my calves protesting.

Never thought I'd hear myself wish for inclines up – I must be off my rocker!

CHAPTER 9

A couple of miles on, I heard a voice from a car coming the other way, 'Morning Mr Heeley.' I knew that voice. It was Richie, Deb's cousin. The girls and the kids had stopped at his house overnight in Bridgwater; next thing I knew, he was running alongside us! Richie ran with us for a couple of miles, and again a change of voice helped us along… before he realised he had left his car two miles back, and his car was currently housing his keys and wallet. He had to leg it back to pick it up, but just before he left, I asked him if he could do me a favour: could he find a single red rose for the finish?

Rosemary joined us at some point, keeping us amused with her many facts, mostly sexual, but Jo could no longer run with us – after yesterday's run, she had picked up an injury to her leg. Another casualty!

The road was long. Why did 26.2 miles seem to get longer each day? Our bodies were tired, exhausted. Our legs were leaden. Karl was feeling the pressure on his body, but from his injuries from his bike fall, he was doing marvellously and we made sure he knew it. We trudged on, counting down the miles. The days, the hours, the miles, the lack of sleep… it was all beginning to show and take its toll, but we cracked on – and I had a card to deliver!

At around ten miles to go Longy had a craving for an apple. And I thought it was Laura who was pregnant? Duggie, hearing this, and in the middle of nowhere, went in search. He came back a little while later, complete with apple! He explained that he rode off, found a pub, and began chatting to the cleaner. On hearing his tale of the challenge, he was more than willing to get him that apple, so Longy munched as we ran. Good old Duggie, nothing too much trouble for our team!

The 20-mile point was passed. Then, with only a couple of miles left, I asked if I could have the card and the rose. To the horror of the lads, I managed to up the pace and with half a mile to go, it felt like we were sprinting! We crossed the finish line at the Lime Kiln in **four hours and 49 minutes** and as I held out the card and rose for Deb, I wished I could have seen her face, just for that second. She was incredulous, saying, 'You've come all the way from John O'Groats, running and cycling, and you still thought to get this organised! I haven't even written your card yet!' But the hug I got was all I needed.

The hospitality at the Lime Kiln, courtesy of Graham Palmer, was superb, mountains of pasta. When Deb and I did the original recce, we would never have believed that her cousin Richie's local would be the marathon stop, but here we were. Tired bodies, tired people, but the banter was still flowing and the whole team were still on a high. It was great to sit and chat but there were only two things spoiling it: Rosie and Longy telling us it was time to get on the bikes.

Bikes and riders primed and ready to go, we had a few photos taken by the *Somerset County Gazette*. We said our goodbyes and set off, with the rain re-joining us. Our route would take us through Taunton and Tiverton before the end in Okehampton. The rain was on and off all afternoon and I'm certain that, contrary to popular belief, the further south you go, the hillier it gets! I reckon the entire country is a slope, and all the hills have slid down from Scotland.

The razor blades were back, the tired legs were back, but the team of riders, with jokes and obscenities flying, rallied each other on. The hills came and the talking gave way to grunting and cries of, 'Oh no, not again!' but the legs kept on turning. We also found that the courtesy shown to us while out running on the road had changed: the cars weren't giving much time for us cyclists, but with the support vehicle and Garry out in front, we managed to combat it and travelled on pretty safely.

The last few miles into Okehampton threw us a serious hill; it seemed like Glen Coe all over again, only split into four. Up, down, the feet pushed, the wheels went round, sometimes slower than others but we kept on pedalling. The last hill up to the Betty Cottles Inn was a killer. We were silent. I was told later that the relief was evident on everyone's faces when we pulled on to the car park and through the finish line. If my legs were anything to go by, the lads were all hurting, too. The support as we finished was, once again, absolutely unbelievable – the Mayor of Okehampton even came out to welcome us!

That night, I actually got to share not only a room with the family but a bed with my wife. Poor Deb got to witness the 'holiday' I was having: showered, kit ready for the morning, tea. It was still after midnight when we got to bed, but dare I mention that I sampled the dream of many a man? Yes, two women in one bed! Yes, there I was, lying in bed with my wife, on our anniversary night, when Rosemary came in to give me a much-needed massage. And then it happened – I fell fast asleep!

Thursday 18 August 2011

How to upset a great night's sleep? A 5am alarm. And poor old Deb saw it all. Rosemary came in first with a gentle massage, Longy with breakfast, then Duggie offering his Jaffa Cakes, Karl afterwards on the quest to borrow toothpaste. Finally, Garry told us it was 'time to rock and roll'. The kids were still fast asleep, oblivious to it all.

Just before 6am, three tired runners, Karl, Longy and myself, were standing under the start line in the pouring rain for the penultimate marathon. I had a comforting smile on my face knowing Deb was waiting to cheer us off. She was standing there, getting wet in her nightgown – this challenge has seen it all!

We kicked off, although very much at a crawl. Longy was still limping, with his new-style trainers cut out at the heel, and Karl was certainly suffering, with his bruising, grazes and his leg beginning to stiffen. I had the feeling it was going to be a very long, very hard, not to mention slow, day. We got to around four miles and thankfully my knee warmed up. Garry and Steve said they were going to fuel up as there was a petrol station at hand and although Longy mentioned that Garry had said for us to stop and wait, Karl and I conveniently didn't hear him; raining as it was, we wanted to carry on. Garry caught us up some ten minutes later and was not amused! It turned out we had passed the turning we needed a mile down the road, and were now off-course. He would have to re-route us, and his words were definitely unprintable. We took the telling off and carried on. Karl had initially dared us to hide behind a tree for a laugh, and as Garry wasn't in a humorous mood, I was pretty glad we hadn't.

We ran on and when we turned right, what a flaming hill! I swear that I was leaning so far forward that I could almost touch the floor with my nose. It was that steep that Duggie's front wheel was lifting upwards as he pedalled. He had to practically sit on his handlebars. The only consolation about this hill was that my calves weren't hurting – though everything else was.

Skirting Dartmoor, I indicated to the lads I was desperate for the loo, but this time, not for a wee. Karl very kindly escorted me on to the moors, about 100 yards or so on, and then left me to my own devices. Sometimes my other senses go into overdrive, and with the wind blowing and the fact that I was somewhere up on Dartmoor, I started thinking of all the creepy things you could possibly think of when you're on your own on a moor: I saw old films and newsreels of moors murders and reports of big cats, and *The Hound of the Baskervilles* sprang to mind. Despite being a grown man, I have to admit I was much happier when I was back with company and running in the rain. Rosemary joined us at this point, and she managed a few miles, but when I stopped to have a chat to Radio WM, she jumped back in the support car and the dry. I can't say I blamed her.

It was a very hard day. The miles were very tiring, the hills kept coming – in fact, I had never known so many hills in a 26.2 mile stretch. The rain was relentless and with the added wind, it was very cold, but we pushed on. Due to the re-routing, we had to run along the A30. Maybe the rain made the cars sound closer and faster, but it sounded terrifying and I was glad to get away from the main road. Payback for me today as it was my turn to try and pull the lads through, especially Karl who was now really suffering. Keeping everyone buoyant, though, had the welcome effect of taking attention away from my own aches and pains.

Nevertheless, when the 20-mile mark was announced, I could have screamed with delight! Those last five miles to the Wilsey Down Hotel, Camelford in North Cornwall, seemed to take forever, but at least the sun had come out and the rain had stopped – one bonus. Deb also took up the running cord in those last couple of miles and ran a short distance with me; so did the kids, until Georgie-Lee fell, grazing her knee. On the run-in, a good mate of mine, Tom, with his wife, Mal, and his mom, who were on holiday in the area, came across to give us some support. The finish line was heaven, with no sprinting today. We staggered across the line in **four hours and 47 minutes**.

The penultimate marathon completed, there was the matter of a 50-mile bike ride before we could move on to the last day, but the warm reception from the team, the family members now among us and the staff at the hotel was fantastic. It was great to meet PC Dave Trout who had kept a watchful eye on proceedings during the marathon, but of course it seemed no time at all before those fateful words rang out, 'Time to go.'

The Mommies' Bus set off for Penzance so they could be there at the finish of the last marathon, while we set our sights on Truro.

The road to Truro was pretty much without incident, unbelievably. The contours were kind, the legs were tired but seemed to keep themselves turning. With the sun out and the end of the challenge becoming a reality, the road to Truro was actually enjoyable. We thought that maybe the locals were fed up with so many bikes on their roads as they seemed reluctant to give way, but with Garry at the helm we sailed safely through to the Donnington Guesthouse in Truro, our home for the night.

It was so nice to have time for once. At the guesthouse, I could chill out on the bed, take a shower, shave and get dressed to go for a meal, all without rushing. I could also have a bit of time to meet up with Tony Ellis, now a good pal. Having just flown in from a holiday in Greece, he would join us for the final marathon. We enjoyed taking time over our meal, too, but we still didn't get an early night. With all the chatter about the final day, and where had the last nine gruelling days gone?, it was well past midnight when we finally made it to bed. Still, at least we're consistent!

Friday 19 August 2011

I wouldn't miss that 5am alarm, but on Friday 19 August, I didn't dislike it so much. After all, it was the tenth and final day of the challenge!

As normal, Rosemary started my day with a gentle massage and Longy with breakfast. Garry bounded in with excitement, telling me, 'We're going to do it, mate!'

'I hope so, Gaz,' I replied, 'I do hope so.'

The morning was fresh as we stood under the start line for marathon number ten. While the minutes ticked away to the start, I dwelled on my thoughts, just like at John O'Groats a lifetime ago. This had been one hell of a challenge, Blind Dave's challenge, but standing here I realised that all that had been achieved was due to a fantastic team that supported me.

I didn't need to see what was happening around me to realise their importance; I heard, listened, took in the conversation, felt the team spirit, experienced the camaraderie, but more importantly, sensed the will for success. Team Blind Dave was like a well-oiled clock, a team that moved as one. Ten days ago we were a team of individuals, wanting adventure but unfamiliar with each other, but now we were friends for life, pulling together. We were desperate for the Top To

CHAPTER 9

Toe challenge to be a total success – for Macmillan, and for ourselves.

For the last time, we stood on the marathon start line: Karl with a broken body, Longy still wincing with his heel, my knee throbbing, and we all shook hands and off we went. We were also joined by Tony Ellis, in what he said was his West Bromwich Albion away top, the red one... The lads were all having a laugh on me when Karl exclaimed, 'But it's got a Man U badge on it!'

Our trusty support team, Duggie, Mike and Dave Sinar followed us on their bikes, dishing out the drinks. Steve and Dave Dourass, along with our glamorous physio, Rosemary, were sitting tight in the support car right behind us, with Garry out front, I can only imagine like a shining beacon. Then there was Andy Williams, Jo Sinar, now brandishing a walking stick due to her running injury, little Ben, the media team from South Birmingham College, dismantling each and every day the start and finish line. These lads and lasses had done so much behind the scenes. It was very, very much appreciated.

Today was the finale but there were to be no heroics. With Karl's leg stiffening to the point of dragging, it was a matter of right leg, left leg, gritted teeth and running through the pain barrier. With the constant pounding, Longy was suffering; my knee warmed up about five miles in but collectively, our legs were so tired but spirits ran high.

Duggie had become our butler on wheels, and today he rode alongside us. Both Dave and Karl described his antics: he had a towel over his arm, a silver tray in hand, on which lay a bottle of Lucozade, a nut bar and a piece of fruit, all secured by velcro. It was also revealed that this was the last Fruit and Nut bar as Steve had devoured my entire stash of sweets – all the Fruit and Nut, the Dairy Milk, the jellybeans and the jelly babies! Still, it made me laugh and took my mind off the aches and pains.

There was no time for scenic descriptions or nonsensical chatter; we simply counted down the miles. I could hear people as we passed by the little towns, I could smell the fresh clean air. The sun was now quite hot. Twenty miles announced, then 22, 23, then 24 miles, just two to go.

Then Garry informed us that we would have to run past the finish line, up to the next roundabout then back on ourselves in order to get the 26.2 miles in, which was pretty demoralising to hear. The last half-mile was so painful: we pushed as hard as we could, but then it happened. All three of us raised our arms as we passed through the finish line. I was enveloped in shouts, screams, hugs, kisses and tears. It was absolutely amazing! We had completed the tenth marathon of ten days in **four hours and 47 minutes** – staggering! The car park at Jordan's café, Marazion, became the best place on earth!

For me, the marathons were certainly the hardest part, but we still had 15 miles to go to Land's End, I had to remind them. Admittedly we could hop, skip and jump from the café, but I firmly believe in the motto never count your chickens. I was quietly confident, but that was all.

Rosemary appeared, but Duggie was busy saddling up the spare tandem to ride in with Longy. Unfortunately no one had thought to bring a spare cycle helmet so off Longy went in search. When he came back, there were shrieks of laughter. The only helmet he could find was a kid's, in bright purple! Sometimes, I cursed, if only I could just see for a moment!

Our cycle team had now grown by one more tandem, along with another 20 bikes from the local cycle club Jerry and Joe belonged to, and we kicked off in search of a finish.

I can't honestly remember the 15 miles or so to Land's End; I even forgot the razor blades! I do remember a slight hill. As we came to the brow, I heard Mike gasp, 'Dave, I just can't believe how many people are here to meet us, I just don't believe what I'm seeing!'

It sounded like thousands of people clapping and cheering. As we cycled towards the Land's End finish, we did exactly as we said we would – ten yards before, we stopped. Halted. Garry turned the bike off, Steve parked the car and Andy the caravan, and the crowd fell silent.

This morning before we started, I had a word with the team. Besides thanking each and every one of them for their fantastic support, I had to say how proud I felt to be a part of the team. The challenge was labelled 'Blind Dave's Top To Toe', but there was no way I was crossing any line without them! So Garry, Karl, Longy, Rosemary, Duggie, Steve and Dave Dourass, Mike, Dave, Andy, along with Jo and Ben, linked arms with me and we crossed the finish at Land's End, as one.

It was like an eclipse, or something. It felt as though the world had stopped. I don't remember any sounds, just the feeling of the team joined together, shaking with exhaustion and adrenalin. Then, as soon as we crossed that line, everything just erupted. We grinned, we hugged, we cried, we posed for pictures; family grabbed us, friends. *We bloody well did it!* I chanted to myself, the words ringing in my head.

10

THE YACHT Inn, Penzance, on the Saturday after the challenge was when the party truly started. It began with me speaking, thanking the team for their utter dedication and their relentless hard graft. Duggie, Dave Sinar and Mike Hopkins had cycled the whole journey, Longy had completed all ten marathons, while Karl ran six marathons and cycled the length of England. I was also keen to thank our friends and family for support, not just during the challenge but also in that incredible build-up, when it pretty much took over our lives.

'And finally, there's one extra special thank-you I'd like to make,' I said, as the crowd hushed. 'Can I ask my wife to come up here, please?'

I felt Deb approach. I flipped open my watch. She was definitely confused – I could feel her silence.

I took out the diamond ring that had been specially nestled into the watch. It had lived with me for the entire journey, from John O'Groats to Land's End.

'We're doing everything backwards,' I told the crowd. 'We're already married but Deb always says I didn't formally ask her, so here's the engagement ring.' She laughed and cried, said yes, and threw her arms round me.

CHAPTER 10

We always said we did things slightly differently: the children, the marriage, and then the engagement.

Then it was Steve's turn, and he proposed to his partner Tracy.

It was a wonderful moment, topped off by Garry who decided, at that moment, to pop the champagne corks Formula 1-style and empty the bottles over me and the team. The kids found it hilarious, diving under the tables to escape the foam. Georgie-Lee ushered us all out and insisted we take a graduation-style photograph by throwing our team t-shirts up in the air.

Much like the Sevens I didn't experience a comedown, or the post-challenge blues, once everyone had dispersed and life returned to normal. I had something else to talk about in my professional speaking engagements, and, in some ways, it was a challenge that had been much more difficult and heavy going. The fundraising had gone pretty well, too.

In the November we held a black tie event for a final stab at topping up the money raised for Macmillan. It would be a big party, too, of course, culminating in the presentation of the money to the charity. However, it soon proved a busy day. I, alongside other Macmillan supporters, had been invited to Clarence House to meet with Macmillan patron, Prince Charles. It was an offer I couldn't refuse, so it meant that I had to dash home by train just in time for the start of our event. We sold corporate tables, Adrian Goldberg and Paul Burrell were the masters of ceremony, and we auctioned off ten bottles of Top To Toe-labelled champagne and – the icing on the cake – the diamond encrusted pendant I had worn for the duration of the challenge. Kindly donated by Steve Quance Jewellers, it was in the shape of the British Isles, with 11 diamonds depicting the route. Businessman, Manny Dhaliwal, made an incredibly generous winning bid – but refused to take the pendant, instead presenting it back to me! What a man! I couldn't believe it. And when the surprise birthday cake came out, too, well, I felt like I'd been spoilt rotten. Once the final sum had been counted, verified, and re-verified, a hush fell across the room. We'd raised £126,271.13.

Our old pal Liz Mabley, who had so generously helped us with health and safety requirements for the Top To Toe, had to leave the night feeling rather poorly. No one realised how poorly, and she passed away a week later. In her memory, we decided to take part in the Wolverhampton to Aberdovey bike ride in June 2012, fundraising for the charity close to her heart, Changing Our Lives. We were joined by Liz's friends and relatives – Paul, Alan, Lissa, Lizzie and Ben Mabley, alongside Simon Day, with Kerry Mabley providing the support vehicle – and the whole convoy wore t-shirts bearing Liz's name. It was a celebratory affair, and a suitably challenging ride.

The ride started out of Wolverhampton at 7.30am, the rain joining us. It was a long, cold, wet ride covering well over 120 miles. On the tandem, Duggie and I attempted the mountain at Dinas Mawddwy in the Snowdonia National Park. We limped up against a force eight gale. The support staff at the top told us that we would need to pedal during the descent, such was the force of the gale. I initially thought it was a strange comment – we would be freewheeling down that mountain, surely? But they were right. The wind was so strong that Duggie and I had to pedal hard down that mountain, barely getting above 15mph! We later found out that cyclists behind us had been prevented from carrying on, such were the treacherous conditions.

The following day, the Liz Mabley contingent decided to reverse the ride, coming back from Aberdovey to West Bromwich. We were supported by many of the Top To Toe team, including Garry and Alison Wells, Karl Moore, and Tony Ellis in his mobile home. It was a really lovely way to remember our Liz, and I think she would have appreciated our efforts.

The Top To Toe caught the attention of the Land's End to John O'Groats Association and I was named the winner of the association's oldest cup, the Griffin Trophy, for the most amount of money raised for charity along the route. Cycling In Sandwell also announced me as their Cyclist of the Year, which was very kind of them. I think it was the tandem that did it.

But perhaps most excitingly, I was to be awarded an honorary doctorate by the University of Wolverhampton.

In the immediate build-up to the Top To Toe, all efforts were concentrated on training and publicising. I used every opportunity I had to promote the challenge, to sing the praises of the team, to celebrate the achievements and need of Macmillan. Deb and I were completely focused: heads down, get on with it.

So I was quite surprised to receive a letter of support from the University of Wolverhampton in June, completely unrelated to the challenge. It asked me whether I would be prepared to receive an honorary doctorate, in recognition of my sporting and fundraising achievements. Of course I would! I was delighted. However, Deb and I were asked to keep quiet until the announcement would be made public, after the Top To Toe, in September. By then we were trained in keeping embargoes, and filed away the letter in the pleasing pile and put fingers to our lips.

On day eight of the Top To Toe, I dialled in to my morning interview with Radio WM. Phil Upton, the presenter at the time, told me, live on air and without any warning, 'And we've just heard that the University of Wolverhampton has offered you an honorary doctorate, too! How do you feel about that?'

Firstly, I hadn't realised that the embargo had been lifted, so I didn't know how to respond. I mumbled a few choice words of humbled thanks, hoping that the station had received the news through all the right channels and I wasn't about to be lambasted for mentioning it. But next, I realised, this did nothing for my street cred. As soon as the interview was over and the lads had got wind of this new development, they christened me 'Doctor Dingle' and I didn't live it down.

The official ceremony took place on 9 September 2011. Deb, the girls, our moms and I went across to the university and I had great fun donning the cap and gown before parading with the other honorary graduates to the Grand Theatre in Wolverhampton. There were a good few of us, including well-known barrister, Constance Briscoe, and – possibly most excitingly – Kevin Rowland of Dexys Midnight Runners fame. And, of course, being in the spotlight in Wolverhampton, I had to make my allegiances known – I made sure my Albion tie was visible for the photo opportunity.

As an Honorary Doctor of Letters, from the School of Sport, Performing Arts and Leisure, I could technically call myself Dr Heeley if I wanted to… which could prove useful one day, I'm sure! I wasn't entirely sure what the role would entail, but it turns out I am now invited to attend an array of university functions, and sometimes I'm even invited to come along and speak to current students, make award presentations, and that kind of thing.

And then another surprise award made itself known.

Just after Christmas in 2011, at the turn of the year, I was invited for a telephone chat on Adrian Goldberg's show on BBC WM; nothing out of the ordinary, just a customary catch-up. The leader of Sandwell Council, Darren Cooper, also dialled in. Out of the blue, he cleared his throat and addressed me.

'Dave, I am going to make an announcement, and I would like an answer, yes or no,' he said.

Adrian went strangely quiet.

'Okay,' I replied, trying to disguise my intrigue and failing.

'I want to make you an offer: would you be prepared to be the 11th honorary freeman of the borough of Sandwell?'

Gobsmacked. There was a heavy, thick silence. I was mindful of the people listening at home.

'Well…' I began, but I was interrupted.

'Just an answer; yes or no,' he repeated. There was a friendly urging tone to his voice.

CHAPTER 10

'Yes, yes!' I laughed, terrified the offer would be taken away from me if I hesitated any further.

'Good,' the leader confirmed.

Of course, I also didn't really know what I'd accepted, either, so once I got home, Deb and I did a bit of research.

In the times of Lords and Ladies of the Manor, when us ordinary folk were subservient to a big cheese in the parish, born into his privilege of power of course, then a working person would need the permission of his or her Lord of the Manor to do pretty much anything. So if I was in West Brom, and wanted to cross the border into Birmingham to sell my livestock at the market, then I would have had to grovel to my Lord for his consent.

A freeman was a very rare, treasured thing: he could roam the country and do exactly as he pleased, grazing his cattle on the best pastures and driving his sheep along any highway and byway.

Of course, that means little now, but I hadn't quite anticipated the formality of the proposition. Once my acceptance had been recorded, it had to be agreed at a meeting of the full council – the mayor, the leader, the chief executive, the full whack, all in their official guises. A few different councillors told me that there had been no opposition; I had sailed through. I would be a freeman of the borough.

I was thrilled. I'm so proud of the area in which I was born and raised, where I live now and have brought up my girls. I love the people, the accent, *the* football club. I relish our self-deprecating humour, our vocabulary, our industrial history.

My fundraising endeavours over the years have allowed me to better know my neighbours, to give me introductions to a whole range of different people from the same area as me that I might not have met in any other situation. I like the fact that when I have my latest calamity stitched up at the hospital, the nurse knows my name. I live in a real community – something we're being told is being eroded in modern times.

Over the years, I suppose I've become an unofficial ambassador of Sandwell, so to cement this, to make me an official ambassador, would be an absolute honour. A joy.

The date for the ceremony was set to be 31 March 2012. I was asked whom I would like to attend and as there was a rather slim number permitted, I had the difficult task of deciding which friends and family members would enjoy the occasion most.

On the day, guests arrived first. Then the mayoral procession – which included me! – was announced by the town crier. We filed in and took our seats. There were speeches, firstly from the chief exec, mayor and leader, and then it was my turn. I gave my heartfelt thanks, and culminated with the explanation of one of my biggest dreams. And I made everyone cry! Georgie-Lee tells me that she still can't think about that speech without crying!

Once I'd finished and the taps had been turned off, it was my turn to be surprised. Georgie-Lee, still wiping the tears from her eyes, stood and presented me with a cuddly sheep – at least I would have one sheep I could drive along West Bromwich High Street! I was very proud of her courage to stand and speak in such a grown-up, formal occasion, especially given that she was only ten years old. She told me later that she had been crying so much during my speech that one of the councillors had asked if she would still be able to make the presentation, and she had nodded, determined to do it.

Once my sheep was tucked under my arm, I was issued with a scroll and an official badge of office. The list of freemen and women that have preceded me is pretty impressive: the likes of Betty Boothroyd, Christopher Graham Collins (or Frank Skinner, as he is better known), Cyrille Regis, Julie Walters, Tony 'Bomber' Brown... what company to be in!

I hoped that being a freeman entailed a council tax waiver and a free pint every time I went into a Sandwell pub, but sadly that's not proved to be the case. It does mean that we're invited to all council events, even the big ones like the mayor making, which has been fascinating – and particularly useful when I'm on a fundraising drive. A freeman of the borough is the highest honour a council can bestow, so I'm always present in a formal photograph or seated at the table along with the mayor, the MP, the chief executive and the councillors. I try to show my gratitude whenever I can, by attending the events I am invited to and speaking about my home town with pride.

The feeling of civic pride continued well into 2012, and it felt as though it spread right across the country.

I was as delighted as anybody to hear that the Olympics and Paralympics would be coming to London in 2012. Not only was I proud that our country would be hosting the Games, welcoming incredible athletes from across the globe, but I looked forward to the inevitable joining together of communities that these events tend to help us do. I hoped we could demonstrate to the world that us Britons are a friendly, efficient bunch able to put on a good show.

And when the Olympic torch relay was announced, I thought, 'Well there's a thing.' I had to admit: I fancied that. Carrying the flame through West Brom would be quite the honour. Had I a chance, I secretly wondered to myself? There would only be 8,000 torchbearers across the UK. I kept quiet.

But it wasn't long before there were a few favourable rumblings from council officials, too. 'Don't worry, Dave, you'll be doing it; it's just a case of when and where.'

'Well, whatever happens, happens; it's not a God-given right for anyone to do it,' I replied, trying not to get too excited. I knew these things were never as straightforward as they seemed. My nomination form was apparently completed and submitted before the deadline on 29 June 2011, but I don't know by whom.

However, on the day that the torchbearers were announced, in March 2012, it seemed that others felt I was in with a chance, too. BBC and Central News crews turned up unannounced at the house, waiting for my confirmation e-mail to arrive. Deb replenished their mugs of tea as I kept refreshing my inbox.

Eventually an e-mail arrived from LOCOG. It told me that my application had been unsuccessful, that the committee had been overwhelmed by the number of applicants, all worthy of carrying the flame. It had been a difficult decision to make.

My heart sank. I was disappointed, but how many other people were disappointed, too? Hundreds? Thousands? I was in good company, and I resolved to get over it and help out where I could. Perhaps I could volunteer? I wanted to experience the Olympic atmosphere, at least.

But our local news stations were having none of it. There was more coverage – speculation, condemnation – on why Blind Dave hadn't got it, than people who had! A Facebook campaign was launched to overturn the decision, and I was even invited to talk on the radio about it. It was very flattering and rather embarrassing.

Two weeks later, I received a letter from LOCOG. The committee had met again and decided to make me a torchbearer after all. I couldn't quite believe it! My place in the relay would be Cobridge in Stoke – which the council also tried to appeal, as it was adamant that I would be torchbearer in Sandwell, my home district.

'Let's leave it at that,' I told the council, 'I'm just delighted to be offered a place at all.'

Next, the details came through. My date would be Thursday 31 May 2012 and I needed to be at the Potteries Museum and Art Gallery at 5am. Nobody would be allowed to accompany me but Seamus. It was intriguing. I didn't know what to expect.

Of course, I did know that those two months would fly by, and they did.

The extended family, as well as Deb and the kids, accompanied me and we all stayed in Stoke the night before, catching a glimpse of the Olympic flame as it arrived at Hanley Park that evening. There was already a celebratory atmosphere, as musicians and contemporary dancers performed on the stage in front of a massive, excited crowd.

Then, at some godforsaken hour the following morning, Deb packed Seamus and I off into a taxi. We were met at the museum and registered, and then I bought my torch. At 6.15am, all the torchbearers were corralled on to a coach and dropped at each of our individual 300 metre intervals, ready for our leg of the relay. Funnily enough, Tony Pulis, then Stoke City manager and now boss of West Brom, was the first torchbearer of the day.

I was number six, so the sixth person to take the torch that morning. I was standing on my spot from 6.30am and although it was a miserable day, with the threat of rain in the air and my tracksuit collar pulled tight to keep out the draughts, the atmosphere was incredible – I couldn't believe the amount of people sacrificing their warm beds to line the streets that morning, including my own family and friends. Duggie, the daft sod, set out on his bike at three in the morning! BBC and Central News had also taken their places beside my starting point.

At 7.15am it was my turn. The noise from the sidelines amplified and I knew that my predecessor, the torchbearer before me, was approaching. Suddenly, Seamus started barking and pulling on his lead. I tried to control him, force him back to my heel.

'What is it? What's the matter?' I hissed through my teeth as he continued to duck and dive, barking his head off.

Thankfully a really friendly chap from LOCOG by the name of Tommy came to my rescue.

'A cat's just decided to wander across the road,' Tommy laughed. 'I take it your dog doesn't like cats?'

He was right. By the sounds of it, that cat enjoyed its moment of glory: taking centre stage, being admired by people and cameras alike, and teasing a great big German Shepherd that couldn't come anywhere near it.

Thankfully, Seamus managed to come to his senses just as the previous torchbearer arrived and performed 'the kiss', as it's called, from torch to torch to ignite my flame. As my torch was lit, a cheer went up from the crowd and Seamus and I took off in the middle of the road – which confused poor Seamus no end. I had only had him six months, and as guide dogs are taught to find the nearest kerb, there I was, asking him to walk us safely down the middle of the road, as deafening cheers rang out from the pavement either side. Tommy kept behind me, carefully notifying me when I needed to move left or move right, but he didn't have to work too hard – I milked those 300 metres like it was a marathon. I'm sure I broke a record that day: for the world's slowest 300 metres.

I also heeded the command of Auntie Mavis, Deb's aunt.

'Everyone's been holding that torch at chest height,' she had said earlier in the week, tutting. 'Will you hold the torch in the air, so people can see it, please, Dave?' It wasn't really a question, it was an instruction. But I did as I was told and held the torch high, high so the world could see it.

It actually wasn't all that easy, holding that torch aloft and trying to walk in a straight line while Seamus repeatedly veered off, aiming to find me a footpath, so I was pleased to be allowed to take my time. I could hear Deb running up and down the road beside me, chanting encouragement; I could hear cameras clicking and whirring. Above the sound of the whooping and cheering was a clacking and clapping from the promotional ephemera the sponsors had given out to supporters, being hit together. I could feel the rain about to burst. I could feel my cheeks cracking from the smile I couldn't help but grin, from ear to ear.

Though I pretended to Tommy that I had cramp and would need to walk slower – he saw straight through that one! – my 300 metres were over in seconds. I kissed my torch with my successor's, and Seamus and I were ushered back on to the bus. Once our team relay had been completed, the bus took us back to the museum for a lively reception where we were presented with medals to mark the occasion. The Lord Mayor of Stoke-on-Trent was in attendance, television and radio crews were capturing the atmosphere… it was manic, but a wonderful manic.

By midday, we were back in the car, heading down the M6 to home. I pinched myself. Did that really just happen? Did I just do that?

I had little time to reflect as Deb, the girls and I flew out to Skopelos, the Greek island famous for its association with the film *Mamma Mia*, the following day for the wedding of Steve and Tracy Dourass. But when we were back, the following week, I found that I had a few speaking invitations waiting for me. People were desperate to see the torch first hand. Olympic fever had hit – especially when one fella offered me money for it! There was absolutely no way I would part with that torch!

It was around this time that I received another e-mail that caught my attention: were there any tandem riders willing to take part in the Paralympic opening ceremony? Naturally, I couldn't think of anything better – after all, I was still buoyed up by the torchbearing experience, and if there was another way for me to sample some Olympic spirit, then I would certainly have a go. I asked Duggie what he thought, and whether he fancied auditioning.

'Well, why not?' he said, simply. 'It's never going to come around in our lifetime again, is it?'

I liked that boy's attitude.

It felt like auditioning for *X Factor*: our queue of other hopefuls snaked round the building. We had our photos taken and we were asked a multitude of different questions. The producers told us that they needed eight tandems – and by pure chance, there were eight tandem couples present. We were in if we wanted it. And we did!

In June and July, Duggie and I were measured up for our costumes and tried out the bike in the studio for size. But it was all very secretive: we weren't told what we would be wearing, or even what we would be doing. We were required to sign documents to promise that we wouldn't reveal what we experienced in rehearsals to family and friends, and any use of photography or social media was explicitly banned. It was exciting.

The majority of August was taken up by rehearsals, and travelling to and from London to the old car plant, not far from Upton Park, West Ham's ground. We made around 15 trips in total, all of which were kindly sponsored by Virgin Trains so Duggie and I didn't have to pay a penny, and Tim Andrews kindly lent us the use of his nearby flat for the days when we needed to stay over. Some days we did half an hour of rehearsing and nothing else; other days were more full-on. Slowly, over time, it all started coming together. We were to be in the 'Gravity' section of the ceremony, where actors and dancers on foot, on rollerskates and in wheelchairs would accompany the tandems. Four tandems started from the north of the arena, while mine and Duggie's starting position, plus three other tandems, was at the south. We were asked to cycle the perimeter first of all, with all the dancers doing their thing on the inside, but as our confidence grew, and the dancers' movements became more certain, the tandems were plotted to weave in and out of the dancers. We needed to cycle quickly, and we hoped and prayed a dancer wouldn't mis-time a step and find themselves in our pathway... Little accidents happened, of course, and teething problems were ironed out, but after a couple of weeks, our rehearsals moved to the Olympic Stadium.

The first time we were let into the stadium was like a celebration in itself, albeit a private one. We were photographed and allowed to explore. We were given our costumes and our bikes were transferred across, on our behalf, decked out in their regalia.

Security grew tighter and tighter. It had been drummed into us that we couldn't say anything about what we were doing, so when innocent bystanders asked us out of curiosity, or when friends and family pumped us for information, we didn't know how to behave or what we could say. We stood awkwardly, muttering the most generic things we could think of. We would bump into other dancers outside of the stadium and ask them, 'Have you had a good day?' and fearful of letting anything slip, they would reply with a short, sharp 'yes'.

On the actual day of the ceremony, 29 August 2012, we were locked into our room. If we needed the toilet, we were escorted, and everything else was catered for in our little room. But we weren't just waiting around for our moment, twiddling our thumbs; it was incredibly busy with a variety of personnel flitting about us, from costume alterations to medical consultations.

The bike was wrapped in green gauze and we were fitted with matching green helmets, after we had requested them – unusually, the original plan was to go without helmets, but we resisted. What kind of message would that give to our viewers? Our bodies were cloaked in a hessian suit that had a border of a thick material a bit like Astroturf. The trousers were three-quarter length, and chunky Dr Martens topped it off. Duggie protested each time we climbed into our costumes, saying that we looked like dorks. In fact, when we were later invited to the BBC *Midlands Today* studio to recount our experience live on air, Duggie said to me, 'There are few occasions when it's worth being blind, Dave, but this is definitely one of them!' I think the costume insulted his street cred.

A few of us sneaked GoPro cameras on to the front of our tandems to capture our moment of glory and some were spotted and duly confiscated. Duggie and I managed to secrete ours beneath a substantial piece of gauze so we got away with it, and I was delighted to be able to share it with the girls when I got home.

The music was deafening and I was so grateful for the earpiece that told us 'tandems ready', then gave us the countdown before we set off. We were the lead tandem on our side and as we went out into the arena, it was an assault on the senses. The crowd was cheering, the music thumping and the earpiece calmly reminding me of the manoeuvres I needed to be doing on the back of the bike: arms out from the body, up, round, back down, repeat. We were out there for just shy of two minutes – that's it – and it passed by in a blink. A whole month of rehearsals, countless trips between West Brom and the capital, and it was over in two minutes.

The finale saw every performer taking to the arena floor to join in with Beverley Knight's song 'I Am What I Am', a rousing anthem to set the scene for the subsequent Paralympic Games. We all sang along heartily, our arms and feet automatically doing the movements we had so carefully and repeatedly rehearsed over the past month. At every pause in the song, the performers whooped and cheered, mimicking the intense noise of the audience. We turned out and faced the crowd in an enormous circle. It was powerful.

After the ceremony had come to a close, the eight tandem couples decided to ride out of the stadium park together, just as a nice final gesture. Admittedly, we probably shouldn't have done that as we got told off by security guards, but it was going to take a lot more than that to dampen our jubilant spirits. We travelled home in our costumes the next day – even Duggie was swept up enough to go along with it.

I think everyone back home was surprised at how quickly our starring roles passed by. Because of the intensity of the lighting, and our camouflage, friends and family had difficulty in picking out which tandem was ours. So when I downloaded the GoPro footage and they could see our path through the dancers, and the tiny corridors that we wove through, they appreciated the amount of rehearsal time that was required. Deb and the girls later found YouTube videos of the ceremony and spent time describing to me the overall narrative, so I could work out where we came in.

CHAPTER 10

Entitled 'Enlightenment', and narrated by Stephen Hawking, the ceremony focused on 'rights' and 'reason'. Our section was just one part of a whole array of different aspects of the knowledge we have today. 'Gravity' was dominated by apples – a nod to Isaac Newton, of course – which were being juggled, thrown and suspended across the arena. Just before the tandems had taken to the stage, a short countdown invited all performers and audience members to take a single bite of the apple they had been handed on the way in to the arena. The sound of 80,000 people simultaneously biting an apple is probably unlike anything I've ever heard.

Some people book a holiday as soon as they return from one, and perhaps I do a similar thing – lining up the next challenge or adventure so I keep focused, keep looking forward, giving my mind and body something to aim towards. It means I rarely experience an anticlimax, the fall from the high of something that has passed. I didn't feel sad or empty once my involvement in the Olympics and the Paralympics came to an end, mainly because there were other adventures already on the horizon.

11

HARRY Moseley's story will no doubt be familiar: despite suffering from terminal brain cancer and constantly being in and out of hospitals, he tirelessly, and fearlessly, fundraised and campaigned on behalf of other cancer sufferers. He was perhaps best known for making and selling his colourful bracelets, which many celebrities sported in his honour. Sadly, Harry died in 2011, aged only 11, but his charity, Help Harry Help Others, goes from strength to strength in continuing Harry's work. In 2015, the charity even opened a cancer support centre in Stechford.

Just a year after Harry's death, on 19 October 2012, Deb and I attended the first Harry Moseley Ball. There, I caught up with two chaps named Gus Lunt and Tim Andrews.

Tim, through his company Hollywood Monster, is well known for charity work across Birmingham and further afield. I'd first been introduced to him through Steve Dourass and he'd kindly agreed to sponsor the Midlands leg of the Top To Toe. He then truly put his money where his mouth was and joined us to run it, too. He'd impressed me: a businessman with a real heart. So this time, when it was his turn to approach me, I listened.

'Dave, we'd like to approach you with a little thing that we're doing,' they began. 'Next year, we're cycling across seven countries in seven days, hopefully covering 700 miles. For Harry, of course. We wondered whether you'd be interested in joining us?'

Of course I was. I'd be delighted, I told them.

It was early days in the preparation for the challenge, but they anticipated starting in Birmingham in the September of the following year, and ending seven days later in Zurich, Switzerland.

I suggested reversing the ride: starting out in Zurich and ending in Birmingham, Harry Moseley's base, too, where our loyal supporters, our families and friends would be waiting. It would have more of an impact, especially where PR was concerned. Gus and Tim agreed.

Tim took the major admin on board and knowing what a job it would be, I offered to help where I could: a few introductions, a few meetings, to help get some beneficial partnerships up and running. But Tim, bless him, he and his company put the show on the road. This was actually quite a pleasant change for me; it was great to take a couple of steps back, be a part of it but not let it take over my life. Instead, I would concentrate on training and enjoy clocking up the miles on the tandem with Duggie – ever keen for a new challenge!

We also took the opportunity to reconfigure the tandem. Throughout the Top To Toe, I had felt like I had purely pedalled and rung the bell occasionally. I wanted more involvement. Though I had a small brake at the back, I asked Duggie if he'd be happy with me having full control of all the brakes and gears.

Duggie drew the line at the brakes, telling me, 'There's no way that I'm sitting at the front of a tandem, doing however many miles an hour, with the brakes being controlled by a blind bloke. Absolutely no way.' He was probably right. But I got my wish with the gears, and I learnt to feel the gradient of the road and when was best to switch gears, meaning that communication between Duggie and me became even more essential. Duggie tells me I get it right about 80 per cent of the time, which isn't bad, eh?

The build-up to the challenge started on Saturday 21 September 2013 at the Baggies. A few of the cycling team went on to the pitch at half-time to drum up support, get the fans ready to watch our progress over the following week and encourage them to reach into their pockets for sponsorship. Of course, it always helps the cause when the home team win, and win we did, beating Sunderland 3-0. That started the week off nicely, ensuring the wind was in my sails.

The following day I said goodbye to Deb and the kids. I'd made Deb promise that nothing untoward would be waiting for me when I got off the plane in Zurich. She had enjoyed teasing me about 'end of life' clinics when she bought that one-way ticket to Switzerland. She reiterated that the only thing waiting for me would be a gruelling 700-mile trip home, and that made her laugh even more!

But then we were off: Duggie and I on the National Express to Luton Airport. By 3.30pm we were on the plane, and 6pm Swiss time saw us settled in the hotel. I'd stayed in touch with our friend Tony, now a regular guide runner following his completion of the final marathon on the Top To Toe, who was providing the support vehicle service with his mobile home. His plan was to drive from the UK and meet us there at the hotel in Switzerland, ready with the kettle already on the boil. But it wasn't his lucky day.

Tony had made his way down to the south coast and pulled in to the ferry queue, ready to board.

'Sorry love,' the ticket inspector told him with a friendly smile as she handed back his ticket, 'but you're not getting on there tonight.' She thumbed towards the ship docked behind her. Tony thought she was joking and smirked. She didn't reciprocate.

'What? Why?' Tony's stomach lurched like a waterlogged football. 'But I'm booked on!"

'Yeah, you're booked on,' she said, pointing to his ticket, 'but it's 22 *October* you're booked on for, not September.'

In his mobile home, Tony had the tandem, all our kit, everything we needed to make the journey and complete the challenge.

Thankfully, though, it all worked out in the end. Tony was able to buy another for the next ferry and although there was a bit of a wait, he made up for it by motoring through continental Europe during the night. In fact, he was waiting for us in the car park when we arrived and had the kettle on as promised – there were just telltale dark circles under his eyes, so I'm told. Not the easiest start to the week for poor Tony!

That evening, the core team of cyclists, around 25 of us, met together to go over the route and discuss what we were to expect. There were nerves around the group, especially as most hadn't done anything like this before and were not sure what lay ahead. We decided that we would naturally fall into three distinct groups of ability: the hares, those that were young, fit and eager to complete within the times they had set themselves; the tortoises, who hadn't done much training or much long-distance riding at all, but were keen just to see it through, feel the challenge and raise a sum in the process; and then there was me and Duggie, named the Double-D. We were fit, we had trained, but we weren't quite as young and spritely as those hares up front.

In the morning, we rose early, showered, kit on. I could hear the nervous chatter, the shaking out of trembling limbs, the psyching up. There were lots of photos, too. God knows who I was posing for, but I was grinning all the same. Then we were off: all 25 of us cycling through the centre of Zurich on cycle paths where we could, but on roads, too. I could hear all the traffic surrounding us, especially loud given we were in the middle of rush hour, but I did find a part of me wondering whether this was in fact West Brom in rush hour – it could have been, for all I knew. I suppose modern-day European traffic does sound and feel the same the continent over: the warm exhausts of passing buses, the shrill hoots of couriers on scooters, and cars cars cars. I did notice, however, that the roads in Zurich were much smoother than back home, wider and more comfortable for riding.

It took us the best part of 30 miles to reach the approach to the border but boy, was it some approach. A terrific hill that climbed for about three miles, a three-mile drag, incessant, unrelenting, something to really get your teeth into. It was quite a relief to get to the top and reach the border.

But unfortunately, I found the border itself to be a bit of an – well, not an anticlimax, but a disappointment. Thirty years ago, visitors to that border would have found it much more exciting: soldiers, stamping of passports, an air of hostility and suspicion. You'd see the Swiss holding their cuckoo clocks, the Germans with rifles in their hands, maybe. But when it was described to me, I was told that the border buildings were still there, but they weren't occupied as such. The searchlights were still there, but if they were used for that reason, it wasn't obvious. It was uncanny – I had my left leg in Switzerland and my right leg in Germany, and nobody seemed to care. I could just walk across, no problem. Nevertheless, we had a few pictures taken to mark the occasion, all of us under the Swiss–German border signs, and then we were into Germany, heading for Offenburg.

The roads were wonderful and we were sailing through, up and down with relative ease. There were a few big hills, and at one point, we enjoyed a very fast descent over three or four miles. At the bottom, when I'd got my breath back, I was told that the sat nav had recorded our top speed: 54.3 miles per hour.

If something had happened at that speed – a dozy driver or a pothole – we would have been history. Thankfully it didn't and we weren't, and I was able to enjoy the experience. For me, being blind, you really do *experience* it, too: I felt the wind whistle past, and I knew we were going at terrific speeds as the wind became fiercer and fiercer.

After our first stop, at Napoleon's Café – and why it's called that, I have no idea – we were aiming for a place called Bad Dürrheim. Apparently it's beautiful, a typical old German town with fantastic buildings centuries old, but on leaving its vintage charm, we were forced right back into the modern age, battling the truckers on a gridlocked A road. Despite it being nose to tail, the drivers were kind to us. In fact, even the truckers were; I could feel their enormous lorries looming up behind us, but they were careful and respectful, their gears coming down well in advance. Nobody tried to force their way past our party, or leant on their horns angrily, chanting at us to get out of their way. We were impressed, and hoped to experience similar tolerance from road users throughout the rest of the week.

Hornburg was the next town we encountered and again, the descriptions I heard were very complimentary. Tony – who we had now nicknamed 'Tony the Gypsy', due to the prevalence of our kit hanging out to dry on his portable washing line – told me that the town was beautifully paved throughout, with a small gorge cut into the paving slabs so that the town's river could flow freely and gently through. It sounded like a nice touch.

Day one's final stop was the city of Offenburg. As traffic built up, noise levels increased and the pace slowed, the city came into view. Our route in was thwarted when we realised that many of the roads we intended to take were closed for repair, so it was a case of us having to go back on ourselves, reverse out of the city and find another entry point. Which, as you can imagine, was a big frustration when the finishing line for the day was so close we all swore we could smell it. Or perhaps that was just our cycling jerseys.

Eventually, us cyclists made it to the hotel, though our support vehicles were still held up in traffic. But it wasn't long before Tony, too, was parked up in the hotel car park and the kettle was on. The hotel seemed a really friendly, supportive place and we were delighted when they offered us space in their conference room to store the bikes. After dinner, we thought we would do the sensible thing and get to bed at a reasonable hour, safe in the knowledge that the first 103 miles were in the can.

Day two would see us cycle the 105 miles to Metz, crossing the Rhine, the German–French border and passing through Strasbourg. And we were pretty pleased with ourselves, Duggie and I, because we kept up with the fast lads, the young pups, and they couldn't seem to shake us. We're plodders, I suppose, we keep going – until I do something daft, usually.

No sooner had we got over the German–French border than my foot slipped off the pedal and kicked the back brakes clean off. We pulled up, which naturally drew the attention of some of our party who wanted to know if everything was all right. As I stood there hopelessly, adding words of encouragement, the lads set to work fixing it, manoeuvring it back into place gently. Fortunately for us, Dean, our resident bike mechanic, pulled up in his Bike Wrench van. Within ten minutes, we were back up and running. I think Dean had just breathed on it, or given it a stern word, or something. He saved a few people's bacon across the course of that week.

Once we were into France, we hit the farmlands and their rolling roads. We passed through tiny, sleepy French villages, each described to me in detail: flowers lining the verges, window boxes at every window, quiet independent brasseries, plenty of grass, trees and fresh air. Admittedly there were some heavy-duty hills upward, but we had a few down, too, to soften the blow. Andy Lamb, one of the other cyclists, found our pace suited him perfectly, so he joined us for good.

As the other challenges will have illustrated, these kinds of adventures also bring with them challenges of a toilet kind and it became the standing joke that whenever and wherever a call of nature should be required, a particularly thorny barbed wire would be nonchalantly leaning nearby. Of course, I was very much reliant on my fellow cyclists for their guidance in these matters – so imagine my perplexity when Duggie and Andy completely forgot and left me standing alone in a cornfield! I dared not move a muscle in case that barbed wire ensnared me.

'We keep forgetting you're blind!' they said when I remonstrated with them, both howling with laughter.

There were times that I had to wander off by myself, so desperate was I for a pee.

'And where do you think you're going?' they'd ask, bounding after me.

'I don't know! Anywhere!' I'd reply as I trotted off into the distance.

It wasn't long after I was nearly abandoned that our front light completely disintegrated, crumbling away from its fittings. Of course, I didn't need it, but it was pretty important to Duggie at the top and tail ends of the day so that was another job for busy Dean.

Tuesday's final destination was university lodgings belonging to the University of Metz. The hares broke their necks to beat the old codgers on the tandem and I understand there were plenty of smug smiles on their faces when we walked in. Once everyone was showered and fed, it was time to anoint the plonker of the day that would wear the hallowed pink t-shirt the subsequent day. Tuesday's plonker was none other than Phil Upton who, upon turning round in his saddle to direct the party behind him, had veered into a gutter and clattered to the floor. During our team talk about what lay ahead for Wednesday, I could hear much shifting in seats – there were obviously some saddle-sore bottoms among us. Some of the lads who had only done 30 miles or so in training were really beginning to suffer, and there were many sore legs slowly stiffening round the table.

The next day purported to be the toughest so we decided to get going at 7am to give us the best chance to get through it.

Experience told us just to get this day out of the way, and I think Duggie and I were the first to get on the road. But even getting out of Metz at that time of the morning meant encountering a surprising amount of traffic sighing and snorting along the dual carriageways. After cycling past the city's enormous Peugeot plant, we were out and heading for Luxembourg. Our first stop was supposed to be at 20 miles but we decided to plough on, promising to meet Tony at the once-Luxembourg border, 31 miles into the day. After a quick cup of coffee in the mobile home, we set off again, into Luxembourg. Of course, Luxembourg is not much more than a city and after 50 or so miles, we arrived at our next designated stop, the Luxembourg–Belgium border. It's crazy to think a whole country can just be 50 miles wide.

One of the more interesting landmarks, so I'm told, was the big underpass we had to travel through, a quarter of a mile long. We had been told that this was something special, and to a degree it was: we hit the underpass with all the traffic, horns blaring, and then the lads told me we were plunged into darkness. 'Welcome to my world,' I said. It was a good steep hill down, then a plateau, then a climb up and out the other side. We reached some terrific speeds, 25–30 miles an hour on the tandem. We popped out the other side and away we went. When we regrouped at the end of the day, however, we discovered that just minutes after our tunnel adventure, something had happened – an accident, possibly – causing the tunnel to be closed off. The other cyclists and support vehicles had to make their way round Luxembourg city negotiating the traffic and avoiding the underpass, inevitably adding a few miles to their clocks.

It was a tiring climb to the Belgian border, 30 miles of drag. It wasn't so much the steepness, just the relentlessness; no respite for the legs. Duggie told me that it was an odd view. To the left was a lovely valley that rolled on into lush greens, but directly on our right was an impenetrable rocky cliff that

CHAPTER 11

rose upward and didn't change, mile after mile. It also seemed remarkably fast for an A road. As I felt another articulated lorry whoosh past in a rush of air, I shouted to Duggie, 'What's the speed limit on this road?'

'I've never seen anything like it before,' he shouted back, '110 kilometres per hour unless it's raining and then you've got to drop down to 90.'

As soon as the border came into view, so did Tony, already parked up on the traffic island opposite, our washing drying in the exhaust fumes. On seeing us approach, he immediately set about cooking us pasta. Nothing was ever too much trouble for him; he kept us well fuelled. At this point, we were approaching the 80-mile mark and there were only another 25 or so left for the day.

It hadn't seemed the toughest day yet, and with the bulk of it over, we began to wonder what all the fuss was about. We told Tony we would see him at the Eddy Merckx memorial, the sculpture dedicated to the legendary Belgian cyclist and five-times winner of the Tour de France, situated along our route up to the city of Spa.

We were enjoying the exhilaration of a large hill down when we could see the support vehicles flagging us down.

'That way! That way!' the chap pointed us to the right, furious hand gestures to push us on.

'But the sat nav is telling us to carry on!' Duggie protested as we slowed.

'I've been told to divert you this way,' the steward insisted, so we did as we were told, instantly hitting a mountain of a short climb. It was straight from big gears to little in just a few revolutions and though it was only 200 yards or so, it was enough to tax our legs to jelly. At the brow of the hill, though, another support vehicle rushed in to tell us that we had gone the wrong way. We had to go back the way we came and turn right – exactly where our initial steward had enthusiastically diverted us.

The original steward looked surprised to see us again, and we gave him short shrift, vowing to follow the pink line on our sat nav from now on – it hadn't failed us yet. Trouble was, the pink line was heavy on the hills. The first was only 150 yards, but it was like scaling a brick wall. It turned a sharp right, then climbed upwards again. It was like cycling standing still, but at least we knew we were on the right track – these were the hills we had been promised!

After these murderous climbs, our sinews stretched and singing, the sat nav took us off road, across sand, gravel and loose earth. We had hit a rural path and before long, Tony's mobile home couldn't go any further. We buried our heads into our handlebars, vowing to trudge on, while Tony went off to explore a more suitable route through to the memorial.

As soon as he left, we realised it simply wasn't safe on the bike. We needed to dismount and walk. Andy and Duggie studied the sat nav: the pink line was taking us into the woods. They deposited me with the bikes while they went ahead to see what was waiting for us and whether it was an infamous case of sat-nav-gone-wrong. There was a path and it seemed kosher, so we followed it on foot, though the terrain was something else – surely only tanks had ever passed through here? We felt rather out of place, dainty with our slim tyres, fancy handlebars and skintight lycra. Before long, we needed to carry the bikes, hopping over pools of stagnant water and avoiding mud that had never seen the sun through the canopy. Overgrowth, undergrowth, thorny bushes of all shapes and sizes… and a blind man that had to be physically negotiated through and around each of these hurdles, told where to put his feet and when to duck and turn his head lest a brambly branch should thwack him in the face. Duggie and Andy found it easiest to guide me up one side of the path first, dodging the worst of the sticky mud, then go back for the bikes once I'd reached relative terra firma. It was 3.45pm and the sat nav told us we only had another 40 minutes before we had reached the day's destination, the hotel in Spa. Though it seemed unlikely, it was just the spur we needed and we kept trudging.

The woods had receded and a housing estate had come into view but there was still no sign of Eddy Merckx. In our best pidgin French, we had asked a Belgian passer-by the way. He told us we were nearby, it was just a case of going down the hill for about six kilometres. But still no sign! We flagged down another couple who told us we had missed it – meaning another climb back up the hill. It had better be worth it, we hissed to each other. Then we realised why we had missed it: on the way down, it was tucked away, unnoticeable; coming up the hill, there it was, as large as life. Cut in the rock, so I was told, the memorial was quite fantastic, detailing all his achievements. Then it was just two final miles to the hotel – though those two miles did happen to be up the hill on which Merkcx would train daily. No wonder he was so good.

So how did I know we had finally reached civilisation? Cobblestones, as big as our fists. Our aching, weary bodies were thrown around as our teeth rattled in our heads, our hands shaken until numb. But finally, the hotel came into view. The tandem was as weary as we felt, its brakes rattling. We later discovered that the brake pads had worn right through – it really had been a hilly day!

We eventually reached the hotel at 7.30pm. And we were first in.

One by one, as the hares and tortoises came in, we realised that everybody, at some point during the day, had been well and truly lost – abandoned by their sat nav or led astray by their instincts, they were so relieved to see us at the hotel, even if we had beaten them to it. And we were the only ones to set eyes on the Eddy Merckx memorial!

Of course, what could top the day off but the hotel from hell? It was so bad that Tony was asked if the others could bunk up with us in the mobile home! One of the cyclists complained that after a well-deserved bath, the muddied, murky bath water appeared in the bathroom next door, home to one of the other cyclists, while wires hung out of the wall in rooms and along corridors. The interior décor was beyond tired – it was dusty, even dirty. The hoteliers obviously didn't care: the city's connections to motor racing meant that Spa was regularly full to the brim with visitors, and why spend on tarting up the place when custom was so captive, so in abundance? And even if customers complained, it didn't prevent the hotel from filling up the next night. I was quite pleased I had Tony's hospitality.

Still, we all made merry that evening as we shared our stories about the day's trials and tribulations. Some had reached the woods and turned back; others had climbed three hills to avoid the wooded path. Most had clocked up far more miles than they should have done. Phil Upton, who had put together the route – well, you can just imagine the grief he had. We all had a good laugh about it anyway; there were no hard feelings, especially when we had been promised that the following day would be the easiest – it was claimed to be completely flat. Duggie, Andy and I, though, were not convinced. As we sat together over a pint, we concurred that we had never had an easy day on one of these challenges, that they simply didn't exist. We decided that we would be ready for the day ahead, just like any other.

We set off with the tortoises at around 8.30am the next day, enjoying having a bit of a rattle with them. That was until we met the descent of a huge hill and the tandem decided to do its usual thing of hurtling off at 200mph, so we bid farewell to the tortoises and we headed into Belgium's backwaters. But with a down, there's always an up – in fact, for the first six miles of Thursday, I didn't manage to get out of the granny ring, the lowest, tiniest gear on the bike. I wanted to grab the guy who had put the route together and show him flat, as this most certainly wasn't it!

Around 31 miles into the day, we came across the American military cemetery, Henri-Chapelle, in Hombourg. It was incredible, a fantastic place. One of 14 sites the Americans have across Europe, the lads described it to me: immaculate and white, the graves uniformly set out in neat columns and rows. It was hushed and sombre. I didn't need to see it to understand the respect the visitors had for the dead.

There was an American gentleman there, Bob, whose job it was to look after the site. He had been in Europe doing so for 35 years. Once I explained I was blind, he very kindly explained everything he could think of – what the cemetery looked like, the kinds of people who visited, the history of the place. It was so humbling. The lads took some footage of the memorial on the GoPro camera I had on my helmet so I could show Deb and the kids when I got home. We nipped in to the chapel to learn a little more, and there were 470 names listed. These were the names of soldiers that had never been found. Over time, when soldiers' remains had been identified, a brass plaque was fastened to their name. Still, there were quite a number who hadn't been found and as the years went on, it seemed less likely.

I'm so pleased we stopped there, even if it meant time out of our schedule. One of the tortoises, a lad by the name of Simon, had kept up with us for the first part of the day, and he had been in the forces, only recently leaving the army. As you can imagine, going to a place like that, for him, was really touching. He had been quiet and contemplative, but on leaving the cemetery and heading back to the bikes, he cleared his throat.

'Lads,' he said. He sounded serious. We weren't quite sure what he was about to say. 'I can't keep up with you, I can't keep up that pace; I'm going back to the tortoises.' We all burst out laughing.

'You go on then, mate,' we said.

After that, we were making our way to the Belgium–Netherlands border where we'd once again meet the faithful Tony and his mobile home. As I always do a quick interview with the RNIB's Insight Radio every Thursday, today was to be no exception. The time came just as we were charging down another dramatic slope so there I was, chattering away on the back of the tandem as I changed gears furiously and the wind whipped my ears. Sadly I lost reception for the latter half, but Garry Wells, back at home, promptly sent me a text message to say that he had been listening and it had been a surreal experience, knowing full well I was hurtling down a hill somewhere in continental Europe! I was just amazed that anyone had been able to hear anything at all!

Once we entered the Netherlands, we were headed for Maastricht. I hadn't been prepared for how big it would be, I'm sure we cycled over 20 miles just to get across it. After leaving the city and the suburbs, we found ourselves on a four-lane carriageway – and not a cycle lane to be seen. The traffic seemed busier, angrier, here, with plenty of hoots and horns, though not in a friendly, keep-it-up-lads kind of way – it was a definite 'get off the road!' I was glad when we turned off and back on to the cycle lanes.

We had to zigzag over the border at this point and after Maastricht had faded into the distance, we re-entered Belgium, taking in lots of small towns and villages before hitting the town of Bree. There, Andy picked up a puncture, but it was a quick and easy fix so there were no concerns. We followed a Belgian canal for a while – probably no different to my own familiar Tipton canal – but the lads told me in surprise that the barges along it were still being used to transport goods.

Tony had dinner well under way by the time we met him again at the border, so we were delighted to tuck in and enjoy those soft, soft chairs for half an hour before getting back in the saddle for the next 15 miles to Eindhoven, our stop for the night. Back into the Netherlands and there were more cycle lanes than we could wish for but they were block paved, meaning they were horribly uncomfortable to ride over. Whether it was to slow cyclists down, we weren't sure, but it certainly seemed a poor design. In scenes reminiscent of Spa's cobblestones, we were shaken numb, our forearms tickling and our jaws aching from being clamped shut to prevent our teeth knocking together. Still, the end of the day was in sight, so to speak, and as we arrived at our resting place, Duggie and Andy let out an irresistible cackle – we were first back again!

The sudden smell of the barbecue in the hotel grounds made me realise how hungry I truly was, and the hospitality of the place certainly made up for the previous night's accommodation. It was right next to a church where the bells pealed every quarter of an hour. I just knew that this was a nice place, a good hotel to rest our weary heads.

We had been right to be suspicious about that day. Though it had proved to be the flattest course in comparison to the others, that meant more pedalling. Of course, hills up are exhausting, but once you're up, you're usually able to give your legs a breather with an enjoyable freewheel down. On the flat, though, there's none of that respite; you've just got to keep ploughing on, and many of the lads found that extremely tiring, myself included.

Friday was our final day on the continent, as it were, and we would be cycling from Eindhoven down to the Hook of Holland where we would catch the ferry back to England. As usual, we had promised to meet Tony at the 30-mile mark and we set off at 8am.

Immediately, though, we encountered a problem – the main thoroughfare for the first part of our route was blocked off for roadworks. The sat nav offered us an alternative, a bridle path around the perimeter of a park, but we soon realised that the path was circular and the sat nav would have us circling forever, it seemed. Sod it, we thought, with Duggie and Andy taking careful looks to the left and right. The road was only blocked off to motorised vehicles, right? Any problems and we could play the daft tourist and blind man card. We dashed down the closed road, avoiding flowerbeds and machine dug pits, the workmen at the far end nodding at us as we passed. They didn't seem at all bothered. It was a joy – why couldn't all roads be as quiet and calm as that?

Once we were back on the route, it soon became apparent that today's course was more an obstacle course than anything else. We circumnavigated a motorway junction, holding our breath as the cars and lorries wheeled and screeched about us, before moving on – to an enormous flight of steps.

'Eh-up,' Andy said, 'surely we can't go up here?' He dismounted to have a closer look. I felt like I had stumbled on to the set of *The Krypton Factor* or *The Crystal Maze*, or something.

'Ah ha!' Andy returned, triumphant. Those clever, bike-loving Dutch – the stairs were fitted with a neat groove all the way up, the perfect fit for a tyre. We could walk up the stairs, push the bikes and not break our backs trying to balance them on our shoulders as we climbed. Genius!

When we met up with Tony, he told us that he had actually gone on ahead to assess the route, only to find more road closures. He suggested that he accompany us along some of the bigger roads for ten miles or so, before picking up the route as planned. Otherwise we would add 50 miles to our trip if we tried to go off-road on the cycle lanes. We agreed, thankful for his insight, but my God, those drivers did not like us being on their roads. I suppose they thought that it was wrong – and ungrateful! – to cycle on their roads when they had such a generous cycle lane network.

After a quick cup of coffee with Tony on a petrol station forecourt – we really did experience the glamorous side to Europe! – we were on our way to Rotterdam. The Dutch's commitment to cycling didn't stop here and the cycle paths were wide, smooth and plentiful. Even motorbikes and scooters of various CCs used the cycle paths here, all controlled by its own traffic light system. I was most impressed. As we approached the city, we cycled past the Feyenoord ground, De Kuip, where

CHAPTER 11

Aston Villa had won the European Cup in 1982 – a begrudging moment of pride for the West Midlands, I had to admit.

But it was the worst time to negotiate Rotterdam on a tandem – turning out time. We negotiated suited pedestrians on their mobiles, gave way to motorbikes overtaking us on the cycle lanes, narrowly avoided cars coming across our path and the tables and chairs set outside cafes which had crept on to the cycle lanes like eager front row spectators. Trams glided past us without so much as a hoot, music blared from shop fronts. The city was deafeningly alive. As Duggie said, 'If we can ride through Rotterdam on a tandem with a blind bloke on the back, we can ride anywhere.'

The cycle paths continued at the other side of the city and the last ten miles seemed to whistle past, aided by the fact that our terrain was so smooth. It was like cycling on glass.

As we reached the port, Tony could be spotted with our cups of tea at the ready. And guess what? We were first back again! Not bad for old codgers.

By 9pm, we were all present and correct, with keys to our cabins, eager to wash away the accumulated sweat, dirt and pollution of the day's ride. At 10.30pm, the boat pulled out of the docks and we were already tucked up in bed, ready to be rocked to sleep. It was an early start and we left the ferry at 6am, taking full advantage of the hour's free parking to congregate in the car park and check over the bikes, get kit on and plan for the day ahead. We took the tandem from the truck.

'Dave,' I heard Tony say, 'your handlebars don't look right. They're too low.' I took my seat. He was right, it didn't feel comfortable.

'Duggie, has your seat altered?' I asked him. My handlebars were connected to his saddle. Perhaps it all needed shifting upward. I heard Duggie squirm in his seat, leaning one way then the other.

'Nope, absolutely fine,' he replied. I dismissed it. It was my mind playing tricks on me.

'No, they definitely don't look right,' Tony insisted, 'you need to pull them up a bit.' He began to wrestle with the metal in front of me. Shhhhh-thrup. He yanked them upwards but overdid it, snapping them clean off the bike. I stood there with half a handlebar in my left hand, half a handlebar in my right. I wasn't quite sure what to do. Poor Tony, judging by the expletives that left his lips, was mortified.

Dean was apologetic, too. 'There's nothing I can do until we can get you to a bike shop.' It was 7.30am. We had a bit of a wait, a real delay to our first day back in England.

'Hang on a minute,' I said. I'd had a brainwave, one of those ideas that pop into your head completely out of the blue, when you didn't even know you were trying to think of a solution. I felt for the width of the tube where the handlebars had split off. It felt about right. It could work.

All week, I had been at war with the towel rail in Tony's mobile home. Whenever I had gone into the bathroom to clean my face, brush my teeth, wash my hands, each and every time I moved a muscle in that small space, I had dislodged the towel rail from its place on the wall and sent it clattering to the floor. I climbed into the mobile home, fetched the towel rail – which pretty much jumped into my hands – and handed it to Tony.

'There. Try that.'

It fitted perfectly, once tapped in and the allen keys adjusted. The lads couldn't understand it.

'How did you know it would fit?'

'How did you even think of it?'

I didn't know, but we all came to the conclusion that I had been knocking that towel rail off every day that week for a reason. I rode all 112 miles that day on a towel rail.

Later that day, a kindly bike shop, after hearing about our challenge and my towel rail predicament, donated a pair of handlebars so I could complete the rest of the challenge in style.

Following Harwich, we were en route to Sudbury, but had promised to stop off in a little village called Clare. Duggie had a friend there who was the village schoolteacher, so we called in to meet the kids and tell them what we were doing before leaving for Cambridge. On our way out of Cambridge, we joined a fast A road. We felt we were being egged on by the other drivers to keep up the pace, and zoomed along to our next meeting point at St Neots – beating Tony in the process! Incredulous at our speed, we checked our sat nav. On that A road, we'd reached speeds of 30mph! It was no surprise, then, that we were first back to that night's stop, Kettering. There was no sign of life at Tony's mobile home though.

'Don't say a word,' he groaned as he begrudgingly opened the door to our knocks.

Of course, West Brom had been playing his beloved Manchester United that day.

'What was the score?' Excitement welled up in my stomach.

'I'll only tell you this once, and then you can shut up about it. 2-1 to the Albion.'

Well, I couldn't let that go, could I? When he served up dinner, I made sure there were two pieces of toast on my plate and only one on his. He suffered that evening, I tell you.

The unexpected result added to the anticipation for the dawning of the final day. Everyone began to forget their aches and pains, and instead looked forward to celebrating the completion of the challenge. Five more cyclists joined us that night ahead of the final day of cycling, swelling our number to 30. As we sat together for dinner that evening, we decided that, for the last day, there would be no hares and no tortoises, no disparate groups finding their own way: instead, we would leave the hotel in the morning as one team, cycling together as a group.

It was a great day of cycling. We took it easier, chatting and celebrating as we rode for the Ricoh Stadium in Coventry. There we would meet over a hundred other cyclists who would join us for the last 27 miles in Harry Moseley's honour, raising the profile of the charity he started, Help Harry Help Others, and fundraising for other brain cancer sufferers.

I knew when the Ricoh came into view. The party began whooping and cheering, the pace slowing to a snail as we were funnelled into the stadium past waiting television and radio crews. Then we entered and the crowd cheered. It was not the macho, guttural roar of football crowds, but something lighter, happier, closer to tears. The hundred new cyclists joined us and we were organised into teams, fastest through to slowest, to make the support vehicles' jobs easier and we set off to the Edgbaston cricket ground, our final stop before the finish line in Broad Street, Birmingham.

I hadn't quite expected what we found in Edgbaston. There were even more people here – families and well-wishers of the cyclists, but also those affected by Harry Moseley's work, both supporters of the charity and cancer sufferers. I could almost hear the smiles on everyone's faces as we rode in. It was such an experience, almost indescribable. But it was intensely emotional, too. A film was playing on the big screens, reminding us all of the cause we had been supporting throughout our week's cycle. Each day of our challenge had been dedicated to a child: one who was currently undergoing invasive, aggressive treatment for brain cancer, or one who had sadly died. In among the cheering and the whooping, I listened to the film, taking in the heartache of the families of the children who had been afflicted by this awful condition.

Someone tapped me on the shoulder.

'Dave,' a woman's voice said, 'I'd like you to meet Jack, who you cycled for on Wednesday.' Jack said hello. It was too much. I shook the young lad's hand as tears gathered at my eyes and threatened to spill over, down my cheeks. I tried to pull myself together. He thanked me and the rest of the lads for our cycling adventure and for raising so much money. It was absolutely nothing in comparison to what he had to face on a daily basis.

At 3.30pm we all assembled in one long parade, the children and their families in an open-top bus and a police escort to mark the occasion. It was quite a sight, so I'm told, with all the

CHAPTER 11

waving and cheering, the weary cyclists given a new lease of life through the collective adrenalin of the crowd.

At Centenary Square, with the crowd bigger still, a stage had been set up with presenter Tom Ross, trustee of the charity, to usher in the participants and warm up the crowd. One by one, to cheers from the audience, we were presented with medals, my hand so enthusiastically shaken by so many different people in such quick succession that I thought it would fall off. Baggies legend, Cyrille Regis, was there to welcome us back and I had my photo taken with him, grinning. So many people came over to give their congratulations, to thump us on the back, to hug us and cheer. Perhaps this challenge hadn't been the hardest I had undertaken, but the finish line was something else, an occasion I would never forget. It was what it all meant, what it stood for and who we had cycled for.

Then there were the challengers themselves – each and every cyclist who started that adventure, finished it. On that first night, when Duggie and I had learnt that some of the team hadn't clocked up 50 miles in their training, had only bought a bike the two weeks prior to the start, we had worried for them – did they know what they had let themselves in for? Could they push through when their bodies didn't stop aching and their eyes had to be prised open in the morning? But we needn't have worried. They were wonderful, a team of heroes. Heroic riding from heroic riders.

Still, Duggie and I had to extricate ourselves before the celebrations went on too long. There was no other way to get the tandem home but to ride it, so we set off for the very last six miles of our journey.

12

THE Marathon des Sables, or the MdS, had been rattling around in my head for a number of years. It was something that intrigued me. It sounded like murder, in all honesty: the fierce heat, the sand dunes, the rocks, the careful planning for hydration, and carrying kit, all food and essentials for the week across the desert. It was more of a scramble, a crawl, than a marathon, so I heard. Tony – of mobile home fame – had completed the MdS a number of years ago and told me it was the toughest thing he had ever done, by far. He said he would never do it again – unless he was guiding me.

Well, doesn't that sound like a challenge?

Since the Top To Toe, and now based in the States, Rosemary had become an endurance athlete herself, completing 50- and 100-milers, and regularly guiding me when she was back in the UK. She and I had completed the London Marathon together, while Rosie and Tony had founded an off-road running partnership, too (something I tend to avoid, given the difficulty I experience coping with the terrain). When I told her that Tony and I were thinking of it, she jumped at the chance. We had ourselves a team.

As my excitement about the new challenge grew, the Albion Foundation came to mind. The Albion Foundation is a fantastic charity that works to provide educational and sporting opportunities for disadvantaged and disabled young people in the West Midlands. I've been mixed up with the foundation for some time now, especially since being made an ambassador in 2010. There are blind football teams, wheelchair football teams, all sorts of disability sports clubs; they work with kids with learning difficulties, they work with underprivileged kids and those that have experienced trauma and help them rebuild their lives or achieve what they hope to achieve. Amazingly, the foundation has recently established a school for kids that have been bullied, excluded or find it difficult at mainstream schools. I gave them a talk not so long ago and I was inspired to hear their stories, and I've also been invited to present awards at their assemblies. The Albion Foundation really is special, and I wondered if my challenge could feature as part of their latest, most ambitious fundraising drive to date.

It was the perfect opportunity, and a cause for which I couldn't wait to dedicate my time. After a few lengthy planning meetings, and numerous telephone calls and e-mails, led by the foundation's director Rob Lake, the Tri Albion Challenge was conceived. In 2015, a cycling team, comprising one of the Three Degrees, the legendary Brendon Batson, GB Blind Paralympian Darren Harris, myself, Duggie and others, would complete a ride from Southampton to West Brom, where we'd pass the baton to the foundation's blind football team. The team aimed to walk to every school in Sandwell, delivering the message about the challenge and raising money and profile as they went. The final leg would be down to Tony, Rosie and myself, in the MdS.

The full challenge aimed to raise £50,000, with me, Tony and Rosie hoping to fundraise £30,000 – a thousand pounds for each of the years the MdS has been up and running, 2015 marking its 30th anniversary.

For some reason, there are plenty of mad lunatics out there who also want to do the Marathon des Sables, and, like the London Marathon, wannabe competitors have to put in applications through a British conduit. Within three minutes of applications opening, all 2015 British places were allocated. Thankfully – or not, depending on whether you would like to run 160 miles in the Sahara desert – Tony called the British supervisor to explain our plight and places were secured.

And then it became a case of working out how to train for a rather long run across sand dunes and in 50°C heat. Funnily enough, there isn't much of that in West Bromwich. We decided to throw the training plans for the seven marathons and the Top To Toe into the pot, but with the addition of carrying weighted backpacks to make it that bit more tricky. We aimed to get more hill work to get the strength in, and enter madcap races like the Gower Ultra 50, which we completed in October 2014. This was the first time this particular race had been organised, and it followed the coastal path around the Gower peninsula. It was the first time I had experienced anything like it. I was completely out of my comfort zone.

The night before the race, we pulled up at the start in Llanmadoc to spend the night in Tony's camper van. Rain hammered down on the roof as we drifted off to sleep, and when we woke up, it was still going. Naturally, such conditions didn't make the next 50 miles very appealing, but our Black Country grit shone through and we told ourselves to get on with it. Sixty-five runners and a handful of walkers were soaked at the starting line, but to our surprise, within ten minutes of starting the race, the rain stopped.

We took to the beach. The sand was flat and wide. Rosie let go of the running cord. 'Go on, Dave, have a run by yourself! You're on your own!' It was a strange feeling. I knew I couldn't injure myself, there was nothing to trip over, but I felt like a dog being let off the lead. A sense of freedom, tinged with trepidation. It was funny, too.

As the sand of the beach gave way, I heard Tony laugh sarcastically up in front. Rosie's response wasn't any better.

She simply groaned, 'Oh no!'

'What?' I said. 'What is it?'

The course we were to follow went up the cliff – right next to the sign warning of the danger of rock climbing and falling boulders. We were to climb upwards. I can only imagine what I looked like, scrabbling around on my hands and feet at a cliff face.

Of course, we were daft to expect a conventional race. There were very few occasions when we could actually run at all. The paths were either very narrow or littered with rocks and boulders. I was told the views were gorgeous but I was far more concerned with stones to request a description. There were big stones, little stones, rolling stones, stones of strange shapes, stones that scratched and dented, and stones that jutted out; all kinds of stones. In fact, the course took us across the river courtesy of stepping-stones. Not much fun for a blind man, I can tell you. My little legs skittered about on the surface of those stones like I was doing the hokey cokey!

The dance continued as we conga-ed up very narrow steep climbs, with my hands on Tony's shoulders in front and Rosemary's hands on my behind. It seemed like this peninsula had every terrain imaginable: gnarly old tree roots hampering our steps downward under the cover of woodland, running along a cliff edge with a 200-foot drop on one side; it certainly concentrated the mind. I did wonder why my guides went very quiet, all of a sudden. Their silence was suspicious, especially chatterbox Rosemary. I later learnt they only told me half of what was going on – I got the full lowdown the next day, when we were safely ensconced in the camper van again.

Up on the cliffs, it was part of the adventure to encounter some animal life. At one point, 50 sheep came running towards us on a path that was only three feet wide. The other side? Oh, only a steep drop to the sea. We managed to tiptoe around their woolly bodies but the cacophony was something else. A little further on and we met some cows, but thankfully they were quiet and stationary, apparently just staring at us as we capered by. I finally got a phone signal to call Deb and as I ran and spoke to her, Rosemary presumed the horse right in front would get out of the way… it didn't, and unbeknownst to me, I ran right in to its rear end, my mouth tasting its dusty rump. If only I could have been kicked to the next checkpoint! Deb laughed. It's not every day you speak to your husband on the phone and listen to him running into a horse's backside!

At the 24-mile marker, I felt the cliff path give way to paving slabs and then our running really started. We arrived at the 29-mile aid station in **nine hours and 36 minutes**, the last in by 40 minutes. The promenade then turned inland along a tarmac cycle path for miles and by the next aid station we were only five minutes behind the last of the field. It was such a relief to run after all that tiptoeing and scrambling.

But we couldn't be content for long. The final leg, by this time in the dark, involved marshland. It was cold and slippery with puddles bigger than the track and we slowed up again. By the last aid station, we made the unanimous decision not to run the last one and a half miles on the trail: the thought of climbing sand dunes in the dark and then back over the rabbit-holed grass to the finish seemed like a recipe for disaster. We couldn't risk twisted ankles when the MdS was only six months away. We told the crew our plans and they suggested an alternative route. They told us that we could take an easy way back to the road by turning off the trail ahead and crossing a 200-metre field of grass. We thanked them for their time and set off, happy to continue and see it through.

But the crew seemed to forget the single file, rocky trail made hazardous by those tricky tree roots and stiles! Still, we enjoyed the chance to run again – even if it was punctuated by stints of walking, tripping and hobbling – and though we ended up going a little further, we came into the finish from the road, having moved up 11 places from the last place we had held throughout.

My first 50-miler felt like a real achievement. If it had just been a 50-mile run, I would have been fine. But the Gower coastline, and all the hurdles it had to offer, was exhausting in body and mind, and the perfect preparation for the Marathon des Sables, for both me and my guides. As a team, we finished in **15 hours and 33 minutes**; joking from the start to the end and knowing we could react well under pressure.

I knew that training on different terrain would be the key to the MdS. Tony had warned that much of the MdS is spent walking, or negotiating unanticipated surfaces, and though I was sure that my muscles could take it, not being able to see what I'm about to walk or run on is difficult for the mind to process. I am never quite sure when to soften my knees or straighten my calf muscles until I'm there, and if I get it wrong, I can injure myself. I needed to get to a point where my muscles weren't bothered by stopping and starting, and a sudden change between horizontal and vertical. The Wrekin, not far from Telford, became our second home. We put in some serious miles across the Brecon Beacons and up and down Snowdon, wrapped up against the snow. Well, it wasn't exactly desert conditions, but we hoped it would help.

And as for MdS climate? Well, I couldn't very well go and sit in a sauna at the local leisure club every week, so I just told myself, 'It will be bloody hot.' I reminded myself of the Top To Toe: we never would have thought to have experienced Scotland's greatest amount of rainfall in one day – in August!

We also used the Great North Run – my 13th time competing – as training. This time, there was a surprisingly large amount of blind and partially sighted runners taking part, and Tony began to size them up on my behalf. We thought we'd give the young, fit specimens a run for their money. Tony suggested we up the pace and we caught them by mile one, settled into our pace and then at around mile three, the Tyne bridge, we were actually leading. Through miles four and five, Tony reminded me that another blind pairing were still behind us. They hadn't gained on us, but we hadn't pulled away any more either. We kept on going, through miles six, seven and eight, and the crowd's noise seemed to intensify. Mo Farah passed us, flashing by as though we were standing still. At mile nine, running round the island and on to the hill, Tony piped up again.

'They're still there,' he muttered, 'the gap's the same but if we can just lift our pace, it will make their task of catching us harder.'

I obliged and stepped on the gas.

'Dave, we have the chance of winning this blind race. I've never won anything in my life. Do this for me! Pick up the pace! It will mean everything to me to come in first!'

Mile ten, mile 11… I pushed hard, heart pumping, legs going like two pistons. Up and over, we hit mile 12, and Tony told me he could see the sea. The pair was still behind us. The gap was still the same but he guessed they would make their move soon. My knees complained as we ran downhill, but I told myself the pain would have to wait.

'Still there,' Tony warned, 'but they're not closing the gap. Just 1,000 metres, five more minutes of pain. Come on!' I focused, determined.

'Which finish line do we run through?' Tony asked suddenly, stopping us dead. I worried about the pair behind us. I told him about the finish line for the masses; the other was for elite competitors only. It felt like we were stationary for minutes, but it had to be seconds. 'Just pick one,' I urged internally. I imagined the blind pair sprinting for the finish line, having seen their opportunity for glory.

I would have given Usain Bolt a good competition, I'm sure. We sprinted for the finish line and as soon as we crossed, I breathlessly asked Tony if we'd beaten them.

'Yes,' he panted.

The relief I felt was enormous. The pain, tiredness and anxiety instantly evaporated.

CHAPTER 12

'How far were they behind us?' I asked, picturing a photo finish.

'I don't know,' Tony replied, 'the last time I saw them was mile five.'

I must have frowned, puzzled.

'I've been winding you up!'

The cheeky sod! He had been teasing me all along! Though my response is unprintable, secretly I was pretty pleased he had done it – a time of 1.41 was worth the wind-up, and a good way to focus on the MdS. I also knew it wouldn't be the last time Tony would use my disadvantage to our advantage.

Fundraising got off to a flying start when I was lucky enough to receive a £10,000 donation in one go. It was at the 2014 mayor making, an event Deb and I are invited to as freeman of the borough. We enjoyed the ceremony, seeing the old mayor go out and welcoming the new one in. Afterwards, I found myself sitting next to the High Sheriff of the West Midlands, Dr Tim Watts, alongside the mayor going out. I knew both.

Deb seized her opportunity. 'Have you heard what he's doing next year?' Without a moment's hesitation, she told them all about the Marathon des Sables.

'Here's my number,' the High Sheriff said, proffering a business card towards Deb. 'I want to know more.'

After a suitable time had lapsed, we tried calling the High Sheriff but couldn't get through. We left a couple of hopeful messages but began to think it was one of those glib comments made in the moment: it's not necessarily untrue, but the arrangement never comes to fruition. It's surprisingly frequent in the fundraising world. But then we had a phone call, asking us to come to Hagley Hall, home of Christopher Charles Lyttelton, the 12th Viscount Cobham, near Stourbridge. We were told two things: the High Sheriff would be there to present me with an award, and could I go to the High Sheriff's head office at Pertemps? He was considering sponsoring me for the MdS.

Of course I could!

'Right, how much do you want from me?' the High Sheriff asked as soon as I walked through the door. It was better to get it out in the open, after all.

'How about a million pounds?'

'Well, you know that's out of the question,' he replied, laughing.

'If you don't ask, you don't get!' I responded. After many years' fundraising, I know that it doesn't pay to be modest where donations are concerned.

'How about a pound?'

'How about two?' I retorted. I had been here before.

'If I was to offer you ten grand...'

'...I'd take it.'

And it was as simple as that: I went along to Hagley Hall for the High Sheriff's awards, and received both an accolade *and* a cheque for £10,000. Pertemps on board as official sponsors and I make sure I wear my Pertemps tie when I do a talk. Win-win, as they say.

It's a funny thing, fundraising: if you don't make as much money as you'd hoped, you feel that you've let the charity down; if you've met or exceeded your target, you're terrified that you won't complete the challenge and you heap this great pressure on yourself to succeed. Only 75 per cent of competitors complete the Marathon des Sables; 25 per cent don't. Still, as with all my challenges, it's a case of how badly you want it.

As the challenge became tantalisingly close, Tony whisked me off to a specialist outdoor pursuits shop. The rules for the MdS are very strict, for health and safety reasons. We were told exactly what we should bring and how it should be packed. We were permitted only one backpack for the full six days, which would be carried by us over the course of the challenge, meaning it needed to be as light as possible. Every participant was required to demonstrate that we had at least 2,000 calories on us per day – 14,000 for the week – and we would be penalised if we did not carry with us the full kit, which was as follows:

- Sleeping bag
- Head torch with spare batteries
- Ten safety pins
- Compass with 1° or 2° precision
- Lighter
- A whistle
- Knife with metal blade
- Tropical disinfectant
- Anti-venom pump
- A signalling mirror
- One aluminium survival sheet
- One tube of sun cream
- Two hundred euros or equivalent in foreign currency.

It was like being back in the cadets, though I wasn't familiar with anti-venom pumps. I tried hard not to think about it. And it didn't matter that the head torch and compass would be completely useless to me – I still had to have it on my person at all times! We would also be supplied a supplementary 'marathon kit' to be provided by the race organisers when we arrived at our first camping ground, or 'bivouac', to give it its proper name. This consisted of:

- A 'roadbook', detailing maps, routes and other race-specific information
- A distress flare
- Salt tablets
- Sachets for the toilets
- ID marks.

The proprietors of the shop knew exactly what to expect and kitted me out to perfection, from the socks on my feet to the hat on my head. A jacket was insisted upon, as 50 degree heat apparently doesn't make nights in the desert any warmer, and we were also given advice about cooking. With gas stoves forbidden, we needed another way round. And much of my new pack consisted of little tiny magic tablets. No, nothing like that – random doping tests would put paid to anyone going down that route – but tablets that purified water or, once water was added, turned into a cloth. Even with everything so small and light, there just seemed so much. Once the straps were pulled tight, the contents sat in my pack as though they were meant to be – although at 12kg, I did worry about its heaviness.

Our final week's training, in early April, was spent at the University of Birmingham where Dr Sam Lucas and Rebecca Lucas allowed us the use of their heat chamber so we could experience running in the intensity of the heat we would be facing for real a week later.

* * * * *

Friday 3 April saw us leave Gatwick at 9am, surprisingly quite a friendly time of the morning for our latest challenge. We arrived in Ouarzazate, the Moroccan city nicknamed 'the door to the desert', in early afternoon. Once we passed through immigration and collected our bags, we boarded the coach waiting for us and spent the next six hours travelling to the bivouac, and our first taste of the Sahara desert.

Rosemary and Tony described everything they could see, from dusty roads and small, dusty villages, to children playing football among the dust. It seemed the desert penetrated the very heart of living in this part of Morocco. Everybody, whether they were newcomers to the 'toughest footrace on Earth' or seasoned professionals, took in the surroundings quietly, wondering what would be in store for them over the next seven days.

The engine ceased and we arrived at our home for the week: a traditional Bedouin tent, number 124. Rosemary told me it was more like a carpet held aloft by four poles, one at each corner. Rough matting lay across the sand and a flap at the front and back marked the entrance and exit. Tony plonked my backpack alongside his and Rosemary's to mark out where we would sleep. Rosie's friends from Dubai, Anna-Marie and Lesley, also joined us, so we were five in tent 124. After some 16 hours of travelling, and a simple dinner provided by the organisers, were rolled out our sleeping bags and experienced our first night in the desert.

It's perhaps no surprise that none of us slept well. The wind whipped round the tent most of the night, sending sand against the tent walls in a loud, disorientating frenzy. It probably sounded worse than it was, I told myself, but it still didn't allow me to sleep. The air-filled mats underneath our sleeping bags crackled like a crisp packet each time we moved position. Rubbed, sore hips seemed preferable to the noise of disturbing my fellow tent residents. And a blow-up pillow certainly took some getting used to.

In the morning, it seemed that everyone's first thought was the same – and the queues for the toilets snaked round our encampment and became quite a sociable affair. I was told that this year's toilet arrangements, shall we say, had been improved a level, from a hole dug in the sand to pure luxury. I wasn't sure about the luxury bit. We were issued with a roll of plastic bags, each being ripped off before use. The toilet consisted of four poles draped in obscure plastic sheeting, with around five of the said constructions lined up in a row for everybody to use. While waiting in the queue, Rosemary issued me with a handful of stones. Then it was my turn.

What I can only describe as a mop bucket housed my plastic bag and I was then encouraged to drop in the stones to anchor the bag to the sand. The next part became, for me anyway, an absolute work of art that needed practice. I stooped, one foot holding down the plastic flap which represented the door, and balanced, squatting, my weight on one leg only, to aim. Performing both a number one and a number two into that plastic bag was no mean feat. And, without being able to see, there was a great deal of hoping for the best. Another little plastic bag held toilet roll and wipes, and there was nothing for it – it had to go in my mouth. But of course, in the heat of the moment, I dropped it. I can assure you that bag went nowhere near my mouth ever again. Once the deed was done, I had to remove the bag from the mop bucket, grabbing all four corners at once, tying a knot in the top, and then deposit it in a bin outside. Rosemary had the unenviable task of helping me find the bin, of course, and gave me very precise instructions, 'Left, right, drop!' I was quite pleased I didn't have the pleasure of viewing that overflowing bin of delights. I just hoped that as the challenge got under way, the amount of water and calories my body would be using would mean I wouldn't need to visit the toilet as often as I would at home... it wasn't a pleasant experience, to say the least.

And less so for poor Rosie, who became my toilet companion each morning. One time, I found I hadn't pegged down my plastic bag quite right. As both solid and liquid descended into the bag, it became unstable and toppled to the ground, spewing its contents. I shouted for Rosemary to come and help me in my situation, but as she entered, she told me, gravely, 'The situation is beyond redeemable.' We had to tell the French men, patiently queuing outside, not to enter, that there was a problem in the toilet and it would have to be cleared up by the team at the end of the day. Lucky, lucky them.

Once that queue was over, we were required to queue again – this time for water rations and breakfast, provided by the organisers for the last time before we became self-sufficient. It's a good job us Britons like a queue! With breakfast digested, we examined our backpacks, ensuring our 2,000 calories were present, alongside the compulsory items. Then it was inspection time. We had to offer our passport, signed doctor's medical certificate and ECG report. Mine passed without issue, and I was given the number 313 for the GPS responder on my bag and ankle. This would allow the organisers knowledge of my whereabouts, but it would also let family and friends back home monitor my progress.

Tony's ECG certificate, however, caused a few French murmurs. His doctors at home had admitted his ECG results were abnormal as he had an unusual heartbeat, put down to the duration and intensity of training he put in. His doctors at home had shrugged and were happy to sign it off nonetheless. But here, in the desert, where race organisers were under such scrutiny to look after their participants in such harsh, unfamiliar surroundings, any deviation from the norm was a worry. Tony's ECG certificate was not right, and race organisers were not willing to take any chances.

We panicked. For a few minutes, it looked as though the adventure would end before it began. Our conversations took on an intense, pleading nature. I would need two guides, we urged, Tony had to be one. Rosemary and Tony were like two extremely important bits of kit in themselves. He was extremely fit, healthy; he'd done it before. Finally, the French doctors agreed Tony could pass – on the proviso that he underwent an ECG test at every checkpoint. We were astounded – a portable ECG facility would be accompanying us in the desert! The complexity of the equipment used by the race organisers demonstrated the gravity of the occasion and the severity of the problems that could go wrong. It began to dawn on me how serious this event was. I was pleased that this was the 30th event; that the organisers had a bank of previous races to draw on.

With formalities over, it was a case of waiting for a heavy sandstorm to subside before we could set off the following morning. We used the time to meet with Sir Ranulph Fiennes. After correspondence through letter and e-mail, and the occasional phone call, we had never met in person. He was attempting the MdS as the oldest Briton to do it, but the conversation turned to the more normal: our families at home. Though we did have a good laugh at the threat of camels catching us. It turned out that once the race was under way each morning, the organisers would set off in pursuit on board a camel train. If the camels caught up with any competitor, then that competitor would be disqualified and sent packing. It was a unique way of keeping the field together, but it would be a sad end for any competitor. Sir Ranulph said he would have a quiet word with the camels, to keep them at bay.

Before settling down for the night, Rosemary and Tony took me round the encampment, to familiarise myself. I had a couple of photos taken with my Baggies shirt on and with the Black Country flag, black, white and red with an illustration of chains as a nod to the industry that made us. We then bumped into a family – yes, a family! – that hailed from Windermere. The husband, wife, mother and brother-in-law, Tom, Shelly, Janet and Jez, were a jolly bunch, and I promised to catch up with them again during one of our frequent trips to one of my favourite places in the UK.

Night time comes early in the desert. The whole encampment quietened quickly, and Rosie took the opportunity to read me letters written by my two youngest, each signed with lots of love and kisses. On previous challenges, I kept a photo of the family with me; this time, I had the imprint of the fingerprints of the three girls and Deb set into a silver ingot, courtesy of jewellery designer Gilly Page. My family would, once again, be with me every step of the way.

I was soon alone in my thoughts. I fretted about how heavy my bag was: 12kg, and I still had a litre and a half of water to add to it. Though race rules permitted bags up to 15kg, it wasn't sensible – the lighter, the better. However, my race number gave me some solace. I must be a superstitious old codger. We flew out on 3 April, and would hopefully fly back on 13 April: 313. Was that an omen? I also realised that my first adventure, the Sevens, ended on 13 April, too. So 313 became quite significant.

CHAPTER 12

Sunday 5 April 2015

As we were now self-sufficient – the organisers providing no more meals or kit – the bivouac awoke at around 5.30am and immediately leapt into action, the whole place a hive of industry. Water rations were fetched so we could boil water for breakfast and drinks. Breakfast, dinner and tea would mainly consist of Extreme Adventure foods over the next week. Freeze-dried, high energy and importantly low weight, a little addition of water would turn these unexceptional packets into a sumptuous meal.

My accompanying little spoon was also very interesting: with no dishwasher, it was mainly licked clean. I soon became accustomed to the taste and texture of sand.

We stowed our kit in our bags, wrapped as tightly as possible, and water was prepared in bottles. We lathered ourselves in sunscreen, and realised that this unfamiliar ritual would become customary each morning for the next seven days.

The tents were lifted from above our heads, quite literally, and I could hear vehicles starting up with the organisers making their way to set up the relevant checkpoints. Though I could hear many different languages spoken, many of which were completely unfamiliar, I could understand their tone and intonation: excitement and adrenalin. As the camp disbanded, competitors started to make their way towards the start line. I could hear the click of cameras.

In among 1,300 other competitors, I was amazed to find myself silent in my thoughts. I wondered how the girls were doing back home, and what they were thinking; I silently sent Tony and Rosie my gratitude, for putting themselves through this to support me. I thought about the Albion Foundation, and how much this would mean to them and the kids they supported, the vast majority facing much bigger, more serious challenges than this every day, involuntarily.

Then, suddenly, I was interrupted. A smug football fan had seen my Albion badge and piped up. 'All right mate,' he said.

I could tell by his voice he was grinning. 'Did you hear? We – QPR – beat you 4-1 yesterday!'

It was news to me. The lack of reception had meant I hadn't been able to get the results of Saturday's games. This guy had managed somehow, though. The withering look from me must have said it all!

To mark the 30th anniversary of the Marathon des Sables, the organisers had put together a little stunt. We were all corralled into a roped-off area and manhandled into position. As a collective, our bodies would form the number 30 from the air. Tony and Rosemary described a fantastic spectacle: a dozen riders, six on horseback and six on camels, rode across the desert towards us. Loudspeakers burst into life and presentations were made and competitor birthdays announced, followed by very loud music. Helicopters flew round, capturing it all on camera. I'm told it was an amazing sight, and it certainly sounded it, too.

I almost forgot the start when it sounded. We were off, and running the 30th Marathon des Sables.

Stage 1: Jebel Irhs to Oued Tijekht, 37k, seven hours 35 minutes

I realised, as the race got under way, that I wasn't actually running on sand. I had imagined the Sahara desert to be soft sand, sending feet flailing deep, left and right, crossing rolling sand dunes, but the ground underfoot initially was hard, rocky, full of camel grass, ridged, as if water had formed ridges and funnels over thousands of years. Our first trek took us a few hours and 13.4k to checkpoint one.

At the first checkpoint, I heard two beeps and this came from the responder on my ankle, checking me in and plotting my position in the race. I soon associated this little beep with sanctuary: the chance of a five-minute rest. Tony pulled into the medical tent for his first of many ECG tests. He wasn't happy but it had to be done. We topped up our water bottles then off we went again, heading for checkpoint two, at 24.8k.

CHAPTER 12

At this point, someone had certainly turned up the temperature gauge. It was ridiculously hot and with the terrain so difficult underfoot, we decided it best to conserve energy and prevent injury by walking. By checkpoint two, we had run and walked over hard stony ground, sometimes with rocks as big as a fist up to the size of a barrel, dried river beds, camel grasses, and sand dunes, all with inclines up and down.

At around 30k or so, we encountered what they call our first real technical ascent. We would call it a mountain. I still hadn't imagined mountains in the Sahara, but I'm told, there they were! Tony explained we were going up and as far as the eye could see. There was a long line of people, looking like ants in the distance, going up the mountain pass between the craggy rocks. Up we went, too, and at the mountain pass, we then became the ants in the distance for the long line of folks behind us. We were puffing and panting, often silent while we concentrated on our feet tackling the rocks beneath, but then Tony and Rosemary gave the welcome news that the finish line for the day, and its encampment, was some 3k in the distance.

It was a long, sandy, hot 3k, but the beeps came eventually, along with the first day's finish line, and relief. But before we could rest, we had to collect our water for the night. Before long, though, we collapsed in the tent. Rosemary did a foot inspection, checking for blisters. She and Tony had collected one or two already but when she viewed mine, she swore profusely at me – I hadn't a single blister!

We swapped stories with Anna-Marie and Lesley. Anna-Marie had done exceptionally well, coming in the top ten women, but poor old Lesley had fallen and damaged her knee quite badly. With our aches and pains, and other war wounds, we slipped into our sleeping bags, but over the next few hours and into the early morning, the wind picked up. The tent didn't quite collapse, but I could hear the poles rattling furiously, and the walls beating like wings. As the sides lifted and the wind pummelled through, I couldn't tell whether I was in the tent or out of it. I feared my meagre possessions would be swept away. I wasn't frightened exactly, but it was unsettling, and certainly disorientating. I must admit that I moaned a fair bit, complaining and asking for updates. Eventually, I pulled the sleeping bag up around me to muffle out the sound and sleep did come eventually – even if it was broken.

Monday 6 April 2015
Stage 2: Oued Tijekht to Jebel El Oftal, 32k, eight hours 15 minutes

Rosemary read the roadbook to me. Today would be the mountain stage. The pair of them knew me well: they knew I wouldn't look forward to the mountain stage, and decided not to tell me until the day had dawned and I could do nothing about it. Rosie had also spoken with another blind chap, a French man who had completed the MdS an incredible 11 times, who had warned her that the mountain range posed real dangers for blind competitors. We were all nervous.

We started at 8.30am and, at first, we got in some good running. Then the first mountain range loomed. It was not horrific, but we certainly worked hard up it. The paths leading to the summit were only wide enough for one person, so I held on to the backpack of either Tony or Rosemary, whoever was in front. My feet collided with the rocks at each step as I fumbled to get a hold. It was not an easy passage up, but at least time flew by and the beeps soon came around to signal checkpoint one at 12.6k.

Tony had forgotten his second ECG test yesterday and had received a stern telling off, so made amends at this checkpoint. As the week went on, he came to relish these checks – for a break, if nothing else!

Within minutes of leaving the first checkpoint, we began to climb. I couldn't believe what was being described to me. Rosemary told me it was one hell of a climb up and then we were confronted with a ridge. She estimated it to be around

CHAPTER 12

2k in length and it looked very similar to a dragon's back, which I interpreted as hard work. Our little team of three, among all the other ants, pulled, pushed and heaved up that mountain and on to the ridge. The ridge was a rocky road, but commanded concentration and flexibility. Sometimes the rocks were close enough, or small enough, that I could stretch over them, with Rosie and Tony explaining where to put my feet and when. Their voices were urgent, commanding, and I listened to them.

They were telling me where to put my feet before they'd even worked out where to put their own. Sometimes I was on all fours, one hand, one foot, one hand, one foot. Tony and Rosie clung on to me for dear life, supporting and guiding me from one rock to the next, heaving and hauling me. Finally, after a painstakingly slow crossing, the ridge gave way to sand and we slid on to it, gratifyingly. At checkpoint two, 24.6k, we filled up on water and a scoop of nuts, dried fruit and Smarties that had been so carefully counted and pre-packed at home. It tasted like manna from heaven.

We set off in search of the finish, but we did have the little matter of another mountain range before, though. I was apprehensive, but I thought to myself, I've done two – it couldn't get any worse.

But how wrong you can be.

The sun was now very hot and after walking for some time, both Tony and Rosemary were trying to see where the ant line was going. I heard a simultaneous 'oh no'. They described a finger of sand, approximately 600 feet up, and then the rock face went sheer. We gulped but joined the queue on that first sand dune, feet going everywhere but up it seemed, three forward and two back. The wind picked up and Tony's hat took the opportunity to blow off into the distance. Though he needed it for protection from the fierce sun, there was no way he was going back down to retrieve it. He decided to take his chances.

We took a diagonal line across the dune, so it was easier to dig our feet in. Then we hit the rocks, and the climbing began. Again, there was no uniformity. Some were three feet in height, some lower; some jagged, some smooth. We scrambled up on our knees, Tony at the front and often turning to pull me up, with Rosemary following by tucking my feet into safe spots.

Then it went vertical.

At this point, the organisers must have realised the seriousness of the climb and had put in some support in the way of rope. I say rope, but to describe it, Tony said it seemed more like a washing line with knots in. But by God it did help some. Tony and Rosemary were really unhappy, though, as using the rope meant that they couldn't keep their hands on me. I felt like it was perhaps more serious than it sounded, especially when stressed to me quite strongly, 'Don't, *whatever you do*, lose that bloody rope!' Rosemary kept encouraging me to lean right into the rock face.

This stretch of mountain range also demonstrated how camaraderie among competitors had grown. A chap we knew as Bernie was firmly on our tails, and Rosemary suggested we let him pass so we didn't hold him up. We were certainly taking our time. The answer that came back was superb, 'We'll stay behind you three, thanks. We can't believe how you are coping with climbing this mountain, so we'll stay behind you just in case you need any help.' That, to us, simply summed up the nature of the other competitors.

It took some time, and some sheer bloody-mindedness, but we reached the top. Tony certainly put a smile on my face when he said, 'You know, Dave, a blind bloke really shouldn't be up here!' At the top, we had a five-minute rest and a sip of water. We gathered our thoughts and plodded on. With all the pulling and hauling, Tony was utterly knackered so Rosie took over. The ground levelled off and, with my fingers clenched round her backpack, we broke into a trot. We managed around 20 yards until the descent appeared. Her explanation was simple but it didn't fill me with any confidence: it was as though someone had got a quarry full of stones and chucked them from the highest point of a cliff. She said that a sighted person wouldn't have too much of a problem, as many of the rocks were large and flat enough to leap across. But I would certainly have difficulty, and so the long, tedious process of sitting and dropping into crevices, clambering up and over, going down backwards, in, out, up, down, began. It took hours and that 2k distance down turned into a nightmare.

I was told that Sir Ranulph passed us, leaping from rock to rock like a gazelle. Sight for a few minutes would have saved us hours, I realised. Dried riverbeds gave us short moments of respite in between precise, orchestrated slips and slithers. I felt like a kid in the back of a car, nagging Rosie, 'Can you see the bottom yet?' The answer always seemed to be no. After about an hour and a half we hit the bottom – and sand. Was I glad to feel that sand?

The heat was up, the sand was soft but I didn't care. We had roughly 3k left to do. The run in – or the half-walk half-trot – took us over a rolling sand dune. Our legs were now battered but it was a pleasing sound when Rosemary and Tony confirmed they could see the finish. And it was even better when I heard the bleeps! Around half a kilometre from the finish we came upon Patrick, a partially sighted French chap with his five guides. We all linked arms and came through the finish line as a French–British convoy.

The day was done. Once we found tent 124, we staggered in and collapsed. Anna-Marie was once again triumphant: she was still in the top ten and slowly moving upwards, but to our surprise, Lesley wasn't back yet. Sadly, it materialised, when she arrived back at camp much later, that she had been forced to pull out. The injury she had sustained from her fall would prevent her from continuing any further.

Lesley's story reminded me of a chap who had attempted the MdS the previous year that had also been a casualty of the second day. He had completed the day seemingly with no problem, until exhaustion brought on a hidden virus that caused him to collapse. He was flown out of the desert and spent the next week in a coma. I remembered Deb was not happy, having heard the story. She questioned my sanity afterwards. It was a story that made me understand why the organisers stuck to such a strict medical regime.

We were gutted for Lesley. All that training and hard work she had put in as preparation had been scuppered, due to an accident that could have befallen any of us. Tent 124 was quiet for a long time. She kindly offered Tony her hat, as consolation.

Once we had eaten and prepared for the morning, Tony and Rosemary set about recounting the day's events. It turned out that they had been rather economical with the truth. Remember that's dragon's spine-like rocky road? Well, either side of that ridge was a 1,500-foot drop. Sometimes the ridge had been eight feet wide, but sometimes only two. If I had misplaced a foot, or stumbled too much to the left or right, I would have been a goner – and probably taken one of them with me. And that cliff face we climbed? There was another drop, of a similar kind of distance. I had been perched on a ledge above the drop, holding on to that tiny washing line without any idea of the danger I faced. No wonder Tony and Rosemary had been so strict in their instructions, so urgent in their tone. And no wonder they were so exhausted.

Tuesday 7 April 2015
Stage 3: Jebel El Oftal to Jebel Zireg, 36.7k, eight hours 27 minutes

We woke to find that our tent was pretty well on its knees, having been battered by the wind most of the night. None of the other tents looked nearly as bad, so I'm told, so we set about making reparations and propping up the poles as best we could.

At the start, birthday announcements were accompanied by the names of the previous day's casualties and it was a surprisingly long list. I hoped we wouldn't be added to that list and although we were tired, I was enthusiastic and confident. As things stood, I didn't think we would be. We had tackled the mountains, after all. The helicopters circled and the loud music blared, and once again, we were off. The roadbook had informed us that today would, primarily, be a sand dune day, which we took to mean a slightly easier day. After patchy sleep and the battering our legs took the day before, I wasn't convinced any part of this adventure was easy.

The sand dunes and camel grasses made for a corrugated terrain and about halfway through to checkpoint one, my foot collided with a hidden root and I toppled over, hitting the ground with a bang. Thankfully, nothing was hurt but my dignity. At 14k, checkpoint one beeped and we relished the five-minute rest in the shade, away from the relentless sun.

The day trudged on, hot and weary. We covered dry riverbeds and even a dry lake and checkpoint two, at 25.9k, was certainly a very welcome bleep. At the back end of the day, we hit what was called a progressive climb: a small sandy mountain. Its descent took us into more sand dunes and those last few kilometres, under intense heat and with heavy legs, seemed to drain the body and mind. Time seemed to stand still and if ever I wanted to hear two solid wonderful bleeps, it was now. The finish line couldn't come quick enough.

We collected our water rations, found tent 124 and flopped down. But I shot up again like a rocket – the tent, after being moved and re-erected, had flattened a thorny bush, whose spines had stabbed my backside with all its might. It gave everyone a great laugh, especially after the day we'd had.

We also had some great news. Anna-Marie had moved up to second place in the women's race, and we surrounded her with backslaps and hugs. She was doing incredibly well.

With trainers off came the obligatory blister check. Tony and Rosemary's feet were now in a shocking state. I still hadn't got one; sore, yes, but otherwise unblemished.

Wednesday 8 April 2015
Stage 4: Jebel Zireg to Jdaid, 91.7k, 24 hours 55 minutes

After another night of high winds, with the sand hurled against the sides of the tent, I found that sleep, once again, didn't come easily – despite my body protesting its need for sleep all day. Why brains can't know what's best for them sometimes, I don't know. So when we roused, with the now familiar pre-dawn ritual, the MdS's longest day in its 30 years stretched ahead of us pretty dauntingly: 91.7 whole kilometres.

Still, the start line was just as jubilant as ever. The birthdays were announced, Aerosmith blared from the PA and the helicopters whirred overhead. The elite men and women had been given a later start and cheered us from the sidelines to give us a great send-off.

The wind hadn't died down. It was just safe enough for us to press on, so we covered the first 12.2k to the first checkpoint accompanied by a sandstorm.

I'm told that the scenery was much the same: dunes and dried riverbeds, and that was about it. But there was one curious addition – Tony and Rosemary suddenly exclaimed that we were passing what looked very much like a holiday camp! In the middle of nowhere! Why anyone would stay there was anybody's guess, as it didn't sound particularly appealing.

Just as we came to checkpoint two, the elite athletes began to pass us. I couldn't believe their speed and stamina – they'd covered the distance in no time at all, and in the face of a ferocious, sandy wind.

After checkpoint two, an unwelcome sight made Tony and Rosemary groan in unanimous disbelief. There was a mountain in the distance, and the pair couldn't decide if the ant-like people were going round – or up and over. As we continued our sandy shuffle and got closer, they both grimaced. 'They're actually going over!' So, not satisfied with almost 100k to complete, we had a mountain to climb, too. Thanks, organisers.

CHAPTER 12

Off we went, climbing and clambering over rocks. There were corridors of rock; at times, the path only allowing single file. By now, we had a system: I would hold on to the pack of the person in front, and the other guide would push me from behind, all the while singing, 'Left, right, left, right, you're in the army now.' It worked a treat and kept our feet in sync, preventing us from tripping up or standing on each other.

But when we reached the top, there was no time to relax. 'Who's going to tell him?' Rosie sighed.

I felt my heart sink. What could possibly be next?

Tony picked up the mantle, describing the descent as a 'long way down, very steep, almost sheer'. He placed my hands on another rope, another washing line, and instructed me to walk backwards and not to let go.

At this point, I was not the only one holding the rope and it was moving all over the place. It was quite disorientating, like grappling with a snake.

Then I was told it ran out – there'd be no rope for the next section. I must admit that I panicked. I knew we would be going down, I knew it was a sheer drop. But quick-thinking Rosemary grabbed me before my palms could sweat or my knees could knock.

'Turn around, relax, dig your heels in. We need to slide.'

She manhandled me and we dropped, skiing through the sand without any control. If I wanted to brake, I couldn't have done. It felt like an eternity, even though Rosemary assured me, once we reached the bottom, it hadn't been longer than 300 metres. I had put my life – quite literally – in Rosie's hands. Thank God we trusted each other.

I wanted to make sure I captured the descent on my GoPro so I turned to face the descent, tilting my head up.

'No, Dave, that won't do it. You'll only get the last third in.'

She tilted my head much further. I was nearly bent double backwards, and it was only then the full extent hit me of what I had just done. It really had been steep.

There was one final rocky road to go until we met checkpoint three at 37.8k and a welcome rest. My legs were jelly.

Checkpoint four, at 50.2k, was deemed the halfway point for the day and instead of counting the checkpoints up, we found it was a psychological boost to be able to count down towards the finish – even if it was still a hell of a long way to go. Many of our fellow competitors decided to set up a makeshift camp at the checkpoint and sleep, but we felt the need to refuel and keep going.

We stopped inside a tent to prepare some tea and I found myself chatting to a French chap who turned out to be a doctor. He told me he had volunteered his medical services to the MdS the previous year, and had decided to compete himself this year so he could experience the event from both perspectives.

He was quick to tell me that although he'd volunteer as a doctor for future MdS, he would never come back as a competitor.

We left checkpoint four as night time had drawn in, a terrific sandstorm already whipping up. In fact, it didn't subside the entire time it took for us to get to checkpoint five. With sand swirling about us, we cracked open our glow sticks to provide extra light for Rosie and Tony, in addition to our head torches. I was told we were making our way across one enormous sand dune. With sinking sand beneath our feet and sand continually pelting our bodies, it was arduous and unpleasant.

Checkpoint five eventually came at 63.3k and 2am, and deckchairs set out by the organisers greeted us. It was incredible just to be able to sit down on an actual chair! I couldn't wait to tear into my specially saved packet of KVE pork scratchings which, I found, were envied by a good few competitors. We weren't all junk food abstainers, it seemed!

But the pork scratchings couldn't revive poor old Rosie. For some reason, this checkpoint brought on real fatigue for her, and she was desperate to sleep. We gave her a stay of 20 minutes so she could get a power nap in, but once we got her up and pressed on, we wondered if she was actually sleep walking… we'd never known her so quiet.

The sandstorm continued, unabated, so Tony kept up our spirits with quizzes: 'Name me 20 John Wayne films', followed later by 'Name me 20 Clint Eastwood films'. This kept us marching along, our minds preoccupied.

We then realised we'd become a kind of Pied Piper. Hundreds of people had swarmed around us, treading in our footsteps and getting really close. Several bumped straight into Tony, blinded by sand and deliriousness, and he grimaced and groaned, annoyance biting him.

All of a sudden, he leapt and shouted in alarm, bouncing into me. I jumped, too, my aching muscles stiffened into action like at the start of a race.

'What is it?' I whispered.

'Oh nothing,' he responded, irritably. 'I thought it was a snake.'

It turned out to be desert grass, snagging his shoes. We laughed. It felt good to laugh.

We allowed ourselves just time to fill our water bottles at checkpoint six, 74.8k, as we could smell the next – and last – checkpoint. We were still crossing that same sand dune, a slow, unbearable incline all the way. Tony said if the gradient increased any more we'd soon be touching the moon. We took to singing our way to checkpoint seven – a few favourites, the most memorable being America's 'A Horse With No Name': 'You see I've been through the desert on a horse with no name…' – where we were greeted by scattered bodies, sleeping intently. Though it was 6.30am on Thursday, we only had another 6k left to do so we couldn't face stopping. As tempting as it was to lie down, I honestly don't think we would have got back up.

I felt the heat rising from the sands. The sun had to be coming up, and I asked Tony to capture it on the Go Pro. I never saw the sunrise, but I was told it was a magical sight, rising above the dark, desolate desert.

Though our roadmap told us this was a good running surface, we didn't think so: our path was littered with boulders and rocks, and I'd shatter my ankles in seconds. Rosie perked up though, as the pace picked up. Tony challenged us to a spelling test, which was pretty hilarious given Tony can't spell to save his life. Suddenly, Tony's phone bleeped. After two days without signal, a text came through from Deb.

'What's taking you all so long? Will you get a move on, please? I'm waiting to go out.'

The cheeky sod. A great big grin crept across my face. Deb, even from thousands of miles away, could still spur me on.

After 90k, after 8pm had come and gone, Rosemary said those wonderful words, 'Dave, I can see the finish line. It's about 1,200 metres away, I'd say.'

She must have said 1,200 metres five times. If she had realised those last metres would be up and down, meaning it felt like five times that, she had kept that to herself. Deb sent another text.

'I'm expecting a little finish dance for the camera.'

We ran, even though we tripped and stumbled, our heads pounding, our knees numb. After 24 hours and 55 minutes, we heard the most amazing two bleeps, the finish line. I did the most ridiculous dance I could muster, with one hell of a smile.

By now, we had quickened our ritual to allow for a better, longer collapse time. I didn't have a blister – still! – but Tony was in all sorts of pain. Rosemary was in agony, and decided to see the dedicated foot medical team to get prepared for the next morning. After she left the tent, we lay quietly, taking it all in and wondering what we had just done.

Rosemary returned a couple of hours later, feeling slightly better and explaining the whole procedure, which once again sounded remarkable, considering where we were. It seemed there were some 190 other people needing attention, and 20 specialist foot medics. Rosie was asked to show her number and sit with her feet up. They were then cleaned with disinfectant and covered in surgical overshoes until the medics arrived.

Rosemary had not looked forward to the nurse's visit, given the screams she could hear. The blisters were cut and sliced, slathered with iodine then taped and bandaged. The detail of the blister on one of her feet made me wince. It was on the heel and she described it as being as big as an orange. Blood spurted out as it was cut.

As competitors continued to finish the stage throughout the day, an exhausted feeling began to permeate the camp. It's hard to explain, but still the mood was high – people felt elated, but exhausted. Everyone knew that, barring an accident, tomorrow would be the very last day. The finish.

We spent the entire day resting, and repacking. I still couldn't believe how heavy my pack remained. I counted the meals I needed for the remainder, discarding whatever I could, but that pack was still heavy. Both Tony and Rosie couldn't understand it; theirs were so much lighter.

The last person came in just before the 36-hour deadline, while we had been resting for over ten hours. I did feel sorry for them. It was an early start the following day and their rest would be nominal. As a bit of a prize, the organisers gave us all a small can of Coke. We decided to save ours for the day ahead and a much-needed pick-me-up.

We zipped up our sleeping bags as the wind and sand began to blow, but that night, I was too tired to care.

Friday 10 April 2015
Stage 5: Jdaid to Kourci Dial Zaid, 42.2k, eight hours 18 minutes

Although I'd dropped off in no time, it didn't stay like that. Sadly, the wind had been so ferocious that we had all been awake, listening to its assault on the tent walls. We were up well before dawn.

After hardly any sleep at all, I sat on my sleeping bag and pulled on my kit. Tony began howling with laughter. 'You don't know where you are, do you?' he laughed. I didn't know what was so funny.

'Not exactly. Somewhere in the Sahara, sitting on my sleeping bag, getting dressed in this tent,' I replied, wondering what the joke was.

'No, I mean you don't know what's happened.'

Tony went on to explain that the tent had actually blown down in the night and Rosemary and Anna-Marie were actually underneath it, using the tent as a blanket. Both Tony and I had been – literally – sleeping under the stars. I did wonder at some point in the night why the wind hadn't seemed quite as noisy, but had put it down to a steady decline in speed. When, really, it had been because it had no tent to blow through!

The morning ritual got under way, only this time with a bit more pain thrown in. Tony struggled to get his trainers on, and poor Rosie whimpered at just the thought – then even more as she tried to put them on. In the end, she had to cut her trainers just to fit her feet in without so much rubbing and chafing.

We didn't mind the 7am start. In fact, it seemed most didn't; everyone just wanted to get going, and get finished. At the start line, the list of those who had been forced to give up had grown longer still, with the sad news that Bernie, the chap from the mountain day, was one of them.

The day proved a real mixture of terrain: hard rutted sand, corrugated sand with small ridges, large ridges, and hard ground with many stones and rocks. We hit our first checkpoint at 12.5k and shared the can of Coke – the hiss tormenting others wishing they had saved theirs, too.

At checkpoint two, 24.6k, we shared and savoured our second can of Coke. It was only a couple of sips each, but it hit the spot. On the way to the third checkpoint – the last of the entire challenge – the temperature ramped up, the sweat in rivulets along my spine. But the last checkpoint, 33.7k, was in touching distance. The sound of those bleeps was something else.

After leaving checkpoint three, we could smell the finish but the ground toughened before we could get excited. With only 5k to go, Tony did his normal attempt at winding me up. As we began to climb a slight incline, with Rosemary in cahoots, he told me that he could see Patrick, the French partially sighted chap, along with his guides ahead of us. It was just the competition I needed. I upped the ante, my legs finding strength from somewhere – my ego, I suppose.

It was at the top of this incline that Tony exclaimed in surprise, 'I was winding you up before, but Patrick is really in front of us now!'

I didn't need any more encouragement, my legs automatically quickened. Rosie warned me not to go any faster; it would be dangerous in the heat, especially after what we had already endured. But we passed Patrick and his crew, Tony filming as we ran and Rosie hanging on to the running cord. I gave my obligatory 'boing, boing' as I realised that this was really, truly the finish.

We crossed the line as one, all bleeps together.

We had completed the 30th Marathon des Sables.

The hugs, the tears, the smile, the daft little dance again. I felt the medal draped around my neck. We had done it; our great little team had pulled together. We had looked after each other when we needed it and we experienced none of the bad words or bad tempers that can sometimes flare and fly when in close company for a few days.

The camp sounded jubilant, claps and congratulations ringing out all round. Tent 124 was a happy place – painful, but happy. Anna-Marie had secured second place, first British woman. What an achievement! As we flopped down, sharing our experiences and congratulations, I put my hand in my pack and found a bulge in the lining. I recognised that bag. It was the coffee, tea and sugar! I thought I'd lost that little bundle on the first day; even Tony and Rosemary had checked my pack and couldn't find it. How wonderful on the last day to taste that cup of coffee! And no wonder my pack hadn't become any lighter!

Later that evening, with all participants home, music struck up from a live band and we grinned and backslapped as the official presentations were made. This was to be our last night spent in the Sahara and tent 124.

Saturday 11 April 2015
Charity day: Kourci Dial Zaid to the departing coaches, 11.5k

But it wasn't to be our last run quite yet.

We awoke to find the tent in the correct position, thankfully, and performed the morning ritual that had started so alien and become completely normal for the very last time. It would be our last breakfast from a packet; no more sand-baked spoon, no more Sahara floor, no more sandstorms, just the obligatory 11.5k charity walk, run or crawl.

Our charity shirts, supporting Unicef, were handed out alongside a brand new number, just for the occasion. At 9am, we set off for the very last time. It was all very casual; even the elite strolled alongside us. Our route took us through, round and over the highest sand dunes in Morocco, the Merzouga sand dunes. It was hard work that we rewarded with the final Coke. I filled a small plastic bag with sand to take back for the kids, and then we filed on to the coaches, ready for the journey back to Ouarzazate.

As a coach filled, it left, preventing queues of sand-beaten waifs from standing around. It was wonderful to sit down on a soft seat and to finally slip off my trainers. I felt incredibly sorry for the driver. A coachful of runners, almost eight days in the desert in the same clothes with no washing facilities to speak of – it certainly tantalised the nostrils. That poor driver; he had six hours of us and our desert odour in a hot, confined space!

CHAPTER 12

Back in Ouarzazate, the British participants were put up in the Berber Palace Hotel and within half an hour I was standing under a shower. It was a wonderful feeling, but it took easily three showers to feel anything like clean.

The next morning, scrubbed and rested from a real bed, I waited in the hotel lobby for our last trip – back to the airport.

'Morning, Blind Dave,' an unfamiliar voice approached. 'I'm a Foxes fan and I just thought I'd let you know that we beat you yesterday, 3-2.'

Brilliant.

* * * * *

On landing back in the UK, I told Tony and Rosie that we needed to show our faces at The Hawthorns first, just to say hello and to prove we were in one piece. Tony, camera-shy and PR-phobic, was suspicious but I assured him it was just a casual courtesy call.

But what did I know?

'Cheers, Dave,' Tony groaned as our car pulled in to the ground. TV and radio awaited our appearance, while our families, friends and other supporters amounted to a rather large crowd. The cheers erupted as soon as we swung our legs out of the car, on to what felt like carpet. 'It's red,' Georgie-Lee and Dannie told me, excitedly. I heard the snap and click of cameras.

Rosemary and Tony joined me and we strode into the stadium like Olympic athletes, clad in our tracksuits. We waved and smiled, posed for pictures this way and that, and had welcome glasses of bubbly thrust into our hands. We were ushered into the Richardson Suite where an enthusiastic piano started and children burst into song: 'I'm Gonna Be (500 Miles)' by The Proclaimers. They'd changed the words, though, to be about us and the MdS. We were thrilled!

'Fantastic!' I found myself repeating. 'Fantastic, fantastic!' We gave the kids from Crocketts Community Primary School a well deserved round of applause when they had finished.

It was then we realised this was more than just an impromptu party: this was a proper awards ceremony, to thank all those who had participated in the Tri Albion Challenge. First, we congratulated the walkers and cyclists who had completed the first two legs, and then it was our turn. However, I'm not quite sure it was the vision that Rob Lake had in mind. Bomber Brown, on duty to present us with some gifts, tripped and fell on to the stage. I'd spoken before I realised I was going to.

'Come on, Bomber, I'll guide you,' I grinned.

Thankfully, the rest of the occasion passed without incident and the three of us were on a high – albeit a very tired one. It was only now, back in West Brom with the staff and young people of the Albion Foundation, that it had begun to sink in – we'd done it. We'd raised over £30k, and the challenge as a whole had raised £73,000. And to think that I thought I'd been offered dessert and ended up in the desert!

13

BY now, you might have noticed a pattern. A challenge ends, the PR wanes – and I'm already planning the next. It's my way of keeping positive and feeling focused, but also maintaining fitness.

Though I love running and cycling, it's difficult to sustain fitness levels if I've nothing to aim for. Restlessness sets in, the pounds pile on, and before I know it, I have to start all over again.

Returning from the Marathon des Sables has proved no different. It was one of the hardest challenges to date, and I've vowed never to attempt it again. But I'll attempt *something* again, I just know it. Turning 60 is now within touching distance, so I've got to find a way of marking it somehow. Though I have been begged not to do any more… Deb's cousin, Richard Harris, told us he didn't see his wife, Mel, during the course of the MdS.

'She was chained to the computer, following your every move and sobbing,' he told me. 'Please, Dave, don't do any more – I didn't eat for a week!'

When my body does tell me that it's had enough and I hang up the trainers for good, I hope that I can still raise the profile of the charities and causes that I care about. It's become a passion: doing whatever I can – whether that's speaking, or going on the local radio station, or tweeting, or putting people in touch – to try and get important messages out there.

It started off with wanting to give something back to a charity that had directly affected me. I had been that blind person in denial, unwilling to do anything about my situation and slowly limiting my lifestyle until a charity, Guide Dogs for the Blind, could show me a better way. If Guide Dogs hadn't the funds to have reached me in the first place, it's possible I wouldn't be as happy and as fulfilled as I am today. As Deb says, I am now comfortable in my own shoes.

Charitable organisations, and their tireless, dedicated staff, are doing the same in their field the world over, reaching out to cancer sufferers, children from disadvantaged communities, people with physical disabilities... Charities can help individuals turn their lives around, improve communities, or make things just that little bit more comfortable, even in the most unpleasant situations.

As long as I remain in the public eye, the suggestions of things to get involved in keep on coming. Tony flies a helicopter and his instructor suggested I come along and have a go myself, while the Albion Foundation is already in planning for its 25th anniversary in 2016, with a cycle challenge already announced, so I'm certain I'll be involved in that somehow. I'm willing to try anything, within reason, and if it helps to raise funds or the profile of a cause or charity, then all the better.

And thankfully, the family expect nothing less. I'm blessed with a loving, happy family that continue to support me in my madcap schemes. There's Grace, my eldest, who is proving to be a talented graphic designer and has recently started doing these mad races where you end up covered in mud and scratches. Maybe she's more influenced by her old man than she realises. Then Georgie-Lee and Dannie, who are in the throes of secondary school, tackling the tests and exams that are routinely thrown in their direction, seemingly every week. They're lively, funny and popular, and make me laugh every day. I think that having a blind dad probably isn't easy, but it has certainly taught Grace, Georgie-Lee and Dannie patience and to be more aware of other people's circumstances. They don't mock people, but they're never patronising or cloyingly sympathetic, either – I'd say that they meet people halfway, and I'm pretty sure that disabled people would appreciate that. I know I certainly do.

Then there's my wonderful Deb, my girl, who takes such good care of us all. She's always there, always providing the logical backdrop to everything. As with everything I do, Deb was instrumental in the writing of this book: giving advice, reminding me of long-forgotten moments, offering clarity and different perspectives. I don't know what I'd do without her.

Reflecting back over my life while putting this collection of words and stories together, it's amazing how sport and charities have had such a bearing on my working life. Redundancy in the 1990s saw me move into the voluntary sector, which, in turn, encouraged me to don the trainers once again. The finish line of the London Marathon led me to a world first, running the seven marathons, which ultimately catapulted me into self-employment.

My role as a motivational speaker has put me in front of many different audiences, in many different countries. In this world of cut and thrust, many disabled people find it difficult to find employment, so for me – a blind old codger from West Brom – it makes me feel very proud that I earn my own corn. I always finish my talks with this simple message: don't worry about what you can't do; concentrate your efforts on what you can do and you will find you can achieve those goals and ambitions. After all, that's the mantra I've stuck to all these years.

My primary reason for writing this all down was to give something for the girls to look back on when they're older. But I realise it's become more than that. I've reached into the furthest corners of my mind, searching for memories, and ploughed back through all the diaries and records of all the things I've done, to set it down on paper. And it's proved to me something that many would dispute or not quite believe: that blindness has been a gift for me. My blindness has encouraged me to see another way, to live life to the fullest, to embrace the mad, daft and dangerous, to make more of relationships, to take nothing for granted, and to realise that, actually, I am one incredibly lucky, fortunate man.

I wouldn't change my life for anything.